The Battle of CARTHAGE

Border War in Southwest Missouri
July 5, 1861

by

David C. Hinze
and Karen Farnham

PELICAN PUBLISHING COMPANY
Gretna 2004

Published by Savas Publishing Company, 1997
Published by arrangement in North America by
    Pelican Publishing Company, Inc., 2004

First printing, 1997
First Pelican printing, 2004

ISBN: 1-58980-223-3

Maps copyright © 1997 by Theodore P. Savas

Printed in the United States of America
Published by Pelican Publishing Company, Inc.
1000 Burmaster Street, Gretna, Louisiana 70053

To Mary,
a remarkable woman, friend and wife

&

To my mother, Jay Dee Farnham,
for all of her love and support

1. Nathaniel Lyon moves upriver and defeats Governor Jackson's wing of the Missouri State Guard in a brief but significant skirmish at Boonville, June 17, 1861;

2. Governor Jackson withdraws his column south (the divisions of John B. Clark, Sr., and Mosby M. Parsons), hoping to form a junction in the southwestern portion of the state with the Lexington wing of the Missouri State Guard;

3. With the Missouri River under Lyon's control, the Lexington wing of the Missouri State Guard (the divisions of James S. Rains and William Y. Slack) also falls back, linking with Jackson at Lamar on July 3, 1861. Sterling Price is ill and not with the column;

4. General Thomas Sweeny's Federals leave St. Louis on June 12. Strung out because of bad weather and logistical problems, the vanguard under Col. Franz Sigel passes through Rolla and Springfield, hoping to find the Missouri State Guard;

5. Sigel moves north, anxious to defeat the Rebels. Jackson moves his men south and meets Sigel on the morning of July 5, 1861, 10 miles north of Carthage.

Theater of Operations

June 12 - July 6, 1861

N

70 miles

Table of Contents

continued. . .

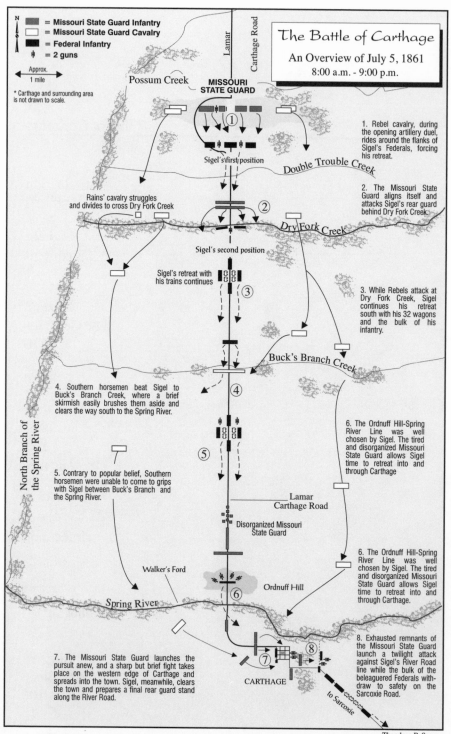

The Battle of Carthage
An Overview of July 5, 1861
8:00 a.m. - 9:00 p.m.

= Missouri State Guard Infantry
= Missouri State Guard Cavalry
= Federal Infantry
= 2 guns

N

Approx.
1 mile

* Carthage and surrounding area is not drawn to scale.

Lamar Carthage Road

Possum Creek

MISSOURI STATE GUARD

①

Sigel's first position

Double Trouble Creek

1. Rebel cavalry, during the opening artillery duel, rides around the flanks of Sigel's Federals, forcing his retreat.

Rains' cavalry struggles and divides to cross Dry Fork Creek

②

Dry Fork Creek

Sigel's second position

2. The Missouri State Guard aligns itself and attacks Sigel's rear guard behind Dry Fork Creek.

Sigel's retreat with his trains continues

③

3. While Rebels attack at Dry Fork Creek, Sigel continues his retreat south with his 32 wagons and the bulk of his infantry.

Buck's Branch Creek

④

4. Southern horsemen beat Sigel to Buck's Branch Creek, where a brief skirmish easily brushes them aside and clears the way south to the Spring River.

North Branch of the Spring River

⑤

5. Contrary to popular belief, Southern horsemen were unable to come to grips with Sigel between Buck's Branch and the Spring River.

6. The Ordnuff Hill-Spring River Line was well chosen by Sigel. The tired and disorganized Missouri State Guard allows Sigel time to retreat into and through Carthage

Lamar Carthage Road

Disorganized Missouri State Guard

6. The Ordnuff Hill-Spring River Line was well chosen by Sigel. The tired and disorganized Missouri State Guard allows Sigel time to retreat into and through Carthage.

Walker's Ford

Ordnuff Hill

⑥

Spring River

7. The Missouri State Guard launches the pursuit anew, and a sharp but brief fight takes place on the western edge of Carthage and spreads into the town. Sigel, meanwhile, clears the town and prepares a final rear guard stand along the River Road.

⑦

⑧

CARTHAGE

to Sarcoxie

8. Exhausted remnants of the Missouri State Guard launch a twilight attack against Sigel's River Road line while the bulk of the beleaguered Federals withdraw to safety on the Sarcoxie Road.

Theodore P. Savas

Table of Contents (continued)

List of Maps and Illustrations

Photos & Illustrations (continued)

Modern photographs of the battlefield:

Introduction

More than 136 years ago, the Battle of Carthage—or Dry Fork, as some sources refer to the action—was fought on a hot Missouri day in early July 1861. The engagement was one of the earliest land actions of the Civil War and the culmination of the war's first large-scale campaign. The importance of the overlooked Southwestern Missouri operation to the war in the Trans-Mississippi is difficult to overstate, for its outcome largely determined the state's course in the war: would it remain under Union control or risk its future with the new Confederacy? Despite its importance to the course of the war west of the Mississippi River, most studies of the region focus primarily on the earlier struggle for the St. Louis arsenal and the subsequent Union defeat at Wilson's Creek on August 10, 1861—skipping virtually everything else in between. This spotty coverage has skewed history's view of what actually transpired in the critical border state sandwiched between Iowa and Arkansas.

Far from being isolated incidents, the affair at the arsenal and the fighting at Wilson's Creek unfolded within organized campaigns designed by Union Brig. Gen. Nathaniel Lyon to either destroy or drive pro-Southern forces out of the state. Lyon's aggressive (and almost successful) plan called for a two-prong movement against the retiring Southerners. One column, under his own leadership, followed and harassed Governor Claiborne Jackson's Missouri State

Guard as it retreated south toward Arkansas, while another wing under Brig. Gen. Thomas Sweeny sliced southwest out of St. Louis via Rolla and Springfield to intercept the militia army. An obscure Union colonel named Franz Sigel led the vanguard of Sweeny's blocking movement into the lightly populated corner of the state.

The dénouement of Lyon's bold effort began about ten miles north of the small village of Carthage, Missouri, on the morning of July 5, 1861. There, Sigel's regiments stumbled upon Governor Jackson's army as it was deploying for battle. The sporadic combat that followed opened with a lengthy artillery duel and lasted from late that morning until well past dark, a series of pitched and running engagements covering miles of rolling prairie. Even though the action was far removed from a major population center, the story garnered front page coverage in the *New York Times* for five consecutive days before being pushed off the cover in favor of the Manassas (Bull Run) Campaign, which was just beginning to heat up. Errors contained in the sketchy reports of the fighting were compounded by the fact that no reporters were present at or near the scene of the fighting.

Two small skirmishes, Philippi (June 3) and Big Bethel (June 10), preceded the clash at Carthage. While more attention has been heaped upon these actions—primarily because they were waged in the Eastern Theater, i.e., near the capital city of each opponent—significant differences set them apart from the early Missouri engagement. Philippi involved smaller numbers of troops than the Missouri fight, no pitched fighting and produced only seventeen total casualties. While the antagonists at Big Bethel possessed slightly more men than did those at Carthage, a majority of the soldiers at the June 10th skirmish never made it into action. Furthermore, Big Bethel was not part of an organized campaign. Unlike either Philippi or Big Bethel, Carthage spawned important consequences that shaped the course of the war in the area in which it was waged. Although secondary sources generally refer to Big Bethel as the first land battle of the war, the short duration of the engagement, coupled with other factors, influenced many contemporary news sources to refer to Carthage as the first "major" battle.

The fighting at Manassas (Bull Run), coupled with the high casualties and heavy press coverage, quickly overshadowed the relatively small Missouri engagement. Interest waned and attention was diverted away from Missouri, where the combat was more fragmented and difficult to follow. The guerrilla war that consumed much of the region for four years following Carthage effectively depopulated the countryside. Many residents never returned to tell of what they saw and experienced during the summer of 1861. Those who remained were too preoccupied with survival to remember much about a single day of the war. As local memories faded, so did the importance attached to July 5, 1861.

We hope this study will heighten interest in this corner of the war. We are certain it will generate some bit of controversy as our interpretations of several aspects of the fighting vary considerably from standard accounts. Historians regularly review materials and reach different conclusions as to how certain events occurred or how well certain officers performed. It has been our intention from the first to base this work, as far as possible, on the battle reports, firsthand accounts and a familiarity with the terrain. After spending years sifting through these documents and walking the prairies where these events transpired, we are reasonably confident our conclusions will stand the scrutiny of others who have plowed this field before us.

*   *   *

Although two authors share the credit for this book, it would have been impossible without the help of many others. We are indebted to each of them, and apologize for anyone we may have overlooked.

John Bradbury of the Western Historical Manuscript Collections in Rolla, Missouri, who gave willingly of his time and expertise; Steve Cottrell and Marvin Van Gilder, two of the first to write about and popularize the Battle of Carthage. Marvin warrants a special note of thanks. His articles in the Carthage newspaper have kept interest about the fighting alive for many years; Jeff Patrick at Wilson's Creek National Battlefield, for his research assistance and fine edited manuscript on Henry Guibor's Battery; Bob Maher for his initial assignment that ignited the authors' interest in the project; Dr. Tom and Karen Sweeney for their interest and assistance; Andy and Dina Thomas for the superb artwork and assistance in procuring pictures for the book; Steven C. Wetlesen for volunteering to read and comment on an early draft of the manuscript; Theodore P. Savas for his numerous maps and editing assistance; and Deena Deason of Savas Publishing Company for the index.

Several libraries and historical societies have generously donated their time, help and guidance through the fragmented records of this early portion of Missouri's Civil War past. We are especially indebted to the following staffs and institutions: the Curtis Laws Wilson Library at the University of Missouri-Rolla for their patience and willingness to go the "extra mile"; Jennifer Richardson and her staff at the Carthage Public Library; the State Archives of Missouri in Jefferson City; the Missouri State Historical Society in St. Louis; the State Historical Society of Missouri in Columbia; the Carthage Civil War Museum; Springfield Public Library; the Greene County Historical Society; the Wilson's Creek Battlefield Research Library; and the Rolla Public Library.

Finally, we are especially indebted to two people, Mary L. Hinze and Theodore P. Savas, for their tireless help and patience in completing this project. Writers require others they can rely on for honesty and encouragement during what is often a grueling process. Mary and Ted provided both.

David C. Hinze
Karen J. Farnham
Rolla, Missouri
May 1997

The Missouri weather continued to ruin the best laid plans of the Union colonel. His small column of two regiments, two batteries of artillery and 32 wagons trudged and rolled north under a searing July sun, the overbearing heat slowing the progress of his gray-uniformed Federals. Normally a dusty trail, the road upon which the men marched remained slippery from recent rains and added to the difficulty of moving the column. The Union infantry was moving from the small village of Carthage, Missouri, hoping to strike the pro-Southern Missouri State Guard militia troops led by the state's displaced governor, Claiborne Fox Jackson.[1]

Thirty-six-year-old Col. Franz Sigel pushed his men forward with old fashioned European discipline acquired from the Karlsruhe Academy in Germany. The short but stocky leader surveyed the ground ahead from the back of his jet black horse. The small well-tended farms sprinkled across the rolling prairie reminded Sigel of European battlefields, where he earned his reputation as a military commander. Local informants told him the Southern militia was camped north of Carthage. How far north and whether the information was accurate remained unclear. Sigel had spent his entire military career attempting to gain independent commands to demonstrate his talents and impress his superiors. But fame and glory on the continent that spawned Napoleon and Frederick the

Great had somehow eluded him. His political connections and experience in Europe, however, enabled Sigel to gain an opportunity to lead the advance Federal strike force into southwest Missouri, where his objective was to capture and destroy the largest group of organized Southern sympathizers in the divided border state. That he did so as a colonel and not a general rankled the feisty German. As the morning wore on he became worried about his inability to find the enemy.[2]

The quiet muggy morning stillness was shattered when Federal pickets opened fire near a small farm house on the left side of the road. Sigel spurred his horse forward to determine the cause of the commotion. In the distance he could see homespun-clad Southern horsemen attempting to contest the advance of his column. The Rebels fired and held their ground, slowing the Federal march. Excited and relieved to have discovered the enemy, Sigel raised his small brass telescope and trained it on the troublesome cavalry. Impatient to clear the way, he ordered two of his 6-lb. artillery pieces forward to add their firepower to his skirmish line. The cannons unlimbered in front of the congested roadway and delivered a few well-placed shots that scattered the horsemen, who melted away into the Missouri prairie. With the road once again clear, the Union column resumed its march.[3]

The men reached a swollen stream that bisected the road, waded into the waist deep water and continued on, trudging up a gentle hill on the far side. When they reached the crest they were rewarded with a good view of the surrounding terrain—and the enemy. The Southerners were taking up a position on the crest of a ridge about one mile to the north. To the confident Federals they appeared as a motley collection of armed men fielding a few pieces of artillery, struggling to align themselves for battle.[4]

After marching blindly through the state, the German colonel had finally found his enemy. Now, perhaps, he would also find the glory and fame he felt he so justly deserved.

* * *

Discontent

Political and military upheaval were nothing new to Missourians. Prior to the outbreak of the Civil War the state was the center of controversy for many years. Even her birth was troubled. The request for statehood evoked nationwide controversy over the slavery issue and threatened to tear the country apart. The enabling legislation quietly went to a House of Representatives committee for consideration in February of 1819. While the bill was under deliberation, first term New York Congressman James Tallmadge, Jr. attached an amendment to the bill with the purpose of gradually eliminating slavery in Missouri. Tallmadge's plan, which may have eventually provided a blueprint to end slavery throughout the United States, banned the transfer of additional slaves into the new state and proclaimed that children of the current slave population would become free when they reached the age of twenty-five. The proposal ignited a firestorm of protest from many Congressmen, while others praised it as an important and far-seeing innovation.[1]

Most Missourians viewed Tallmadge's proposal unfavorably. The early French and Spanish settlers had introduced slavery into the territory, and by 1820 slavery was imbedded in the state's economy. By 1840 slaves comprised one-sixth of the state's population. Many Missourians viewed the Tallmadge Amendment as simply "Yankee meddling" in their affairs. Anti-slavery groups in the North gathered to secure the passage of Tallmadge's measure. Throughout the South, counter demonstrations and meetings denounced Northern attempts to shackle the spread of their "peculiar institution." Southerners understood that if the Northern population continued to grow, Southern political clout in Congress would diminish. They also understood the implications of losing control of the Federal Senate if Missouri entered the Union as a free state. Maintaining a balance of power in the Senate, where each state wielded two votes, would allow Southern politicians to counter anti-slavery policies.[2]

When Congress reconvened in December of 1819, Missouri's application for statehood dominated the session. Although Tallmadge was defeated in his bid for reelection, his colleague, John W. Taylor, reintroduced the controversial amendment. The measure snarled the legislative process in both houses of Congress. During the impasse a northern district of Massachusetts—Maine—applied for statehood. There was now an opportunity to play Maine against Missouri by allowing the former to enter the Union as a free state, and the latter as a slave holding entity, thereby maintaining the balance of power in the Senate. The Speaker of the House, Kentuckian Henry Clay, together with Senator Jesse B. Thomas of Illinois, fashioned the compromise to grant both territories statehood under those conditions. A key provision of what became known as the Missouri Compromise involved a dividing line drawn at latitude 36° 30', along the southern boundary of Missouri. Slavery was prohibited north of the compromise line, but the institution remained legal below Missouri's proposed southern border. Anxious to avoid serious conflict, Congress passed the Missouri Compromise by an overwhelming majority. The crisis involving slavery forced the antagonists in Congress and the nation to compromise over the problem of black servitude, but Missouri, a state born out of controversy, faced a divided future.[3]

For thirty years the Missouri Compromise remained in effect. Missouri's geographic location, however, propelled the state into the national spotlight again during the middle of the turbulent 1850s. Once again the overriding issue was . . . slavery. The expansion of black chattel into the Nebraska Territory (in what eventually became the state of Kansas) brought the issue to the forefront of public attention. A second politically negotiated settlement known as the

Compromise of 1850 failed to solve the nation's problems. The violence in Kansas and Missouri that followed passage of the agreement presented the country with a glimpse of the approaching war that would soon engulf the nation.

The controversy began in earnest when the Nebraska territory, on Missouri's western border, was divided into two sections, Kansas and Nebraska. The division was part of the compromise over the route of a transcontinental railroad. Without gaining something in return, Southerners refused to assist Stephen A. Douglas, Chairman of the Committee on Territories, in realizing his dream of building a railroad across the midwest. Southern politicians demanded the abrogation of that section of the Missouri Compromise that forbade slavery north of the latitude 36° 30', thereby allowing the extension of slavery in the newly-created Kansas territory. Douglas, in response, crafted the controversial Kansas-Nebraska Act. The new law called for a repeal of the Missouri Compromise and the introduction of popular sovereignty into American politics. A reluctant Congress passed the bill and President Franklin Pierce signed the legislation into law in May 1854. The politicians seemed oblivious to the future hardships the new law would create. Indeed, the Kansas-Nebraska Act cast the border territories into a terrifying period of confusion and violence.[4]

Stephen Douglas' Popular Sovereignty allowed the citizens of a territory to decide the slavery issue by voting to accept or reject the institution in a general election. Douglas and other politicians failed to understand how this issue's emotional impact would play to those clinging to the radical fringes of the political spectrum. Exterior meddling by the several factions involved turned a basic exercise in democracy into a heated controversy with the potential for bloodshed. As a result, Kansas and Missouri became the first battlegrounds over the issue of extending slavery.[5]

Although Kansans went to the polls in 1855 to decide the future of slavery in their new territory, the election results failed to reflect the wishes of the voters. This was largely because slaveholders from the western counties of Missouri crossed the border and voted illegally. As a result, the pro-slavery block in Kansas was provided with a "victory" that lit a fuse on a powder keg that had been simmering for some years.[6]

Violence erupted between the pro-slavery and anti-slavery Kansas factions. Missourians responded to the bloodshed by crossing the border to assist the beleaguered pro-slavery contingent. Their raids into Kansas included the sacking of Lawrence, the center of the anti-slavery coalition. The continued violence inspired both sides to form guerrilla units, which repeatedly raided farms and settlements along the Missouri-Kansas border. The increased violence forced both governors to muster their state militias to patrol the border. It was hoped the presence of armed militia units would dissuade the roaming guerrillas from striking. By 1858, a period of relative calm was restored to the frontier. The deep-seated animosities and blood feuds created over a span of several years, however, continued to bubble just beneath the surface. The violence of the 1850s remained vivid in everyone's memory as the region looked to the turn of the decade.[7]

Despite the growing disorder on Missouri's western border, the remainder of the state continued to grow and prosper. Eastern Missouri continued to develop business ties to the growing Northern economy, while the western half of the state remained sparsely settled and agriculturally based. The population around St. Louis steadily became more cosmopolitan and diverse. Before long residents with predominantly Southern roots, whose families had relocated from Tennessee, Virginia and Kentucky, found themselves in the minority. During the early 1850s these families comprised Missouri's political and economic elite. As the decade wore on, waves of immigrants from both across the country and the Atlantic Ocean arrived. Their presence challenged the preeminent position of Missouri's older and more established Southern families. Tensions increased throughout the state.[8]

By the middle of the decade the traditional Southern power base in Missouri was crumbling, even though the changing situation remained hidden to many observers. New settlers from a variety of ethnic backgrounds rushed to enjoy the economic prosperity in the eastern portion of the state. The newcomers settled by the thousands in the St. Louis area and the Missouri River's fertile valleys. The most recent wave of settlers came from Germany, fleeing the Revolution of 1848 and the consequences that swam in its wake. They remained so strongly committed to the failed revolt that they still identified themselves as "forty-eighters." Missouri politics slowly but steadily became more diverse, as the quarrelsome factions fought for control of business and society.[9]

In many ways the presidential election of 1860 characterized the changes underway in Missouri. Just a few months prior to the election Missourians sent Claiborne Fox Jackson to the governor's mansion in Jefferson City. The charismatic Jackson, a Kentuckian by birth, moved to his adopted state at the age of twenty. After immersing himself in a variety of business endeavors, he was elected to the Missouri House of Representatives and thereafter to the state senate. The years following the Mexican War found the young politician ardently championing the extension of slavery into the new territories. His rise to the top of state politics arose during the turmoil of the 1850s, which conveniently tossed Jackson up as the consensus candidate for governor in 1860. The schism in the national Democratic party that year, however, caused him great anguish. Although he was politically closer to John C. Breckinridge's wing of the party, he remained loyal to the Stephen A. Douglas faction—but only to insure his own election to the state house. As a result, he openly campaigned across the state in favor of saving the Union, successfully painting himself as a pro-Union politician. Behind the scenes Jackson remained in close contact with Southern politicians and planned to utilize these connections if and when the opportunity arose to pull his state out of the Union. Jackson, according to one of his aides, "[was] the most conspicuous leader of this movement." A Southerner by birth, he was "a true son of the South, warmly attached to the land that had given him birth, and to her people, who were his own kindred." Missouri's new governor quietly let it be known in his close circle of friends that he hoped Missouri would do her duty when the time came and stand by her Southern heritage.

Once elected he spoke his mind at his inauguration, publicly proclaiming that Missouri would join and assist any states if the North attempted military action to restrain secession. Thomas L. Snead, a chronicler of the early months of the Civil War in Missouri and friend of the governor's, described Jackson as "tall, erect and dignified; a vigorous thinker, and a fluent and forcible speaker, always interesting, and often eloquent. . .with positive opinions on all public questions, and the courage to express and uphold them." His

Claiborne Fox Jackson
Missouri Historical Society, St. Louis

physical appearance—complete with long hair swept to one side and a thick beard that gave him a biblical countenance—radiated confidence. But Jackson's failure to accurately represent his core political beliefs to the general populace exacerbated the level of discontent within the state.[10]

The gubernatorial election was not the only political debate raging within Missouri in the autumn of 1860. The national presidential election included all four candidates on the state-wide ballot. Vice-president John C. Breckinridge represented the Southern Democrats, while John Bell of Tennessee headed a new political entity called the Constitutional Union Party. Neighboring Senator Stephen A. Douglas of Illinois represented the Northern Democratic Party, and remained extremely popular throughout Missouri. The Republican Party, participating in only its second national election, ran a virtual unknown at the head of its ticket: Illinois politician Abraham Lincoln. The four candidates represented a cross section of political opinions.[11]

The most vocal of Missouri's citizens involved in the campaign consisted of a small faction of pro-Lincoln and anti-slavery German immigrants. Lincoln's supporters organized, marched and gave exuberant speeches on their candidate's behalf. They managed to carry the areas where the Germans dominated the population base. Outside of the German sphere of influence, however, seventy percent of Missourians voted for either Douglas or Bell. When the final results were posted, Douglas gained the largest plurality of Missouri's votes. His margin in the badly-splintered victory was narrow, 58,801 votes to Bell's 58,372. Breckinridge managed 31,317 votes, while Lincoln ran a distant fourth with 17,028 votes.[12]

The results of the vote demonstrated that Missourians as a whole wished to steer a moderate course through the nation's growing sectional strife. The positions espoused by Douglas and Bell appealed to the state's citizens, who desired to avoid radical solutions to the state's—and the country's—problems. Many viewed Douglas as the only candidate who could heal the widening national rift. While the "Little Giant," as Douglas was popularly known, was Missouri's choice to lead the nation, Lincoln carried the more populous Northern states and gained an anemic electoral victory. His success, which galvanized the opinions of the radical elements in

Missouri and across much of the South, initiated a call for secession from the Union.[13]

The majority of Missourians were appalled by the Southern demand for the destruction of the country. The state's geographical location in the middle of the nation, coupled with its diverse citizenry, political and otherwise, classified it as a border state. A string of states from Delaware to Missouri separated the squabbling factions. Inevitably, the divided loyalties in these areas turned them into early political and eventually military battlegrounds. If Missouri joined the South and added her star to the Confederate flag, her proximity to the major Northern city of Chicago would force the North to position thousands of troops west of the Mississippi River. If the state fell under Union control, it would provide a solid anchor for the Federal western flank and a convenient invasion route into the Trans-Mississippi Confederacy.

By this time a collage of mixed feelings and bad blood had spread across the state. Throughout Missouri Unionists' counties lay next to areas of pro-Southern sympathy. Within many counties there were islands of divided sentiment. Some towns displayed the stars and stripes while others, a few miles distant, flew only the state flag—a sign of Southern loyalty. This fragmentation created a difficult situation for the politicians attempting to lead the state and the military authorities charged with maintaining order within its borders. Not all of the residents had declared their loyalty by late 1860. Many remained neutral and hoped to avoid the coming turmoil. It would not be long before virtually everyone's lives would be touched by the chaos and bloodshed about to be visited upon Missouri's rolling prairies.[14]

Like the nation itself, the main issue dividing Missourians was slavery. By 1860, the state's peculiar institution was no longer the potent economic force it had once been, although it retained a strong psychological hold on the citizenry. The largest pockets of black labor were concentrated primarily in the counties along the Missouri River, from Jefferson City west to the frontier settlement of Kansas City. Local citizens referred to this area as "Little Dixie," because of the Southern background of its residents and its agricultural base. Slavery in Little Dixie provided a much-needed labor force in a region perpetually beset by labor shortages. Governor Jackson's political base of support was centered in these counties. The eastern portion of the state, contrarily, with its expanding population enjoyed a plentiful work force. Immigrants supplied the rapidly growing manufacturing and shipping industries with steady workers. Missouri's diversified economy became less reliant on slavery and agriculture, which in turn added to the growing debate over the future of the institution within the state.[15]

With the election of a Republican president and an emerging controversy over slavery, Governor Jackson decided to call a special state convention to discuss the issue of secession. Missourians elected 99 delegates to convene in the Cole County court house, located approximately in the center of the state. The delegates, who found the small meeting room cramped and unsuitable for their needs, accepted the offer of the Mercantile Library and its spacious facilities and moved the convention to St. Louis. This proved helpful to the pro-Union men in the delegation because the scene of the meeting shifted away from Little Dixie into a more neutral or pro-Union environment. In retrospect, the Union men need not have feared meeting elsewhere, for Missouri's citizens selected primarily Unionists from their congressional districts to attend the meeting. Missourians hoped to remain more objective in the debate over slavery and secession than the conventions meeting in the deep Southern states. Economic survival for the majority of Missouri's population, after all, did not depend on the continuance of slavery. Transcripts of the meeting reveal that the convention attendees participated in heated debates on the slavery problem. In the end the delegates voted to keep Missouri neutral and remain in the Union.

The decision was a blow to those who hoped Missouri would join other Southern states that seceded from the Union after Lincoln's election. The momentum for secession, if any existed, was temporarily stalled.[16]

The Germans

The Federal soldiers who participated in the campaign that culminated in the Battle of Carthage were composed primarily of
German immigrants. Many Missourians questioned why these recent arrivals were so eager to fight to keep their new country united,
especially when so many natives either remained neutral or joined
the Confederacy. Their motivation was largely a result of their participation in the failed revolt that had swept across the European
continent in 1848. Many Europeans, especially in Germany, attempted to overthrow governments viewed as autocratic in the hope
of installing more liberal, democratic regimes. The monarchies used
military force to strike back against the revolutionaries. The conflict
was short and vicious, and the defeated rebels were forced to either
flee their homelands or risk being thrown in jail—or worse. Many of
the defeated revolutionaries migrated to America, attracted by its
comparatively liberal democratic principles and the economic opportunities it presented.[1]

Missouri and other midwestern states with a history of rugged
individualism attracted large numbers of the failed "forty-eighters."
Most of them arrived in St. Louis in the 1850s, a period of great
change in both the country and Missouri. Just as manufacturing and
industry had altered the face of St. Louis, the new arrivals changed
the demographics of the town. By 1860 Missouri's German popula-

tion of 88,000 ranked sixth in the nation. The majority lived and worked in the eastern half of the state. The families who made the long and hazardous trip to the region were following the advice of Gottfried Duden's enthusiastic newspaper accounts of the area. Duden, himself a recently-arrived immigrant, claimed the hills and valleys of the area reminded him of their fertile homeland and the Rhine River valley. The new arrivals brought their hard work ethic and failed dreams of the 1848 Revolution to their new home. According to the 1860 census, there were more than 50,000 Germans in and around St. Louis. Most lived in enclaves or neighborhoods that reminded them of the Old Country, parochial close-knit communities that preserved their language and heritage for themselves and their children. The sheer size of the German population and homogenous background gave them political power in their newly adopted communities. As the country moved toward disunion, the German's used their new-found political voice to speak out on issues important to them.[2]

Slavery was a key issue with Missouri's staunchly-abolitionist German population. As the German's rallied and railed against the institution, slavery's economic underpinnings were being eroded by the industrialization and modernization of Missouri's eastern counties. Railroads and steamboats linked St. Louis' bustling economy to eastern markets, transforming the region and making it less dependent on trade with the South and the western part of Missouri. Reliance on slave labor lessened accordingly. Emotional ties with this issue proved more difficult to cut. Sixty-seven percent of Missouri's population traced its roots to Southern states, and many still had family members living south of the Ohio River and below the Mason-Dixon Line. Secession, however, would cripple St. Louis' expanding economy. Businessmen in St. Louis knew that the state was rich in natural materials, including lead, coal, granite and limestone. Secession would isolate Missouri from the Northern industrial states and thus sever markets for these products.[3]

The attitude of the Germans toward slavery was not difficult to understand. They had only recently arrived from a country whose political and social conditions reflected, in many respects, the slave's plight in America. The immigrants perceived slavery as a tear in the social fabric of American society. Throughout the midwest German newspapers assaulted the institution. Congressional passage of the Kansas-Nebraska Act in 1854 resulted in a political realignment of the German population in the St. Louis area. Initially, the refugees supported the Democratic party, but many Germans changed affiliations when the party supported popular sovereignty in Kansas. To many Germans, it appeared Congress was attempting to break a promise on an issue already settled with the 1820 Missouri Compromise. The fear of slavery's expansion rallied the immigrants to support anti-slavery causes throughout the country, which included support for the containment policies offered by the fledgling Republican party.[4]

The new political organization quickly flourished amongst the tight-knit refugee community. Prominent men within the German neighborhoods were soon deeply involved in Republican politics. Prior to the election of 1860, Missourian Frank Blair, Jr., a native Kentuckian and prominent Missouri attorney, rallied the local German population and organized it into a powerful political force. Blair gained control of the Republican party in St. Louis when he returned from the Chicago nominating convention after helping Lincoln onto the Republican party ticket. His rhetoric held the German-dominated audience spellbound, and they eagerly responded to his calls to support the new party's nominee.[5]

In St. Louis, the Republican message quickly became identified as the German position. The same anti-slavery message fell largely on deaf ears in the remainder of the state. The immigrants formed caravans to take their message outside of St. Louis but were met by jeering and sometimes violent crowds. In response the German politicians formed local clubs called "Wide Awakes." These groups were similar to traditional associations in the German community known as "Turner Clubs"—local organizations that provided entertainment, meeting places and athletic competition. The main headquarters of the Turner Club in St. Louis and their local branches quickly became hubs of Republican activity.[6]

The formation of the Wide Awakes had significant ramifications because it was the initial step in transforming the power of the Germans from a political movement into a military force. Many of the men who answered the early call to arms in July of 1861 came from this organization. Fearing that the Wide Awakes' supporters and their deeds were too closely aligned with the local Republican party—and would thus tarnish its reputation—the St. Louis Republican leadership split off a segment of the more radical members into a para-military organization. Approximately 500 volunteers responded to the call to arms. Marching with carved wooden rifles, they began to secretly train in local Turner Halls. Military veterans from the failed revolution served as drill instructors for the new recruits. Weekly gatherings labeled "Preservation of the Union" meetings added military training to their agendas.[7]

In addition to these closely guarded weekly gatherings, where only German eyes could hear and observe, full-scale military drills took place in the dead of night. Sawdust spread across the plank floors of the Turner Halls deadened the heavy boots that stamped out military drills in preparation for war. To outsiders, however, these new cabals appeared merely as patriotic groups with little or no connection to the Republican party. While the names of these organizations, such as "Union Clubs" or "Home Guards," did little to obscure their political leanings, the Germans managed to largely hide their activities from the local political leaders who failed to share their enthusiasm for Republican politics. On the surface, Missouri, and especially St. Louis, remained calm.[8]

*   *   *

While the Germans secretly prepared for a military confrontation, secessionists in St. Louis developed their own organized military units. Pro-Southern men began forming "Minute Men" organizations, named after the patriots who answered the early call to arms in the American Revolution. Composed of area natives, Minute Men organizations were not as subdued in their operations as the German-supported Union Clubs. The Southern-leaning groups employed local state militia organizations to identify and recruit members into their association. The Southern sympathizers were led by local leaders who felt it their duty to resist the growing abolitionist power in St. Louis. Political leadership on both sides concluded that a confrontation was close at hand, and that military strength to support their respective political points of view was a necessity.[9]

As both camps continued to recruit and train members, they discovered that assembling enough weapons and other military equipment to arm them was a difficult task. Each side smuggled in muskets in small quantities, hoping to obtain enough weapons to equip a single regiment. The governor of Illinois, Richard Yates, illegally assisted the pro-Union camp by ferrying weapons across the Mississippi River. By early 1861 the German factions were able to field a reasonably well-armed and competently drilled regimental-sized body of troops. The men proudly considered themselves combat ready, and their test of arms would not be long in coming.[10]

The need for weapons remained acute, especially for the Southern organizations. Tempers flared across the state when the Federal arsenal in the western part of Missouri near Liberty was broken into and ransacked by Southern partisans. Its commander, Maj. Nathaniel Grant (a relative of Ulysses S. Grant), faced a large gathering of militia who patiently listened to the major's speech concerning the impropriety of stealing Federal property. When Grant completed his lecture, 200 men from the surrounding counties stormed through the old iron gate and pilfered a large quantity of flintlock weapons and gunpowder. In addition to the small arms, several howitzers, largely of the 6-lb. variety and used by the Missouri militia during the Mexican War, also changed hands. These antique weapons, which were quickly distributed to the local militia throughout Clay, Cass and Jackson counties, would resurface a few months later in the hands of the Missouri State Guard.[11]

While the Liberty arsenal was being sacked, the state's political leaders continued to escalate their involvement in military matters. Forty-year-old Frank P. Blair, Jr., a member of an old and distinguished St. Louis family known for its rough and tumble style of frontier politics, played a leading role. Blair's father, Francis, had been an advisor to President Andrew Jackson, while Frank's brother Montgomery was the Postmaster General in the Lincoln cabinet. Although the family owned slaves, the Blair's fought against the spread of slavery into the lands acquired from the United States' defeat of Mexico. The junior Blair entered Congress on the Free Soil ticket in 1856 but was defeated in a bid for re-election two years later. As the critical election of 1860 approached, the Blair family strengthened its political hand by allying itself with Abraham Lincoln. Lincoln rewarded this support with key appointments and the ear of the president-elect on critical issues.[12]

Continuing the family's political tradition, Frank Blair Jr. ran for a congressional seat again in 1860. Relying heavily on pro-German support, Blair was swept into office on the Union party ticket. His concern over the simmering situation in St. Louis, however, delayed his departure for Washington, D.C. Blair feared the more openly militant Confederate-leaning Minute Men would either make a dash for the critical supplies at the Federal arsenal in St. Louis or unduly influence the city's political leadership. Not one easily intimidated, Blair decided to counter the bold Southern demonstrations of military strength by allowing the Germans to display their military prowess. Before long, the main Turner Hall at 7th and Chestnut Streets assumed the appearance of a barricaded fortress, complete with stockpiles of gunpowder and ammunition. The Missouri politician continued to aggressively raise funds across the area, successfully purchasing another 70 rifled muskets for his loyal followers.[13]

The political and quasi-military chess match continued. Southern Minute Men responded to the escalating situation by drilling in St. Louis' old but still handsome two-story Berthold mansion, located just behind the court house. The building became a rallying point for the community's pro-secession men, who congregated about the imposing structure to boast how they would whip the lop-eared Dutchmen if only an opportunity to do so presented itself. The Berthold mansion was a natural place to gather for those unhappy with Blair's rise to power. The manor previously housed Democratic party headquarters, and the current occupants were continually frustrated with the Blair family—especially after the Republican victory in 1860. By the time violence exploded in the streets of St. Louis, nearly five companies of Minute Men, over 400 citizen-soldiers, were ready to defend pro-Southern ideals in the divided city.[14]

Both sides continued to train even though a lack of weapons remained a problem. The shortage caused both factions to covet the large cache of armaments stored in the St. Louis arsenal, a sprawling 56-acre complex south of the city. Surrounded by a wall ten feet high, the facility's storage buildings housed 60,000 muskets and 90,000 pounds of gunpowder, together with more than a million cartridges and other valuable military items. Whoever controlled the Federal arsenal would be able to equip an army of followers and control the state. Both sides hungered to get their hands on this valuable prize, yet each realized that a pre-emptive strike against a Federal institution could turn public opinion within the state against their cause. As a result, the Minute Men and the Union Clubs impatiently awaited the outcome of a statewide convention being held in St. Louis. While Missourians debated the prospects for secession and the possibility of war, the St. Louis arsenal sat squarely in the center of the developing maelstrom.[15]

Despite his recent precautions, Frank Blair expended considerable emotional energy fretting over the possibility of the St. Louis arsenal falling into pro-Southern hands. He had every reason to be concerned. Across the South state governments were seizing control of Federal property—including several arsenals. In Jefferson City, Governor Jackson outwardly remained calm, showing little or no sign that he was preparing a move against the St. Louis' munitions depot. A different story was being played out behind closed doors. The opportunistic Jackson, waiting for the spark that would allow him to move against the arsenal, ordered men to be prepared for just such an event. Jackson also knew he had an advantage over Blair because of his friendly relations with Maj. William H. Bell, the keeper of the arsenal. Widely rumored to have Southern leanings, Bell regularly kept the governor informed of the current status of the complex. In a deft countermove, Blair arranged for a squad of soldiers to be stationed at the barracks inside the compound, neutralizing somewhat the cozy relationship between Jackson and Bell. The Missouri legislature passed a resolution against Blair's action, but it failed to gain the removal of the troops.[16]

On January 24, 1861, the brigadier general of the Missouri State Militia, New York native Daniel M. Frost, rode to the arsenal to hold discussions with Bell and explain Governor Jackson's views on the simmering controversy. Frost, an 1844 West Point graduate and Mexican War veteran, was openly supporting the Southern cause. He surveyed the situation at the arsenal for the governor and quietly negotiated an agreement with Bell that state rather than Federal authority would take precedence if the Federal government attempted to place more soldiers in the compound. Returning to Jefferson City, Frost reported his successful trip to Jackson. Both men realized they must be ready to strike quickly and decisively if an opportunity to gain control of the arsenal presented itself.[17]

Frank Blair was outraged that a pro-Southern sympathizer was in command of a Federal arsenal. The problem was further agitated by Bell on January 22, 1861, when he refused to allow more of Blair's men into the arsenal, ostensibly to assist in its defense. The next day Blair telegraphed Montgomery, his well-connected and powerful brother in Washington, D.C. Three days later, on January 25, a politically-inspired ax severed Bell from his command of the facility. Rather than accept a new assignment—Bell was heavily invested in local real estate—he retired from the military and moved out to his farm in St. Charles. He was replaced by Brevet Major Peter V. Hagner, a man without known Southern leanings. Blair's blood pressure, meanwhile, continued to climb when pro-Southern forces in Arkansas seized the Little Rock arsenal in February and another group waylaid supplies destined for Fort Smith. The arsenal in Fayetteville, Arkansas, fell on April 22.[18]

While the thus far bloodless struggle for the St. Louis arsenal continued, Frank Blair faced a crucial decision about his future. As a Congressman-elect, Blair needed to depart for Washington to take his seat in the House of Representatives. With his political connections, however, Blair believed that he was the only person able to prevent the city—and possibly the state—from falling into Southern hands. During this period a series of rumors circulated through the city of an impending attack on the arsenal. With the compound only lightly defended, Blair, through his brother Montgomery, strongly urged lame duck President James Buchanan to send troops to deter an attack on the complex. Blair knew his plea was likely to fall on deaf ears. While Buchanan fiddled, military groups in the newly seceded states continued to confiscate Federal property. Buchanan seemed unwilling to take decisive measures to stop the illegal action. Thus Blair was mildly shocked when President Buchanan approved the transfer of a small contingent of troops from Kansas to aid in defense of the St. Louis arsenal. This action, although outwardly nothing more than a minor reshuffling of soldiers, triggered a series of events that few could have imagined.[19]

Nathaniel Lyon
John Bradbury Collection

*   *   *

With commanding general Winfield Scott's orders in hand, red-headed Capt. Nathaniel Lyon disembarked his squad of blue-uniformed men from the Union Pacific railroad depot on the night of February 7. Lyon's command swiftly marched south of town to the arsenal. Neither its commander nor his men had any real understanding of the tumultuous political situation they were entering. The small contingent of soldiers settled into the arsenal's cold stone barracks, where they began familiarizing themselves with the compound and its defenses.[20]

Nathaniel Lyon was not the type of man to come into a situation and calm discontented waters. He was outspoken and obstinate about his anti-slavery views, and cooperation with others always seemed an elusive trait for the hot tempered man from Connecticut. A West Point graduate with the class of 1841, Lyon had denounced the country's participation in the Mexican War, as did many of his fellow New Englanders. Nevertheless he followed orders and served in the conflict, picking up a wound along the way and earning a brevet rank in the process. Lyon's views against slavery hardened during his 1854-1861 tour of duty in Kansas. Although he had been a non-abolitionist Democrat, Lyon became an ardent Republican when he witnessed the breakdown of law and order on the frontier over the issue of human bondage. Congressman Blair, who was seeking a dedicated and impassioned personality to help him gain control of the precarious situation within the city, had found his man.[21]

The day following his arrival was a sobering one for Lyon, who was taken aback when a survey of the arsenal revealed the immense quantity of arms and munitions it housed. The captain busied himself with the security of the facility, but within a few days found himself mired in the political machinations of the fractionalized city. By the end of his first week in St. Louis, Lyon, primarily through Blair, had made many pro-Union contacts. In his mind, Southern sympathizers were the enemy.[22]

Besides angering some of the town's people with his staunch pro-Union views, Lyon became involved in a struggle for command of the arsenal with Major Hagner, who had assumed control of the compound from Bell but a few weeks prior to Lyon's arrival. Seeking to differentiate their respective and likely conflicting roles, Hagner steadfastly maintained that he controlled the actual compound, while Lyon only commanded his troops from Kansas. A series of disagreements concerning dates of rank, temporary or brevet ranks and other similar matters spiraled out of control between the two men. As he was wont, Lyon's temper flared over the disputes and he stormed off to see Brig. Gen. William S. Harney, commander of the Department of the West. By the time he stomped into Harney's St. Louis headquarters, Lyon was convinced matters would be settled in his favor. Harney, who remembered the hot-headed captain from their previous service together at Fort Scott, Kansas, stunned Lyon by denying his request for command of the entire arsenal. Defeated in his behind-the-scenes grab for power, Lyon's gaze shifted to the Blair camp. He was finally coming to understand that no one in the city had more power than the rough and tumble politician. Attaching his future to Blair's obviously rising star proved to be a shrewd move.[23]

It was not long before Blair introduced Lyon to the Committee of Public Safety, a group dominated by the Congressman-elect. The Committee, responsible for keeping the peace in St. Louis, had somehow managed to remain broadly popular with a wide cross section of the townspeople. Many St. Louisans would look to the Committee to choose the proper side if a conflict broke out, and Blair wanted that body and Nathaniel Lyon to take each other's measure. Much to the dissatisfaction of the Southern men of the city, Lyon bonded easily with the group and soon became part of the inner circle of decision makers in St. Louis. In Lyon, Blair had found a man similar to himself. They shared many common personality traits, including a passionate anti-slavery sentiment. More importantly, they shared an eagerness to fight for their beliefs. It was during one of their frequent visits together that Blair quietly informed Lyon of the sixteen companies of men secretly organized in the German community.[24]

Throughout February, encouraged by Blair's support, Lyon turned his attentions once again on gaining full control of the arsenal. Rumors circulated that Hagner and Harney possessed pro-Southern sympathies. Although no substantive evidence of such leanings accompanied the rumors, they raised suspicions in a city already divided along sectional lines. The gossip focused public attention on Harney, a strict disciplinarian and no nonsense army veteran of forty-three years. Harney's wife, a St. Louis native from a prominent wealthy family, saw to it that the general enjoyed socializing with those who possessed a Southern outlook on the current state of affairs. The veteran's wife was responsible for his choosing to be stationed in St. Louis, for she liked the city's culture and wanted to be close to her friends. Although Lyon desperately sought information that would bolster this unfounded hearsay, he could not find any evidence to justify Harney's removal from command. Nevertheless, the rumors damaged Harney's reputation among pro-Union men and increased the tension between Lyon and his superior.[25]

Late in the day on April 12, word arrived that Southern forces in Charleston, South Carolina, under the command of Gen. P. G. T. Beauregard, had bombarded Fort Sumter. The open act of aggression outraged pro-Union sympathizers, while Southerners rejoiced at the news and paraded through the streets of St. Louis, raising the Southern national flag side by side with Old Glory. Throughout the state, especially in pro-Southern Little Dixie, few could have guessed the consequences of the action or what would happen to a divided Missouri.[26]

Three days later President Lincoln reacted to the attack on Federal property by asking for 75,000 volunteers to put down the rebellion. His call to arms created a flurry of activity in Missouri. Members of both the Minute Men and the Union Clubs paraded through the streets, voicing either pleasure or disdain for what had transpired in Charleston harbor and Lincoln's consequent reaction to the bombardment. Governor Jackson promptly rejected Lincoln's call for Missouri to contribute soldiers to attack sister Southerners:

> Your dispatch of the 15th instant, making a call on Missouri for four regiments of men for immediate service, has been received. There can be, I apprehend, no doubt that the men are intended to form part of the President's army to make war upon the people of the seceded states. Your requisition, in my judgment, is illegal, unconstitutional, and revolutionary in its object, inhuman and diabolical and cannot be complied with. Not one man will the State of Missouri furnish to carry on the holy crusade.[27]

Jackson's harsh response widened the substantial political gulf that already divided the citizens of Missouri. Some pro-Union members of the St. Louis militia resigned, believing that the organization represented Southern sentiments. The majority of the militia remained loyal to the governor. In St. Louis, Nathaniel Lyon seethed with anger when he heard the news concerning Fort Sumter. Jackson's reaction to the president's call to arms simply confirmed his opinion that the governor and state militia were traitors. The leader of the state militia, Daniel Frost, also troubled Lyon. On the afternoon of the attack on Fort Sumter, Frost paraded through the streets openly promoting Missouri's secession. Now that fighting had broken out in the east, would Frost organize an attack against the arsenal? Lyon made it known to his pro-Union friends that he was more determined than ever to keep the arsenal—and thus the city and perhaps the state—under Federal control.[28]

The days following Fort Sumter's capitulation were busy ones for Lyon. Plans were developed to arm newly-recruited Illinois troops with muskets from the stockpiles inside the arsenal. Lyon contacted Illinois Governor Richard Yates and discussed an elaborate scheme to transfer the majority of the facility's ordnance to Illinois. He hoped this would make the arsenal a less inviting target for Frost's militia. Despite his recent attempt to fortify the arsenal, Lyon harbored few illusions about its defensive capabilities. A determined attack, he believed, would capture the facility.

Not everyone agreed with that assessment. The local German language newspaper *Angzeiger des Westens* reported to its readers the fine state of readiness inside the compound:

> The courtyard of the arsenal is enclosed by a high wall which is easily defended by a scaffold recently erected behind it. Sentries keep watch, and one shot would call up the entire force. Each of the gates is guarded by a sixty-four pound howitzer, protected by earthworks, and any column that would try to force entry would suffer ruin and death. The cannoneers of these guns are protected from shrapnel. Other cannon are situated to control the railway causeways so as to make an attack from that quarter quite impossible, and others control the walls, so they could destroy an enemy who has taken the walls.[29]

As Lyon attempted to maintain control in St. Louis, reports from the western part of Missouri began to trickle in via telegraph. A flag pole, reportedly 125 feet tall, stood in the center of Kansas City proudly flying the Southern national flag. Throughout the small community Southern flags dotted the buildings—including important public ones. A correspondent from the *Westliche Post* in Jefferson City reported a large pro-secession rally in Boonville. The paper declared it was the largest to date held in favor of the Southern cause. Other newspapers substantiated the ominous news seeping in from the western fringes of the state. The *Mississippi Blatter* received a report from the northwest corner of the state from a St. Joseph citizen who supposedly witnessed "The flag of the secession cause carried through the city and hung in the market square with no opposition." The Kansas City *Business Journal* reported the "feeling in the western portion of Missouri was for secession."

These reports alarmed Blair and Lyon and they became more fearful of a local attack on the arsenal. As a result, security was heightened around the facility. While the citizens watched the tug-of-war played out in the state, the Federal leadership in St. Louis fought one another over control of the coveted arms.[30]

While Lyon entangled himself in the unseemly command dispute, Frank Blair, who had finally vacated St. Louis in favor of Washington D.C., returned with permission for Lyon to arm the German regiments. Instead of simply distributing weapons to the Union Clubs, Lyon disobeyed orders and contributed his after-duty time assisting in the training of new officers. Typical of the officers who signed on to support the Union cause was a former German revolutionary-turned-school superintendent, Franz Sigel. Like the majority of the German population in St. Louis, Sigel had aligned himself with the anti-Southern forces and was anxious to assist his adopted homeland.[31]

Nathaniel Lyon's efforts paid dividends. His prestige within the German community rose as recruits rallied to the Union cause. Even though they remained at personal odds, Lyon finally convinced a reluctant General Harney of the need to strengthen the arsenal's defenses. Soldiers sandbagged the tops of walls, installed artillery at key positions and built ramparts to allow for the placing of additional field pieces. By early April 1861, portholes were cut through the 3' thick walls and nearby trees were removed, creating open fields of fire for the compound's defenders. Munitions were hauled within the walls at Jefferson Barracks, a military encampment south of the arsenal, for fear the material would fall into Southern hands. Lyon restricted the traffic in and out of the facility by instituting a strict pass system under his sole authority. He successfully transformed the lightly defended arsenal into a strongly-held fortress. His decisiveness impressed Union sympathizers and caused considerable distress among the Minute Men.[32]

It was not long before Lyon became embroiled in another dispute with his commander. To avoid surprise, Lyon had posted nightly patrols outside the walls. The Southern-dominated Police Board demanded an end to this illegal patrolling, but Lyon refused. On April 18 Harney backed the Police Board and confined Lyon's men to the arsenal grounds. Harney also ordered Lyon to cease issuing arms without his approval. Disgusted by this turn of events, Blair and Lyon sent wires to Washington D.C. on April 18 and 19, demanding Harney's removal. Blair also sent a wire to Secretary of War Simon Cameron through a trusted friend, Andrew G. Curtin, the governor of Pennsylvania. The message was quickly relayed and later in the day a telegram arrived in St. Louis detailing Lyon to, "Muster in troops at St. Louis and use them for the protection of public property."[33]

Nathaniel Lyon acted quickly. Within a short time he recruited Lt. John M. Schofield, a former West Point graduate, as a mustering officer to swear German regiments into Federal service. Lyon and Blair also organized the best of their units to fill Lincoln's request for four regiments to fill the state's quota. It did not take long before word of these actions spread through the streets and the Germans reported to their local Turner Halls. Enthusiastic cheers erupted when they learned they would be allowed to join the United States Volunteer Army. As midnight approached on April 21, Lyon received more good news: Harney, his long-standing nemesis, had been relieved of command. Lyon could now proceed with his plans without undue interference. By day's end nearly 300 Missourians were sporting the uniform of the Union army.

Lyon and Blair worked feverishly throughout April 22 to muster in an additional 700 enlistees, primarily from the Union Clubs. The new recruits were housed inside the arsenal barracks, substantially strengthening its defense. More welcome news crossed Lyon's desk later that same day. Peter Hagner, Lyon's competitor for independent command of the arsenal, was transferred to Fort Leavenworth to await further assignment. Both Frank and Montgomery Blair, together with Attorney General Edward Bates—also a Missourian—had masterfully used their combined influence in the capital to recall troublesome and politically suspect officers from the state. These key events made it easier for Lyon to solidify his military base in St. Louis, while at the same time shifting the balance of power in Missouri in favor of the Union.[34]

General Harney boarded a train on April 23 destined for the nation's capital. As the day progressed the First Regiment Missouri Volunteers were officially organized and the 1,220 men promptly elected Frank Blair as their colonel. Eager recruits arrived daily at the arsenal's iron gate to muster into the Union army. Additional regiments were created as a result of this ground swell of support. The Second Regiment Missouri Volunteers elected Henry Boernstein as their colonel, while Franz Sigel accepted the colonelcy of the Third Regiment. The Fourth Regiment, 1,207 strong, was commanded by Nicholas Schuettner, a former carpenter. The muster rolls demonstrate that primarily Germans enlisted in Lyon's new regiments, but there were also a smattering of Bohemians from across the river in Illinois, mixed about with Irish surnames.

On May 18, Lyon received orders to organize a fifth regiment, and another 962 men were enrolled in the army with former revolutionary Charles E. Salomon as commander. Sensing that the community was willing to assist in the enlistment of additional soldiers, Lyon encouraged the War Department to grant him permission to enlist a reserve corps. A few days later he received a telegram permitting the formation of the Missouri Reserve Corps, which would become locally known as the Home Guards.[35]

Lyon moved as quickly as possible to turn St. Louis into an armed Union camp. With Harney removed from the situation, he used his newly-acquired authority to dispatch an additional 10,000 rifled-muskets across the river to arm Illinois volunteers. The mass transfer of small arms freed up space in the arsenal for the growing contingent of troops gathering inside its walls. Lyon had orchestrated a remarkable turn of events in St. Louis. A once vulnerable arsenal was now well defended with the original 40-man force expanded into a respectable five regiments.[36]

Governor Jackson reacted to the events in St. Louis by penning an April 17 letter to Jefferson Davis, president of the Confederacy. The letter requested artillery from the recently captured Baton Rouge arsenal be secretly shipped to St. Louis. Davis concurred and agreed to send the weapons. Bolstered by the president's assistance, Jackson boasted that "Missouri can and will put 100,000 men in the field." The governor also called the legislature into session and demanded the body "take measures to perfect the organization and equipment of the Militia and raise money to place the state in the proper attitude for defense." The largely pro-Union legislature, still unwilling to pass a bill that would in effect take Missouri out of the Union, turned down Jackson's demand, which would have led to an armed rebellion within the state. Like the majority of Missourians, the cautious politicians adopted a wait-and-see policy instead of openly choosing sides. Able to read the writing on the wall, the astute Jackson could see that the situation was slipping away from him. The state, he decided, must be taken out of the Union, and he began to formulate plans to affect such a result.

His immediate problem was a lack of troops to confront Lyon, who was unlikely to stand by without a fight and watch Missouri slide into the Confederacy. Frustrated with the balky legislature, Jackson relied on the Militia Act of 1858 to summon part of the state militia to St. Louis for its annual training session. His motive was to gain access to the arsenal and thus control of the political and military situation in the city. Jackson set May 6 as the starting date for militia service.[37]

General Daniel Frost impatiently waited in St. Louis to begin implementing Jackson's plan. Frost, the architect of the 1850s act authorizing the creation of Missouri's militia, planned his strategy carefully. His design was to deploy the militia on the commanding terrain overlooking the western face of the arsenal, dominating the compound in the process. When he arrived to examine the position Frost found the ground occupied by Lyon's field pieces. The frustrated state general had to make do with a sloping piece of terrain at Lindell Grove, two miles from the arsenal on the western edge of St.

Louis. Demonstrating considerable foresight, Lyon continued to anticipate the moves of his adversaries.[38]

While the ground was not of his choosing, Frost managed to pack it with over 800 loyal supporters. Lindell Grove was officially re-designated "Camp Jackson," in honor of the governor. The men drilled in large open fields and marched on "P. G. T. Beauregard" and "Jefferson Davis," two aptly named thoroughfares running through the camp. On May 9, the steamer *J. C. Swan* arrived with four boxes labeled "marble." The crates were quietly removed to the corner of the militia camp, where they remained unopened. Lyon's intelligence network later informed him that the crates held captured artillery pieces and small arms taken from Baton Rouge arsenal.

Lyon maintained a keen interest in the internal operations of the Lindell Grove encampment, insisting to all who would listen that it was nothing more than a nest of Southern traitors. The New England firebrand contended that only swift and decisive action would stop an insurrection. Lyon's appeal to the Committee of Public Safety about moving on the camp, however, was promptly rebuffed. The committee members reminded him that the gathering was entirely legal and most citizens felt the militia failed to pose any more of a threat to the city than did the 8,000 Germans Lyon himself controlled. Dissatisfied, Lyon left the meeting more determined than before to find a way to close Camp Jackson.[39]

Late in the afternoon on May 9, in an incredible display of intelligence gathering, Lyon disguised himself as Frank Blair's blind mother-in-law and boarded a carriage for a drive through Camp Jackson. The steady drilling of troops and the Confederate names on the avenues, to Lyon's way of thinking, were clear signs of treason. Armed with this information, he again attempted to persuade the Committee of Public Safety of the need to close the camp. The only way to ensure that these obvious traitors would not upset the situation in St. Louis, argued Lyon, was to mount a raid on Camp Jackson. After a prolonged and heated discussion, the committee acquiesced to his demands and endorsed Lyon's bold plan. The first significant step in the direction of open warfare within Missouri's borders had been effectively set in motion.[40]

With the blessing of the Committee, Lyon realized he needed to act promptly. Information reached him that Harney was to be reinstated to command in St. Louis and was scheduled to arrive on May 11. On the morning of May 10, Lyon assembled his army inside the arsenal walls. Although spies informed Daniel Frost of unusual movements occurring in the Federal camps, the militia general ignored the warnings. Precisely at 1:00 p.m., seven columns of troops emerged from their assigned locations near the river front and began to march toward Camp Jackson. The largest segment of the strike force left from the arsenal marching parallel to the river. In a well-organized movement, each regiment turned west on different streets and made its way toward the militia encampment. The results of the rigorous training of the regiments reaped dividends for Lyon, whose troops surrounded Camp Jackson at 3:15 p.m.[41]

With the rapid encirclement of the camp complete, Lyon sent in a message demanding the unconditional surrender of Frost's militia. Conferring with his subordinates, Frost decided there was little alternative and accepted the humiliating terms. The militia marched northeast out of the camp through the Channing Gate and turned east onto Olive Boulevard. The men were ordered to stack their weapons and take an oath of allegiance to the Union. A handful accepted and stepped forward, while those who refused were held as prisoners by Lyon's infantry. "This camp is to be surrendered to General Lyon and we with it as prisoners of war," one Southern captive remembered. "We are to be marched to the arsenal tonight and God knows what will become of us."[42]

The swift and bloodless capture of Camp Jackson was a major coup for Lyon, who hoped to use the victory as a bold statement to the pro-secession element in the state. In a bid designed to add to the humiliation of Frost's militia, Lyon decided to march them through the streets to the arsenal, where they would be held for a undetermined period of time. Word of the raid on Camp Jackson quickly spread through the city and a large crowd gathered to observe the surrendered Southerners. Curious onlookers from all quarters of St. Louis, including two soon-to-be-famous Federal generals, Ulysses S. Grant and William T. Sherman, witnessed Lyon's attempts to maneuver the throng of prisoners through a sympathetic crowd. The ill-conceived move proved a recipe for disaster.[43]

Many of the on-lookers were drunk and jeered the Federal soldiers with anti-German taunts. As the march proceeded, Lyon ordered Blair's troops to open their ranks to allow the prisoners to squeeze between them, and the throng of men moved fitfully down Olive Street. The terrain around Camp Jackson favored the onlookers, many of whom occupied a gentle slope rising from the street level north, an excellent vantage point from which to view the procession. At first the Federals encountered nothing worse than verbal epithets. When the column came to a halt a block away from Camp Jackson, more prisoners were shoved into place between the Union soldiers that lined each side of the street. The entire movement threatened to break down completely when Colonel Sigel's Third Regiment blocked the road, but the colonel moved his soldiers, clearing the thoroughfare. The column repeatedly started and stopped, fitfully shuffling toward the arsenal.[44]

The crowd continued to grow, fed by wagon loads of people anxious to witness the spectacle. The throng of humanity pressed in around Lyon's soldiers, who were attempting to navigate down what by now was a very crowded Olive Street. Without warning members of the crowd began pelting the Germans with rocks, bricks and bottles. Before anyone could stop the violence, fighting broke out between individual soldiers and civilians. "The mob first began by insulting our men, without retaliation," wrote Lt. William S. Stewart, Company F, First United States Volunteers, in a note home to his parents:

> Then they threw stones hurting some soldiers, yet the soldiers stood it until the mob began firing pistols, killing one or two and wounding others. Then our men opened fire mowing down about 30, among 15 or 20 of who were killed on the spot. The firing lasted several minutes and the bullets whistled around us in a perfect shower, most of them going over our heads. Our company stood it bravely, ready all the time to engage in the firing, but it did not become necessary.[45]

One teenager in the mob, Philip D. Stephenson, witnessed the chain of events from a different perspective. From his vantage point the Federal soldiers instigated the riot. Stephenson watched as delays in moving the prisoners caused the crowd to press in on the soldiers. At that point, he remembered, a young boy hit Capt. Constantine Blandowski in the leg with a dirt clod. The Federal captain uttered an exclamation mistaken by his men as a command to fire, and the soldiers from his company raised their muskets and discharged them directly into the crowd.[46]

When the breeze finally lifted the smoke, Olive Street looked like the war zone it had become. Twenty-eight of the local citizens, two of the Federal soldiers and three of the militia lay dead in what came to be known as the St. Louis Riot. The civilian casualties included a boy of twelve and a girl just turned fourteen. "We went over to the grove immediately after the occurrence," wrote a reporter for the *Missouri Republican*, an anti-Lyon paper, "and a more fearful and ghastly site is seldom seen." Fearing a wider outbreak of violence, a large number of civilians fled the city.[47]

News of Camp Jackson's surrender and the debacle that followed swept across the telegraph wires. In Jefferson City, a stunned Governor Jackson called the legislature into a midnight session. Many of the lawmakers sleepily stumbled into the chamber, some dressed in their night clothes, others carrying weapons at their sides. Rumors of Federal troop movements up the Missouri River to the capital prompted a mild hysteria among the citizens of Jefferson City. Within fifteen minutes after being gaveled into session, the Assembly passed the Military Bill they had previously rejected. The new law gave Jackson widespread power to react to the military emergency. One of his first actions was to appoint Sterling Price, a former governor and Mexican War hero, to command the State Militia.

As the early morning session drew to a conclusion, Jackson realized there could be no more waiting: he needed to move against Lyon forthwith. Lyon, meanwhile, was actively consolidating his gains by posting guards at key locations throughout St. Louis.[48]

* * *

One day after the Camp Jackson affair, Gen. William Harney returned to St. Louis and discovered a decidedly different situation than the one he had left on April 23. The general somehow managed to convince his superiors that, despite his Southern leanings, he could keep the peace in St. Louis. Harney hoped to prevent additional violence by removing the Home Guards from their duty on the street corners. While he reestablished relations with Governor Jackson, he failed to return the military situation in St. Louis to its pre-Camp Jackson–St. Louis Riot status. Harney's moderate solutions, aimed more at preventing further violence than righting perceived wrongs, angered many of his Southern friends. Recently chastised for being pro-Southern, however, Harney was not about to meddle with the outcome of recent events.

Lyon's preemptive strike against Camp Jackson had drained much of the fighting spirit from the pro-Southern faction inside the city, but the fighting ignited the anger of citizens outside of St. Louis. Much of this hostility stemmed from the fact that many viewed Lyon's move against the militia as the beginning of war in Missouri—and thus the end of their attempt to prevent fighting in the state. Lyon released the captured militia men the day after their arrest because of the cramped conditions inside the arsenal. By late afternoon the majority of the captives had sworn an oath to preserve the Union and not take up arms against the United States. Many secretly believed, however, that an oath given under duress was not an oath at all, and refused to honor their word. A substantial number of those released left town and joined ranks with the governor.[49]

While Lyon freed his prisoners and Jackson weighed the additional powers granted him by the state's legislature, General Harney attempted to mediate the spreading dispute. On May 20 Harney called Sterling Price to his office on Tenth Street in an effort to patch together an accord agreeable to both sides.

"Old Pap," as Price was known by his former soldiers, was a hero in the western portion of the state and considered a moderate by most Missourians. One year on the wrong side of fifty, Price was born into a wealthy Virginia slave-holding family that relocated to Missouri in 1830. Elected to a seat in Congress fourteen years later, Price vacated office to command a regiment in the Mexican War. His prominent military career preceded his single term as Missouri's popular moderate Unionist governor. "Well born and well bred, courteous and dignified, well educated, and richly endowed with that highest of all mental faculties, common sense," was how one acquaintance described Price. "Tall, straight, handsome, and of a commanding presence—he was also a parliamentarian by instinct." While Price's political skills were prodigious, the same can not be said for his military acumen. It was his ability to compromise and bring individuals together, however, and not his aptitude for strategy or tactics, that Harney was seeking. After a lengthy discussion the two men reached an understanding known as the Price-Harney Agreement. Under terms of this arrangement Price was given "full authority over the Militia of the State of Missouri. . . to maintain order within the State." Harney promised not to "make military movements, which might otherwise create excitement and jealousies."

The arrangement was a simple if naive blueprint for keeping order in the state largely by keeping the antagonists apart. According to the document, Missouri would maintain order within the state's boundaries and Harney would make sure the Federal troops stayed away from confrontations of any type. Both men left the meeting feeling considerably better about the future. Sadly, they failed to realize a moderate path for Missouri was no longer possible after Lyon's raid on Camp Jackson.[50]

As if to prove that point, Governor Jackson utilized the period of calm offered by the Price-Harney Agreement to upgrade his militia, which was no match for Lyon's better supplied and drilled regiments. While he also hoped Price could teach the volunteers the rudiments of soldiering, he realized that his primary dilemma was a lack of weapons to place in the arms of his fellow Missourians. With the arsenal firmly in Federal hands, both Jackson and Price discovered it was no simple task obtaining the guns needed to equip a large gathering of eager recruits. The surrounding countryside produced little more than useless antiques, shotguns and squirrel rifles. Most of the Missouri militiamen assembled unarmed, sporting only high spirits and the bold confidence that they could whip the Dutch if given the opportunity.[51]

While the Price-Harney Agreement may have pleased some Missourians, it failed to impress either Frank Blair or Nathaniel Lyon. In their minds the arrangement was little more than a thinly-veiled form of appeasement with the enemy. Seeking a way to break the truce, Blair sent telegrams throughout the state asking Unionists to report any violations of its terms by Southern sympathizers. Reports of statewide harassment of pro-Union men soon littered Blair's desk, who in turn forwarded the telegrams to Harney and key

Sterling Price
John Bradbury Collection

authorities in Washington, D. C. Blair's wires to the nation's capital were accompanied by his continued requests for Harney's removal.

During the last two weeks of May, considerable pressure mounted on Harney, who had reached the conclusion that the German troops at the arsenal were the cause of tension inside the city. On May 26, the general dismissed a group of men who had presented themselves to him for governmental service. Lyon was upset when he heard about the incident and pleaded with Blair to remove the general. Blair consulted with Washington and on the evening of May 30, Harney received a letter from the War Department relieving him of command. I have been "relieved from the command here. . . in a manner that has inflicted unmerited disgrace upon a true and loyal soldier," he wrote Washington authorities a few days later. The stunned old soldier left his post and eventually retired to his farm in Jefferson County, south of St. Louis. Nathaniel Lyon, elevated to the rank of brigadier general and now firmly in control of St. Louis, had won a major battle for the control of Missouri.[52]

General Harney's removal forced Sterling Price and Claiborne Jackson to rethink their timetable for action. Both men believed that Lyon was planning a strike against Jefferson City, much like the stealth attack he had launched on Camp Jackson. The governor desperately needed more time to prepare the state for actual secession, and Price required more of everything to outfit and train the militia. Privately, Jackson sent word to his nine militia district commanders to prepare for action, but his public demeanor and statements were intended to calm the public.[54]

As the excitement of May slipped away, most Missourians anticipated an eventful June. To almost everyone's surprise, the month began quietly. Moderates throughout the state made one last attempt to head off the approaching violence. Jackson and Blair agreed to meet at the Planter's House Hotel in downtown St. Louis to discuss their dispute. On June 10—the day of the engagement at Big Bethel, Virginia—Governor Jackson and Sterling Price arrived in the city, mildly optimistic the meeting would forge a compromise that would prevent the domination of the state by Federal authorities. Both men hoped that the Price-Harney agreement would be extended, although neither believed that it would be acceptable to

Blair. On the following morning Lyon and Blair met the Southern faction in an ornate meeting room. The conference started slowly, with Blair doing much of the negotiating for the Federals. The debate was difficult and after several hours of discussion over complex and thorny issues, Lyon reached his breaking point. The Connecticut officer interrupted the conversation in a highly agitated state. "Governor Jackson," he shouted, "no man in the state of Missouri has been more desirous of preserving the peace than myself." The outburst probably surprised everyone, and all but guaranteed that the meeting would end without an amicable resolution.[55]

Lyon jumped to his feet and continued to harangue Jackson:

> Previously, Missouri only felt the fostering care of the Federal government, which has raised her from a feeble French colony to that of an empire state. Now, however, from a failure on the part of the chief executive to comply with constitutional requirements, I fear she will be made to feel her power. Better, sir, far better, that the blood of every man, woman and child within the limits of the state should flow, than defy the Federal government. This means war! In one hour one of my officers will call for you and conduct you out of my lines.[56]

As if to punctuate his declaration, Lyon ended his tirade by slamming his fist onto the table top. The meeting ended abruptly with each side filing quietly out of the room. Shaken by Lyon's unexpected tantrum, Jackson and Price returned to the train station without waiting for the promised escort and boarded the governor's private coach for a hurried trip back to Jefferson City. Fearful of pursuit, the party stopped and set fire to the Gasconade River bridge. Arriving in the capital about 2:00 a.m. on June 12, Jackson called another legislative session, his last in the state house. Once he had assembled the sleepy legislators, Jackson called for the raising of a 50,000-man army, which he grandly dubbed the Missouri State Guard, to repel the expected Federal invasion of the state. The governor also sent Price's son, Edwin, together with a small contingent of militia, to finish destroying other railroad bridges and the telegraph lines linking the capital with St. Louis.[57]

Later that same morning Jackson's subordinates began to enroll volunteers into the State Guard. The development of this armed contingent would spell the difference between success and failure for Jackson's plans for Missouri. While on paper the State Guard appeared to possess many of the necessary fundamentals of an army, its ranks were unorganized and most of its officers unschooled in warfare. Most of the "organized" units within the Missouri army had been little more than social clubs before the war and their members completely lacked the skills necessary for soldiering. During the secession crisis a few companies were organized and had drilled the volunteers.[58]

After several days of formal recruiting, disappointment wafted through the air amongst the State Guard's high command. Both Jackson and Price were discouraged (and perhaps somewhat embarrassed) by the paucity of volunteers that rallied around their banner in Jefferson City. Less than a thousand men had assembled near the Missouri River landing to welcome Price. Despite the rabid enthusiasm of his new soldiers, Price had little confidence in his ability to defend the city. Although the surrounding hills made it a potentially strong defensive position, Price was understandably uneasy about the large German population within the capital's limits, not to mention that a sizable portion of his command was unarmed. The Mexican War hero decided to abandon the capital and move his men northeast (upriver) to Boonville, deep in Cooper County.[59]

Across the state troops were either in motion or drilling in preparation for war. The time for compromise had ended just as surely as Nathaniel Lyon's fist had crashed into the tabletop between the negotiating parties. The past two months of political maneuvering, open hostilities, back room machinations and enflamed rhetoric inexorably moved the two combatants toward open conflict.

Unfortunately for the Southerners, the only weapon Jackson and Price could field was the hastily organized Missouri State Guard. If the paucity of recruits was an indication of things to come, they must have harbored serious reservations about Missouri's future.

Boonville

After his successes in St. Louis, Nathaniel Lyon prepared to move against Governor Jackson's state-sponsored militia. Lyon's German volunteers had fought and marched well, but how successful would they be moving into hostile territory against an enemy of unknown size and strength? The campaign would be substantially more difficult and complex than the easy raid on Camp Jackson. Just the logistics of such a move were daunting. Lyon, who had been promoted to brigadier general of Missouri volunteers on May 12, was made a brigadier general of United States Volunteers five days later. He had already demonstrated an aggressive spirit and the fortitude to formulate and pursue his goals. But could he deliver a major victory for the Lincoln administration?

* * *

It had not been an auspicious beginning for the vaunted State Guard. By June 13 Claiborne Jackson's private army was retreating from Jefferson City to Boonville. Unable to field a credible force and uneasy about the large and disciplined German regiments, Sterling Price had but little choice in the matter other than to conduct the strategic withdrawal. Desperate for soldiers, Jackson urged the leaders of the state's nine militia districts—all popular men appointed by

Jackson in the hope their reputations would draw recruits—to raise as many men as possible and march them to Boonville and Lexington. Price, meanwhile, dispatched the army's artillery, under the capable leadership of Missouri state Brig. Gen. Mosby M. Parsons, to Tipton, about twenty miles south of Boonville, where Parsons was to await further orders.

On the same day Price retreated from the capital, a mere twenty-four hours after he and Jackson returned from their meeting with Lyon and Blair at the Planter's House, the governor and his political followers boarded a steamboat to meet "Old Pap" at the newly established rendezvous. While Price marched and the politicians steamed upriver, small groups of men throughout the state slowly made their way to Boonville over muddy and badly rutted roads. Brigadier General John B. Clark, an experienced Indian fighter, former Missouri congressman and the commander of a military district north of the Missouri River, reached Boonville shortly after Price to assist with the organization of the arriving volunteers. Many militia members had heard of the riot in St. Louis and had not waited for their local commanders to call them out. The Federals were coming and they believed it was their duty to try and stop them.[1]

Boonville appeared to be a good location to raise, equip and train the growing State Guard militia. It also had valuable strategic advantages. By holding the Missouri River line at that point, Sterling Price hoped to squeeze a few weeks' time to coalesce an army at Lexington and train those camped at Boonville. This would secure, in western Missouri, a line of communication between the northern and southern halves of the state. Without such a link,

Brig. Gen. John B. Clark, Sr.

Missouri Historical Society

the northern Missouri River counties, with potentially thousands of recruits, would be lost.

Boonville was also a friendly place for the militia army. The citizens of the small Cooper County town, nestled up against the Missouri River, heartily supported the Southern cause. In 1856, the county raised money and supplies for the pro-slavery sympathizers in Kansas. The region boasted one of the highest concentrations of slavery in Missouri—thirty-five percent of its population according to the 1860 census. Abraham Lincoln's presidential showing in the county was so poor that the few citizens who voted for the Republican candidate were noted in the local paper "as a matter of curiosity." In addition to its political leanings, Boonville's bluffs and hilly terrain afforded Price a solid defensive position, especially if Lyon chose to transport his troops to the city via steamboat. Still, rallying the Missouri State Guard at Boonville posed some risk. A quick strike by Lyon would likely catch the Southerners before they were ready to take the field. A defeat and the consequent loss of control of such a vital portion of the state could crush Southern morale and seriously damage Southern fortunes in Missouri. Could Price and Jackson raise and train their eager recruits fast enough to meet Lyon in a pitched battle?[2]

*   *   *

The initiative, as both Jackson and Price realized, rested with the Federals. Lyon realized this as well and was not about to mark time in St. Louis. He had heard rumors of the Missouri State Guard moving to Boonville, and grasped the strategic importance of the town. If he could defeat the enemy anywhere in Little Dixie, he could force Jackson and his private army away from its primary base of supplies and the richest recruitment area of Missouri. An early Federal success would also severely cripple the Confederacy's effort to keep the critical border state out of the Union. Concerns other than just Price's gathering army also had to be dealt with. Reports were beginning to filter in that a small Confederate army of perhaps 5,000 well-armed troops was in northwest Arkansas, poised and ready to move into southwestern Missouri. Even though he had no absolute confirmation of the truth of this information, Lyon decided to assume the offensive and move against the enemy rather than allow Southern forces to dictate strategy.[3]

His complex plan—which he apparently formulated and executed without Washington's knowledge—demonstrated a solid grasp of grand strategy. Instead of limiting his attack against just Jefferson City or Boonville, he decided to risk a knockout blow designed to end Southern resistance in the state and prevent the Confederate army in Arkansas from entering Missouri and disrupting his operations. Gathering his subordinates at the arsenal, Lyon presented an ambitious two-pronged advance into enemy territory. Lyon would command the first line of the Federal movement, a thrust up the Missouri River with a fleet of steamboats loaded with about 2,000 troops. His objective was Jefferson City and the defeat of the State Guard militia wherever it could be found. While Lyon proceeded into Little Dixie, securing a large portion of the Missouri River in the process, Brig. Gen. Tom W. Sweeny would lead a column of regiments southwest out of St. Louis deep into the far corner of the state. Sweeny's thrust was designed to prevent the junction of the two Southern armies and possibly allow Lyon to catch the Southerners in a pincer movement. As Lyon later informed his superiors, he "ordered a movement. . .to Jefferson City and in the direction of Springfield. . .for the purpose of breaking up the hostile organizations which I had reason to believe had been formed in those parts of the State to resist the authority of the Government."[4]

Euphoria swept through Lyon's veins. To his staff he boasted that Jackson or Price would either stand and fight and be defeated, or turn and retreat in an attempt to gain time to train and equip their men. The fiery general fully expected his campaign to effectively cripple his Southern opponent. To gain a strategic advantage, Lyon decided to make use of two modern forms of transportation: the steamboat and the railroad. Although neither side was fully trained for battle, he was enough of a soldier to intuitively grasp the value of a surprise strike against an unprepared enemy. From small arms to artillery the Federals were better equipped than their opposition. The outcome of the campaign would rely on his army's ability to turn discipline and firepower into victories.[5]

On June 13 troops and supplies were loaded onto steamboats impressed into service by the Federals. The wharves of St. Louis bustled with chaotic activity as the steamers were stuffed to over-flowing with the accouterments of war. Within a short time the ships eased into the river's channel and smoked their way against the current toward Jefferson City. In his wake Lyon left behind a logistical nightmare and a column of infantry scrambling to ready itself for a difficult march into southwest Missouri.[6]

Confusion marred the preparations of the men who composed the overland column, the second prong of Lyon's sweeping strategic envelopment of the Missouri State Guard. Sweeny's wing, which including Home Guard troops, began its campaign by rapidly packing equipment and baggage onto wagons for transport to the Pacific Railroad depot. Sweeny's orders were to ride the railroad to Rolla, debark, and proceed overland to Springfield. As with every troop movement, the plan looked more feasible on paper than it proved to be in reality. The expedition was Sweeny's first independent command, and it would try the soul of the one-armed officer.

Problems confronted Sweeny from the outset. A paucity of wagons, horses, mules and rail cars delayed his departure to Rolla. Logistics were so poorly coordinated that Sweeny was forced to act as his own quartermaster. Plugging himself into the minutia of army logistics, however, made it all the more difficult for Sweeny to fulfill his obligations as the column's commanding general, a fact that would evidence itself later in the campaign. Supply headaches were only part of his concern. Once he moved beyond the railhead in Rolla, it would be difficult to effectively communicate with Lyon. How would the two widely-separated columns coordinate their movements? Sweeny's column was also bereft of cavalry, a severe handicap that would limit his ability to scout the countryside and protect his column. At this early stage in the war the Union army in Missouri could not field a sufficient number of horsemen to meet the demands of the moment.[7]

Hampered by these and other problems, Sweeny worked tirelessly to overcome them. Hard work was not unknown to the foreign-born officer. Born in Cork, Ireland in 1820, Sweeny emigrated to America with his recently-widowed mother in 1832. After working for a publisher of legal materials, he felt the itch for military service and in 1843 joined the Baxter Blues, a New York militia unit. The Blues served in the Mexican War as Company A in the 2nd

Brig. Gen. Thomas Sweeny

Generals in Blue

New York Volunteers with Sweeny as its second lieutenant. At the Battle of Churubusco he received a severe wound that eventually required the amputation of his right arm. His actions in that battle earned him a brevet promotion to captain and a silver medal from New York City. Despite the crippling nature of his wound, Sweeny recovered and accepted a commission in the 2nd United States Regular Infantry three years later. For the next thirteen summers he fought Indians on the plains while sectional turmoil was ripping the country asunder hundreds of miles to the east.[8]

On January 19, 1861, the Irish soldier was promoted to captain in the United States Regular Army. Still stationed on the frontier, Sweeny was assigned to St. Louis and placed in command of a regiment of volunteers. It did not take long before the wisdom of that appointment became apparent. The enlisted men, who quickly adapted to Sweeny's rough-and-tumble way of doing things, responded well to his leadership. Tom Sweeny understood the temperament of the volunteer soldier. His ability to communicate with them was aptly demonstrated when he pinned up his empty sleeve and twitched his stump while speaking in a high pitched voice to make his men laugh. He cared little that his rough personality, hewn from years of army life on plains, clashed with the clique of West Point graduates who surrounded him in St. Louis. The campaign into southwest Missouri offered Sweeny substantial field experience and was an opportunity every soldier dreamed of having. He was determined to make the most of it.[9]

After unsnarling his supply and transportation problems sufficiently to begin his advance, Sweeny ordered his lead regiment to move out on the 23rd of June, ten days after Lyon's steamboats had left the St. Louis docks. However slowly, Nathaniel Lyon's ambitious plan was beginning to take shape.[10]

*   *   *

The Missouri State Guard, meanwhile, remained in Camp Bacon just east of Boonville. Things were not going well. Sterling Price had taken ill with a severe case of diarrhea, a recurring malady from his Mexican War service. Totally incapacitated, the former governor made but a brief stop at Boonville before proceeding upstream by steamer on June 13 to recover at his farm in Chariton County. Command of the militia temporarily devolved onto Gen. John B. Clark's shoulders. Before his departure Price ordered the town held as long as possible—without risking the army's destruction. An effective delaying action, he reasoned, followed by a twenty mile withdrawal south to Tipton to link up with Parsons' men and guns seemed to be the best solution of the moment.

The loss of the popular Price left a gaping command void that Governor Jackson scrambled to fill. Soon after Price left for home, Jackson—leaning heavily on his nephew, Col. John Sappington Marmaduke—assumed a quasi-joint command of the fledgling army forming along the banks of the Missouri River. Neither was qualified for the position. Jackson had no military training of any kind, while Marmaduke, an 1857 graduate of West Point with but limited military experience, was only slightly better prepared to lead the militia. The pair set about the task of creating an army from the volunteers who wandered into Camp Bacon at all hours of the day and night. About 1,500 men were organized by June 15, although most of these were so poorly equipped and armed they could hardly be called soldiers. All of them, however, were anxious to prove themselves in battle.[11]

*   *   *

Nathaniel Lyon had heard rumors that Jefferson City had been abandoned but, intent on seizing the state capital, refused to believe it. His steaming Federal flotilla of about 2,000 men was comprised of Col. Frank Blair's First Missouri Regiment, nine companies from the Second Missouri under Col. Henry Boernstein, Lyon's own Second Infantry (Company B), two companies of general service recruits under Lt. W. L. Lothrop of the Fourth Artillery, and Capt. James Totten's light artillery battery. Totten, a Mexican War veteran, suffered the humiliation of having to surrender the Federal arsenal at Little Rock, Arkansas, a few months earlier in February. The artillery commander presented quite a contrast to his tight lipped and intense superior. Unlike Lyon, Totten was a profuse conversationalist who enjoyed a good game of cards and whose heavy drinking habit earned him the nick-name "bottle-nose."[12]

As darkness fell the Federal steamers dropped anchor at St. Charles, resuming their ascension of the river at first light on June 14. As it turned out the rumors were true. A stunned Lyon landed his troops in Jefferson City without incident that morning. "I arrived on the 15th about 2 o'clock p.m." reported Lyon, "and found the governor had fled and taken his forces to Boonville, where, so far as I could learn, a large force was gathering." The Federal regiments marched unopposed into Jefferson City and unfurled a large American flag over the State House. Anxious to press on after the retreating enemy, Lyon did not allow his men time to celebrate the capture of the capital. Leaving about 300 behind under Colonel Boernstein to garrison the city, he withdrew the balance of his men to the steamboats.

As the newly-promoted general readied his men for the next phase of the campaign, one must wonder whether the rumors circulating through Jefferson City gave him pause. Even Lyon admitted that a "large force" was coalescing before him, and the gossip swirling about that thousands of Southerners were waiting to meet him at Boonville seemed to confirm it. While the likelihood of meeting a superior enemy did not dissuade him from the task he had set for himself, he was concerned about the possibility that the State Guard might emplace artillery along the shores of the Missouri and shell his flotilla from the riverbanks—a tactic that could inflict serious injuries and cripple his small army before it landed. As the steamboats chugged away from the Jefferson City wharves, Lyon did his best to protect his men. He sandbagged the open decks and posted riflemen to quickly respond to any threat they might meet.[13]

* * *

News that Lyon was approaching prompted a round of bickering between Governor Jackson and his generals about the feasibility of making a stand at Boonville. One of their many concerns centered around the paucity of the State Guard's artillery. The few guns available would never be able to either block the river or drive back the determined general. Jackson, realizing how badly he needed his cannon, reacted by ordering up Parsons and his 6-lb. howitzers to Boonville. Many of Jackson's officers, especially John Marmaduke, who did not believe the State Guard was ready for action, wanted to abandon Boonville altogether and retreat southwest to the Osage River near Warsaw. The terrain there was better suited for a defensive stand, they argued. In addition, the move would draw Lyon away from the Missouri River, which served as his supply and communication lifeline back to St. Louis. Other officers vehemently disagreed with this advice, arguing that a retreat to Warsaw was unwise. They predicted a withdrawal without a fight would dishearten the troops and send the wrong message to local Southern sympathizers, besides damaging further recruiting efforts in Little Dixie. The men were willing to fight for their homes and loved ones, went the argument, and they should be allowed to do so at Boonville. Sterling Price, who harbored few illusions about the ill-training and poor discipline of the State Guard, was cognizant of the political ramifications of abandoning the pro-Southern river counties. While he had ordered Boonville held as long as possible, he knew it was not the place for a decisive show of arms. Much like Lyon, Price believed the critical battle for control of the state would take place in southwest Missouri. Governor Jackson listened to the arguments and decided against withdrawal. The army would make a stand at Boonville.[14]

If the officers of the State Guard were of mixed opinion about confronting Nathaniel Lyon's imminent attack, the rank and file were generally united in their determination to stand and fight. The volunteers were primarily local men whose pride would not let them return home without attempting to throw back the Unionists—even though they knew next to nothing about either enemy numbers or the condition of Lyon's army. To them, the impending battle was as much a fight about honor as politics. Wild rumors about the Federal army circulated through Camp Bacon. The size and strength of the approaching Federal column grew with each passing hour as the men discussed and gave credence to the rumors. If the strain of waiting for the battle rattled some of their nerves, a local preacher's sermon may have helped salve them. Reverend Frank Mitchell circulated among the troops on the Sunday preceding the fight, passionately exhorting them to do their duty as their cause was just and God was on their side.[15]

*   *   *

Lyon's steamboats drew near Boonville on June 16 and anchored for the night off shore from Providence, in Boone County, about fifteen miles down river from the Southern encampment. That evening the Federal commanding general shared his plans with his subordinates. Surprise and speed were the twin cornerstones of Lyon's strategy to defeat what he believed was a superior (at least in numbers) enemy. A reporter for the *New York Herald*, Thomas Knox, reported that the atmosphere was one of excitement and anticipation. Most the the men were "full of enthusiasm and eagerly anticipating" the main event. General Lyon, however, remained locked away in his cabin, "quiet, reserved, and thoughtful." Lyon appreciated that fighting meant killing, a reality driven home to the reporter when the surgeons laid out their tools of the trade in preparation for the morrow.

The steamers got underway again before sunrise on the 17th. By 7:00 a.m. they had edged behind a large channel island for protection from anticipated shore fire. Lyon, together with Frank Blair and John Schofield, walked across the small piece of land and surveyed the landing site on the river's far bank. Before them stretched a mile and one-half of bottom lands, bordered on the north by the river and on the south by steep bluffs. A narrow river road, known locally as the Rocheport Road, ran near the river's edge for some distance before turning inland toward Camp Bacon. After confirming that the riverbank was devoid of Rebels, Lyon disembarked his army on the southern bank around 8:00 a.m., three miles below the Southern encampment. Why hadn't the State Guard contested his landing? Lyon wondered. Before striking inland Lyon left Capt. Henry

Richardson's company of the First Missouri, together with an 8-inch howitzer, to both protect the boats and steam upstream and shell the Rebel camp, thought to be a few miles distant. Two companies of Maj. Peter Osterhaus' Second Missouri, Company A under Captain Schadt and Company B under Captain Kohr, led the way as skirmishers "with excellent effect," Lyon later reported. With little fanfare about 1,600 Federals moved up the sandy Rocheport Road in search of the Missouri State Guard.[16]

After a quiet march of two miles the Federals stumbled into a small group of Southerners near where the river bottom narrowed and the road ascended into the hilly wooded bluffs. The Rebels, John Marmaduke's advance pickets, opened fire on Osterhaus' skirmishers, who were collected and deployed on the right side of the road. The Second Infantry's Company B balanced the front rank of advancing Federals by deploying on Osterhaus' left, from which point they returned fire. Two guns from Totten's battery were unlimbered to add their metal to the developing engagement and additional infantry companies were deployed as well. The outnumbered militia fell back to the west.[17]

Governor Jackson learned of Lyon's approach shortly after he landed and had ordered his field commander, John Marmaduke, to move his men east and engage the Federals. Jackson was hoping to hold back Lyon long enough for Mosby Parsons to arrive from Tipton with his battery of artillery. While Marmaduke disagreed with the orders he readily obeyed them, marching about 500 militia out of Camp Bacon. Oddly, Jackson had withheld, ostensibly as a reserve, his only organized and disciplined unit, Captain Kelly's company of infantry.

Marmaduke and the main body of the State Guard were waiting for Lyon about a mile from where he was initially forced to deploy his regiments. The main line of battle was aligned along a narrow dirt path that ran north toward the river and bisected the Rocheport Road at a right angle. On the northeast corner of this lonely intersection stood the William M. Adams house, a brick structure that would soon suffer the heavy hand of war. Several of Marmaduke's best riflemen already occupied the home. The rest of the state troops faced east behind the residence, extending north and south across the road. Some enjoyed the shelter of a rail fence, while others were

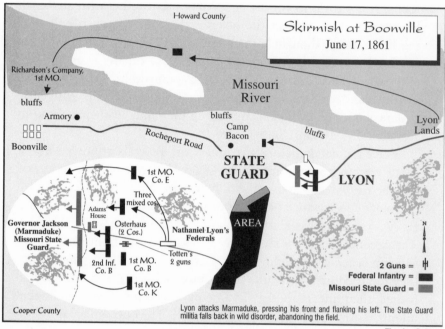

Skirmish at Boonville
June 17, 1861

Howard County

Missouri River

Richardson's Company, 1st MO.

bluffs

Armory ●
Boonville

bluffs

Camp Bacon
●

bluffs

Lyon Lands

Rocheport Road

STATE GUARD

LYON

1st MO. Co. E

Three mixed cos.

Adams' House

Osterhaus (2 Cos.)

Nathaniel Lyon's Federals

AREA

Governor Jackson (Marmaduke) Missouri State Guard

2nd Inf. Co. B

1st MO. Co. B

Totten's 2 guns

1st MO. Co. K

N

Cooper County

2 Guns =
Federal Infantry =
Missouri State Guard =

Lyon attacks Marmaduke, pressing his front and flanking his left. The State Guard militia falls back in wild disorder, abandoning the field.

Theodore P. Savas

aligned in a field of wheat or deployed in a belt of woods. As one researcher of this battle noted, Marmaduke's carefully selected position allowed him to "not only intercept any advance along the river road, but. . .subject it to enfilading fire from both sides."[18]

"After proceeding about one mile," wrote Lyon, "the enemy was discovered in force." Studying the Confederate dispositions, the Federal commander strengthened his left with the addition of Capt. Thomas Maurice's Company B, 2nd Missouri Volunteers. Lyon also unlimbered Totten's two pieces of artillery, which lobbed several rounds of 6-lb. case shot into the state troops. The iron shot splattered against the walls of the Adams residence and unnerved some of the inexperienced militia unlucky enough to be within range. "Captain Totten's battery here did effective service," Lyon reported, "and our troops on both flanks steadily advanced."

In an effort to flank Jackson's line, Lyon sent Capt. Nelson Cole's Company E, First Missouri Volunteers, to extend his right flank. For a time Marmaduke's men held their position and delivered a return fire, probably much to the surprise of their field commander. Several volleys rang out across the fields and through the woodland, the minies and round shot "flying thick and fast," according to one participant. The absence of artillery to counter Totten's fire, however, was demoralizing for the Southerners, especially those stationed near the house. Two shots from Totten's well-handled guns broke through its brick walls, sending the sharpshooters scattering for other cover.

As the firing increased and Lyon's infantry closed the distance, the superior discipline of the Federal troops began to take effect. Knots of Southerners began to abandon the field without orders. Watching the fight from a nearby hill, Jackson and his staff realized they could not hold their ground and that the battle was already lost. The governor issued a general order of retreat, conceding the field to Lyon's superior firepower and discipline.[19]

The State Guard's withdrawal was anything but orderly. Many threw down their weapons and took to their heels. A portion fended somewhat better when it slowly retreated over a fence and through the wheat field to a small rise, where it attempted to make a determined stand. After taking a few moments to reorganize, the thin line advanced several paces and opened fire on the approaching Federals. "In falling back the enemy took advantage of sundry points to deliver a fire and continue retreating," was how one Federal officer described the withdrawal. Lyon's infantry maintained steady pressure against the beaten Rebels, letting loose a volley at close range. The months of drill and weapons training carried the day, and the Southerners fell back once again, this time in utter confusion. At one point Marmaduke was heard to yell at a group of cowering troops, "If the Yankees catch you in here, they'll kill half of you. Orders are to retreat, and every man take care of himself." The major's words were enough for them, and they joined him in the hunt for the rear. One State Guardsman recalled the brief skirmish as a "helter-skelter, pell-mell sort of affair." The entire action had consumed only about fifteen or twenty minutes.[20]

The defeated Rebels sprinted in every direction. Many ran back to Camp Bacon to gather possessions and evacuate the area. Others continued into Boonville, swam the river into Howard County or disappeared into the countryside. The second phase of Lyon's plan, however, effectively sealed the victory. Captain Cole's small band of men from the First Missouri had slipped around Jackon's retreating left and moved in behind the rear guard at Camp Bacon. As they moved on the camp site, a steamboat carrying Capt. Henry Richardson's company of the First Missouri opened fire with the howitzer, scattering the already dazed and demoralized Southerners. By the time the water-based contingent of Federals came ashore the defeated Rebels were on the run again, stunned by the swiftness of Lyon's multi-pronged attack. Correspondent Thomas Knox derisively labeled the panicked retreat as the "Boonville Races."[21]

The victorious Unionists plundered Camp Bacon. The substantial haul of military booty included "500 stand of arms of all sorts," two iron 6-lb. artillery pieces, "considerable camp equipage" and "about 60 prisoners." These supplies, which included a large cache of shoes, would be sorely missed by the fledgling militia army.[22]

Lyon's troops reformed their ranks and continued to the fairgrounds on the eastern edge of town, where a small band of Rebels stretched across the road in a vain attempt to defend a crude armory established by the state. The confident Federals charged the grounds and easily scattered the militia. "This fair ground had been taken by the State for an arsenal," Lyon wrote in his report of the Boonville fight, "and a considerable number of old rusty arms and cartridges were found." Leaving behind a company to control the place, Lyon marched unchallenged into Boonville. Acting Mayor James H. O'Brien and District Judge G. W. Miller met with the general and quietly surrendered the town to the victorious Federals. Lyon promised no harm would come to the civilians.[23]

The first land fight on Missouri soil was over. The entire affair had lasted less than three hours, with the actual combat consuming barely twenty minutes. The Federals lost two killed, nine wounded (two mortally), and one man missing, while State Guard casualties were reported as three killed, five to nine wounded and 60 captured.

The skirmish demonstrated Lyon's capacity to plan and execute a swift and bold strike on ground of the enemy's selection. He had skillfully deployed and handled his troops against an enemy force of unknown size and had committed his men to the action in a concerted fashion. Lyon displayed the ability to use his aggressive nature to win victories—albeit over a weak and untrained enemy.

In retrospect, Major Marmaduke was correct, the state troops were not ready for battle. While he had performed as well as possible under difficult circumstances, the battle revealed that Governor Jackson's multiple talents did not include good generalship. Popular opinion deemed the entire affair a first class embarrassment for the Missouri State Guard and fixed responsibility for the loss directly on Jackson. If he intended to fight at Boonville, his artillery should have been called up in time to participate. Similarly, Captain Kelly's company should have been offered to Marmaduke instead of held far in the rear where it could do no good. Newspaper accounts were quick to question why Jackson had not led his men in person instead of watching the battle from afar.

Lyon's quick advance on Boonville forced the ill-trained State Guard to fight a battle it could not win and in the process exposed several glaring weaknesses. "From a military standpoint," wrote Col. Thomas L. Snead, Jackson's aide-de-camp, "the affair at Boonville was a very insignificant thing, but it did in fact deal a stunning blow to the Southern-rights men of Missouri, and one which weakened the Confederacy during all of its brief existence." To Colonel Snead,

It was indeed the consummation of [Frank] Blair's statesmanlike scheme to make it impossible for Missouri to secede, or out of her great resources to contribute liberally of men and material to the South, as she would have done could her people have had their own way. It was also the most brilliant achievement of Lyon's well-conceived campaign. The capture of Camp Jackson had disarmed the State, and completed the conquest of St. Louis and all the adjacent counties. The advance upon Jefferson City had put the State government to flight and taken away from the Governor the prestige which sustains established and acknowledged authority.[24]

While Boonville was indeed a Southern disaster, the fighting offered important lessons to those willing or able to heed them. Would Jackson and his officers learn from their mistakes?

4

Advance

Governor Jackson and the remnants of the defeated Missouri State Guard withdrew south in disarray from the Boonville battlefield. When Mosby Parsons learned of the defeat he wisely withdrew his artillery command to the southwest, away from Lyon's victorious troops. The pair eventually managed to link up a few miles west of Tipton in the Syracuse-Florence area. When they learned that Lyon had dispatched a small force to capture the governor, the combined state troops retreated southwest toward Warsaw, where John Marmaduke had wanted to fight all along. It was a bitter and sad retreat for the proud State Guardsmen.

While Jackson was shepherding his men out of harm's way, a steamboat carrying Sterling Price docked beneath the bluffs of Lexington, about fifty miles west of Boonville. Weakened by illness, the heavyset Price plodded down the gangplank only to be confronted with news of his army's defeat. While the swiftness of Lyon's advance surprised him, the outcome of the fight at Boonville did not. The loss of Boonville held serious ramifications for Price, for with Lyon in control of the river Lexington could not be held. The town was originally chosen as an assembly point for the gathering recruits because of its geographic and logistical advantages. It was also centrally located between two important districts and the Missouri River offered a means of transporting men and equipment downstream should the need arise. "Old Pap" boarded a wagon and

Brig. Gen. William Y. Slack

Generals in Gray

headed to the outskirts of the town to confer with his district militia brigadier generals, William Slack and James Rains. Both of these men had been actively recruiting from the counties near the Kansas-Missouri border, where anti-Union sentiment was strong. The newly-appointed state brigadiers were typical of district-level militia leaders in Missouri, and both would work hard for the Southern cause.[1]

William Yarnel Slack was not a native Missourian but a Kentuckian. Born in Mason County on August 1, 1816, the Slack family had moved near Columbia in Boone County, Missouri three years later. Little is known of Slack's younger years other than that he studied law and eventually began a practice in Chillicothe. He was pleased to be reunited with Sterling Price, his former commander in the Mexican War. Slack had served as captain of the 2nd Missouri Mounted Volunteers for fourteen months before returning to Chillicothe to resume his law practice. He successfully ran for attorney general and continued his service to the state as a senator in Jefferson City. As the likelihood of civil war increased, Slack was a logical choice to become a militia general in his district. The aggressive and highly partisan senator, described by one contemporary as "an officer of energy and decision," had regularly debated Unionists on the floor of the Missouri Senate. Now he was prepared to carry that dispute to the battlefield.[2]

Tennessee-born James Spencer Rains, who came into life on October 2, 1817, had spent most of his adult years around Sarcoxie, deep in the southwest corner of Missouri in Jasper County. Rains served as state senator of the twenty-fifth district, and his rise in

Brig. Gen. James S. Rains

Civil War Photograph Album,
LSU Libraries,
Louisiana State University

politics was assisted by his marital ties to a prominent family. In 1845 President James Polk appointed Rains as an agent for Indian affairs for the Neosho Agency in northeast Oklahoma. The adventurous Rains traveled to California in 1850 and served as a general in that state's militia, where he also spent time as a forty-niner. Finding that mining gold was not all he had hoped for, he returned to Missouri two years later. Election to a state senate seat followed, and he served in that capacity from 1854 through 1861. Rains' popularity continued to rise. Even though he lacked military experience, Governor Jackson appointed him a militia leader in the Eighth District—primarily because of his fiery oratory skills and ability to persuade men to join the Southern cause.[3]

Thus far both brigadiers had lived up to expectations. They had managed to successfully recruit a combined total of 2,000 men in response to the governor's call to arms. Endemic to the Missouri militia movement, however, was the arms, ammunition and equipment shortage. Uniforms were virtually nonexistent and many men arrived shoeless. It is also somewhat remarkable that in an era when nearly every household owned at least one gun, significant numbers of recruits arrived unarmed. Some had simply left their weapons at home to provide for the defense of the homestead and put food on the table, assuming they would be armed by the state. No one would mistake the large collection of unarmed and indifferently clothed men camped outside Lexington for an organized and effective military force.[4]

The news the two militia generals shared with Price was disheartening for all three. Rumors were circulating that two columns of Federal troops, one from Kansas and one from Iowa, were bearing down upon Lexington. The effects of the Boonville defeat were also significant. "Lyon's conquest," wrote one astute observer, ". . .closed all avenues by which the Southern men in North Missouri could get to Price and Jackson [and] made the Missouri River a Federal highway from its source to its mouth. . ." Considering these factors and the ill-state of the army's readiness, the two generals recommended "Old Pap" abandon Lexington as soon as possible and fall back to a more defensible position.

Price listened carefully to his field commanders and heeded their advice. The best strategy for this portion of his army was to retreat south and form a junction with Jackson's column of the Missouri State Guard. "Price had, indeed, no alternative now but to retreat in all haste to the south-western part of the State," Thomas Snead later observed. Price determined to unite the segments of the army at the small town of Lamar, in Barton County, about 110 miles to the south.[5]

Rains and Slack readied their commands for the difficult march. Price, only partially recovered from his debilitating bout with diarrhea, decided to move alone and in advance of the retreating columns in an effort to reach the Confederate troops massing in Arkansas. He hoped to personally persuade Brig. Gen. Ben McCulloch to come to the aid of the beleaguered Missourians with weapons and reinforcements before Nathaniel Lyon pushed the Southern sympathizers out of the state completely. Price realized that turning over large portions of Missouri without much of a fight was a gamble, but he was willing to trade territory for the survival of the State Guard until it became a more capable fighting unit.[6]

Since James Rains had recruited the majority of the men stationed at Lexington, Price gave him command of the retreating column of troops. It took two days for the poorly organized force to gather itself sufficiently to begin the journey south, and the undisciplined gathering suffered during the early days of the march. None of the men from either State Guard column were conditioned to march long distances, and straggling was a problem from the start. Nor were they yet hardened to other ways of army life, such as sleeping on damp ground rolled up in quilts brought from home. Only a few of the soldiers were fortunate enough to find shelter in wagons, barns or homes of Southern partisans along the march. Martyn Cheavens, a school teacher from Fulton and recent recruit, struggled on the wet roads even though he was mounted. A few friends "gave me a white woolen blanket," he remembered. "I got a Mississippi Rifle and a Bowie knife, and started after the army in earnest." After several days in pursuit of the retreating militia, he and several of his comrades came upon Rains' column as it slogged its way south. Since he was mounted, Cheavens joined Capt. John Stone's cavalry company, Col. Benjamin Rives' regiment, Slack's Fourth Division. Since the ad-hoc army had almost nothing to offer its new members, he had been fortunate to acquire his rifle and knife along the way.[7]

Uncharacteristically for Missouri, the rains of May continued into June, turning normally dusty roads into quagmires and shallow streams into roaring torrents. The western portion of the state was on the edge of the frontier in 1861. Few if any bridges spanned the numerous streams and very few ferries were available to aid in crossing the deeper rivers that cut directly across the path of the State Guard's line of retreat. The withdrawal carried the Missouri-

ans south out of Lexington through Warrensburg toward Clinton. According to Cheavens, normally placid fords claimed the lives of several men, many of whom were swept away by the currents while attempting to cross the streams.

Pvt. Martyn Cheavens

Missouri Historical Society

Others camped near creek banks nearly drowned when sudden downpours caused the water to rise, soaking men and equipment alike.[8]

*   *   *

Nathaniel Lyon was a happy man. His military star was in its ascendancy and his actions west of the Mississippi River captured, albeit temporarily, the attention of the Eastern press. A reporter for the *New York Times* traveling with his column reported back to his paper that "General Lyon is. . . evidently the right man in the right place."[9]

Indeed it seemed to be so. His easy and clear victory at Boonville had sent the governor, his private militia and members of the State Senate and House of Representatives fleeing into the southwest corner of the state. In the process Jackson—and Price in Lexington—were abandoning northern Missouri, a strategic recruiting ground and logistically valuable area. The energetic Lyon, cognizant that Confederate forces were gathering in northern Arkansas, had no intention of resting on his laurels. He realized that his next best move was to cut off and destroy the fleeing enemy, and the plan he had designed to ensnare Jackson and his soldiers—the duel pincer movement with his own column and Sweeny's wing marching southwest from St. Louis—was more viable then ever. General Sweeny's regiments were moving by railroad from St. Louis through Rolla. With any luck, Lyon would be able to harass the rear of the Southern column and perhaps bring it to battle—or crush it against the anvil provided by Sweeny's regiments, his own command playing the part of the hammer.

His ambitious operation, however, hinged on a difficult logistical feat. Thus far he had fed and equipped his column by boat along a supply line stretching from St. Louis up the Missouri River to Boonville. His design to march after Price and Jackson would take him away from the river and extend his line of supply overland. On paper the shift from a waterborne base of supplies to one dependent upon wagons and mules appeared viable and easy to implement. Reality was a different matter altogether.[10]

Lyon's hasty departure from St. Louis left a myriad of logistical details unsettled in his wake. Southern sharpshooters regularly harassed the two steamboats that arrived daily at Boonville's limited docking facilities. The entire system to supply Lyon had to be invented nearly overnight, and shortages of everything, from munitions to food, resulted. Lyon planned to get his wagons and mules from the local citizens, but so far his patrols had returned with little usable stock and few suitable wagons. Unable to provide the basic necessities for the army, Lyon's inadequate supply arm left him and his men stranded in Boonville. Most of the blame fell upon Chief Quartermaster Justus McKinstry, a quintessential bureaucrat whom Lyon's subordinates cursed for his failure to effectively move supplies upriver to support the planned pursuit of the defeated Southern army. McKinstry was angered by Lyon's non-regulation methods of requisitioning supplies and confiscated all the wagons destined for Lyon, discharged the drivers and mangled the entire system. This action forced Lyon to piece together a make-shift transportation pipeline to carry his army after the State Guard. Although McKinstry would eventually be court-martialed for his actions, his meddling did nothing to soothe Lyon's temper as he and his victorious soldiers languished in the Boonville mud. "Our operations are becoming extensive," he wrote near the end of the month, "and our staff officers must keep up with our emergencies."[11]

Alexis Mudd, the assistant quartermaster traveling with Lyon, attempted to untangle the supply snarls back in St. Louis with scant success. His efforts to procure needed wagons and mules to transport the baggage, artillery, ammunition and other supplies suffered because the State Guard had pilfered the best wagons and horses when it evacuated the region. Transportation was not the only necessity Lyon's troops were lacking. The shoes clinging to the feet of his soldiers were nearly worn through, uniforms were tattered and he did not have enough ammunition stockpiled to effectively mount a second campaign.[12]

As Mudd worked to clothe and supply the men, Lyon used the telegraph to effectuate a larger campaign against the retreating Rebels. Major Samuel Sturgis, at Ft. Leavenworth, Kansas, was ordered to advance his troops into Missouri in a move designed to link his force with Lyon. The movement included the First and Second Regiments Kansas Volunteers, four companies of regular infantry, four companies of cavalry, two companies of dragoons, one company of Kansas Mounted rangers and one four-gun battery of artillery. Sturgis' 2,300 soldiers would double the size of Lyon's army. The Kansans were eager to come to Missouri. They had suffered from the cross-border attacks of the mid-1850s and were anxious for revenge. Lyon also confirmed via telegraph that a column of soldiers from Iowa was advancing toward Boonville.[13]

While attempting to control these far-flung columns, Lyon consolidated his gains throughout the state by establishing a series of small outposts, garrisoned by Home Guards, in central and southeast Missouri. On Tuesday, June 18, he issued a proclamation to the citizens of Missouri offering amnesty to anyone who had rebelled against the Federal government by taking up arms. Since casualties thus far had been light, he reasoned, perhaps the gesture would soothe bitter feelings. On the other hand, the large and bloody battle he was planning (and hoping for) would permanently divide the state's residents. Either way, the loss of the capital at Jefferson City and Federal control of the Missouri River assured that the important border state would remain in the Union for the foreseeable future.[14]

Lyon's impatient and involuntary sojourn at Boonville gave him time to reflect on his recent victory over Jackson. The Rebels, even though fighting to defend their homes, failed to impress him. His artillery had unnerved the raw militia recruits and turned the tide of battle at Boonville; perhaps he could use the strategy in the future. The weapons carried by the Southerners, based on what he had experienced on the field and captured at the make-shift Boonville arsenal, were old and unreliable—another advantage he could exploit.[15]

*   *   *

While the defeat at Boonville had far-reaching ramifications, it was not a total loss for the leadership of the State Guard. Word of Lyon's victory spread across the region and galvanized many of the men who were previously undecided as to which side to support. As the two parts of the Governor's Missouri army slogged their way through the rain, recruits slowly but steadily began to appear in increasing numbers.

*   *   *

The newspapers of St. Louis were filled with stories detailing the success of the German troops at Boonville and Thomas Sweeny's movement into southwestern Missouri. The *Mississippi Blatter* proclaimed that "the specter of the rebellion has dissolved into smoke." The paper continued on in praise of ". . .our brave brothers who have sallied forth to stomp on the head of the serpent of rebellion."[16]

With Lyon victorious but temporarily stalled at Boonville, the focus of the campaign shifted to Sweeny's movement southwest toward Rolla. Dubbed the "Southwestern Column" because it was marching in that direction from St. Louis, the Irish brigadier's command consisted of the following troops: Franz Sigel's Third Missouri, Charles Salomon's Fifth Missouri, John McNeil's Third Regiment Home Guards, Gratz Brown's Fourth Regiment Home Guards, and Franz Backoff's battalion of artillery (two batteries under the command of Theodore Wilkins and Christian Essig). The Home Guardsmen were along to help guard the rail line against guerrilla attacks and protect the wagon road from Rolla to Springfield. Sweeny's marching orders reunited Sigel and Salomon, who were veterans of the 1848 Revolution in Europe.

Sweeny, however, faced a supply problem similar to Lyon's situation at Boonville. He had planned to use the railroad to advance quickly to Rolla, over 100 miles southwest of St. Louis. Once safely ensconced in Rolla, the small strike force would be obligated to switch to ground transportation because Rolla was the end of the rail line. Assembling the necessary wagons, horses and mules to move over 2,000 men proved to be more difficult than anyone had assumed. Despite this major handicap, Sweeny set a departure date of June 23. Working diligently he managed to exceed his own schedule by twelve days. Intent on solving his logistical problems, Sweeny remained behind when his column left St. Louis. Colonel Franz Sigel, as the column's senior officer, assumed direct command of the movement.[17]

The first group of soldiers to depart were from the Third Missouri Volunteers, a well drilled group led by Sigel. With their new regimental flag flying at the head of their column, 300 of Sigel's men marched through the German neighborhoods to meet the train.[18] The St. Louis *Missouri Democrat* related details of the movement to an anxious audience the following day: "The First Battalion of Colonel Sigel's regiment, the Third Missouri Volunteers, was ordered to get ready for an instant march; and the Second battalion to prepare to follow on the morrow." The Union men quickly broke their camps and ". . .at 11:00 p.m. the First battalion, Lieutenant Colonel [Francis] Hassendeubel commanding, arrived at the Fourteenth Street depot and entered some seven cars. A heavy amount of freight and several field pieces were laden on freight cars." With the tracks officially cleared the Federals began the movement to intercept the State Guard. The next day, June 13, the Second battalion of the same regiment left the Fourteenth Street depot at 9:00 p.m., and proceeded to take possession of various stops along the railroad. This train carried five additional companies of infantry, two rifle companies and Major Bischoff's artillery battery.[19]

Cheers resounded throughout the German areas of the city as its men marched off to war. Lieutenant Colonel Hassendeubel and Franz Sigel acknowledged the crowd's enthusiasm by saluting the cheering throng of people as the train chugged away from the station. As the cars rolled slowly through the German dominated communities on the way to Rolla, more welcome ovations were delivered by civilians that had turned out to line the tracks. The small battalion arrived on the outskirts of their first destination early on the afternoon of June 14 when word reached Sigel that Rebels occupied the community in strength. The German officer wisely deployed his men in line of battle and cautiously approached the town. The rumor turned out to be false, and the only sign of a Southern presence was blowing in the breeze above the town—a Rebel flag flapping from the courthouse flagpole. The pro-Southern militia men from the surrounding counties controlled the town for a few days prior to Sigel's arrival, but evacuated the area rather than fight the numerically superior Federals.[20]

To the Germans, Rolla was a town of stark contrasts. While they admired the new two-story courthouse that dominated its skyline, they found the remainder of the town to be "nothing more than hillbilly shacks." Like most of its structures, Rolla's residents also failed to impress the German troops, who were used to the bustling life of St. Louis. "To Northern city soldiers," one observer noted, "the natives appeared lackadaisical, long, & limber. Many were barefooted." The *Anzeiger des Westens* newspaper in St. Louis reported that the appearance of Sigel's column in the streets of Rolla caused ". . .a state militia unit, about 180 strong, to vanish in a cloud of dust." German pride, swelled by news from the front, boosted morale in the town and aided in the recruitment of additional soldiers.[21]

Rolla's value to the Federals lay not in her appearance but her location. The town was essentially the mid-point on a line drawn from St. Louis to Springfield. The termination of the Pacific Railroad in Rolla made it a natural location for Sweeny's supply depot. It was also the point where Sigel's men would transfer to the waiting wagons and horses to continue the trip overland to Springfield. Although Sweeny encountered logistical difficulties, he had managed to stock Rolla with the transportation Sigel required, a fact that pleasantly surprised the German native. Within two days Sigel organized his column and marched out of Rolla southwest into the Missouri countryside. A small garrison was left behind to guard supplies and the vital railhead for the arrival of the Fifth Missouri and the additional troops that would follow.[22]

Late on June 15, while Sigel's Third Missouri soldiers occupied Rolla, Lt. Col. Charles Salomon, together with the Home Guard units, began loading his men onto the rail cars at the depot in St. Louis. According to one account, Salomon's Fifth Missouri, over 800 strong, left the arsenal just before midnight, accompanied by half a dozen pieces of artillery. Sweeny's entire column was now on the move.[23]

As the rear coil of Sweeny's expeditionary force arrived in Rolla, Sigel's men left the rail head for their journey to Springfield, about 105 miles to the southwest. Without the luxury of the railroad, his companies slowly picked their way over a rutted, muddy road. Skirmishers were deployed across the column's front and flanks to prevent an ambush. As the Federals tramped deeper into enemy territory, Sigel established a series of small outposts at Waynesville and Lebanon to guide the remainder of Sweeny's army toward Springfield. Despite the rigors of their maiden campaign, the majority of the volunteer soldiers endured the march fairly well. By the time the column reached Lebanon, however, the grueling trek had taken its toll on one of the companies of Home Guards. It members refused to advance another step until they were paid and received new equipment. Acting decisively so that the mini-rebellion would not spread to the rest of the men, Sigel disarmed the 80 "mutineers" and sent them packing back to Rolla.[24]

While complaining men posed a potentially serious problem, rising streams presented the most difficult obstacle. The skies refused to clear and the rains continued to pour, saturating the ground and everything above it. In addition to having to ford the flooded waterways, the Missourians spent much of their time freeing wagons from the deep mud and pushing them through the fast running creeks. The farther south the soldiers marched, the more the rain fell. Up to this point Mother Nature had been more troublesome than the Rebels.[25]

On Sunday morning June 23, eight days after departing from Rolla, Sigel's men arrived on the edge of Springfield. The town's citizens watched out their windows as a group of Federal infantry led by an officer on horseback approached. The men had been sent by Sigel to reconnoiter the town for Rebel sympathizers. If any were present, they kept their politics under wrap. The local newspaper thought that the arrival of Sigel's men presented a grand spectacle in the small Ozark city. "[The] wind shook the banner, which, when unfolded showed the familiar stars and stripes in all their splendor!" waxed the *Springfield Mirror*. "Just then the band struck up a tune. The cry throughout the town was, 'they are coming, they are coming!'" If anyone in the crowd asked who was coming, the response was "the Yankee Dutch!"[26]

It is open to speculation whether the exhausted Federals felt the same as the local paper. The fatiguing journey from Rolla to Springfield had worn them down. The last few days of the march had been conducted through a driving rainstorm and ankle deep mud. Private John T. Buegel recounted the difficulties of the march and the less than grand spectacle his unit made upon its entry into Springfield.

"The majority of the regiment was in deplorable condition," he admitted to his diary:

> We resembled a rabble more than soldiers. Each wore whatever clothes they chose to wear. They had become torn on the march. In place of trousers they had slipped on flour sacks. Others had no shoes and were walking on uppers or going barefoot. Still others had no hats and used flour sacks for head coverings."[27]

While Sigel's small column paraded through the streets, a squad of men hurried into town and surrounded the Christian Church (known locally as the Disciples of Christ Church). Acclaimed as a hotbed of secessionist activity, the place of worship was operated by two outspoken ministers, Carleton and Joel H. Hadean. Known throughout the region for their fiery sermons, the brothers justified slavery by selectively quoting from the Bible. Church was in session as Federal soldiers approached at 11:00 a.m. One of the brothers was in the process of preaching when a burly German officer stepped inside the church door and barked out in broken English: "Inder name of mine adopted country, der United Sdades of Ameriky, und der the President, und der the army; und der by the orders of Franz Sigel, you are mine brisoners of war! Pass out your mens, une to mine headquarters in der gort house, right away quick! Forwart! March! Der laties mat go home."[28]

The congregation wisely heeded the order and disbanded while the troops searched the church and its grounds. Finding little of military value near the place of worship, the soldiers widened their investigation. Before long they discovered a fair quantity of gunpowder in a barn owned by a "Mr. Campbell," who was removed to the courthouse (which doubled as the jail). Through the remainder of the afternoon local Home Guard units assisted Sigel in rounding up men of secessionist sympathies. It did not take long before the courthouse was bulging with Missourians allegedly guilty of plotting against the Federal government. Sigel also deployed pickets on each road leading into and out of the city. With Springfield tightly within his grasp, Sigel dispatched his paltry Home Guard cavalry west into the countryside to gather information about the State Guard's retreat and to determine whether Confederates were advancing from Arkansas.[29]

The arrival in Springfield significantly improved morale, and the men in the ranks were glad to see a town where they could outfit themselves with clothes and shoes and seek shelter from the rain. Springfield's population was about 1,500. A key agricultural center and transportation hub, the community was an island of Union sympathy floating in a sea of secessionist hostility. The German troops warmed to the rousing welcome given them despite the pelting rain. Little did the Federals realize that just a few days prior to their arrival tensions had nearly exploded into conflict when the Springfield Home Guards paraded through the town square along with the local contingent of Minute Men. Remarkably, no shots were fired and by the end of the day the Stars and Stripes was the only flag hanging in the center of town.[30]

Four days after Sigel's soldiers secured the town, Colonel Salomon's well worn Fifth Missouri Volunteers marched into Springfield after a grueling tramp from Rolla. Salomon's arrival swelled Sigel's ranks to a small brigade-sized force of 1,100 men. While Sigel mulled over his options, rumors swirled through Springfield of a retreat by the defeated State Guard toward the southwestern corner of the state. Sigel's primary task, in addition to securing Springfield, was to prevent the unification of the State Guard and the Confederate troops in Arkansas. The arrival of Salomon's regiment boosted Sigel's numbers and made him more confident of hurrying off to implement his plan.[31]

Sensing an opportunity, Sigel decided to assume the initiative. Leaving Home Guards behind to hold Springfield, he marched his small column in the rumored direction of the State Guard. The German commander hoped to stall the retreat of Governor Jackson's troops and allow Nathaniel Lyon to catch the retreating Rebels from the north. The move also offered Sigel the opportunity for independent command he so passionately desired.[32]

On June 23, the same day Sigel triumphantly entered Springfield, General Sweeny finally left St. Louis for Rolla with about 300 men. Unfortunately, his logistical problems were not behind him. His arrival at the railhead the following day was greeted with the unwelcome news that the local transportation he was promised had failed to materialize. Once again McKinstry, Lyon's quartermaster, had canceled the wagons that Sweeny worked so hard to procure. A search of the surrounding area found it devoid of both wagons and animals. Knowing that another lengthy delay could doom the expedition, Sweeny made sure that Col. Gratz Brown's unit was up to the task of guarding the rail head and hastily pushed his remaining men forward, carrying what he could with him.[33]

Exactly what transpired over the next several days remains somewhat obscure. According to one source, when Sweeny's column was a few days south of Rolla it was intercepted by three riders from Springfield expressing concern about the safety of their town. The prominent Springfield citizens were worried that their city might fall under Rebel control without the presence of the Union army. Sigel, they announced, had abandoned Springfield and was marching southwest in search of Sterling Price, who was rumored to be operating in the vicinity.[34]

The news of Sigel's departure supposedly stunned Sweeny. This was the first inkling he had that his two regiments were not where he assumed they were. The riders also related to Sweeny rumors of an impending invasion by Confederate troops in Arkansas. Justifiably concerned and all but helpless to immediately change or influence matters, the Irishman could only urge his men forward at a quicker pace over the muddy roads, establishing small garrisons along the way.[35]

Sweeny arrived in Springfield on July 1 and established his headquarters. Sigel and Salomon had indeed departed. The delays and supply difficulties experienced earlier in the campaign were now seriously impacting Union fortunes. Sweeny and Sigel were separated by some 80 miles, and Lyon was still stranded north around Boonville. Sweeny's line of communications with his superior was virtually nonexistent, and inadequate transportation still hampered Sweeny's efforts.[36]

Federal hopes for a successful campaign in southwest Missouri now lay in the hands of the former German revolutionary and his 1,100 immigrant soldiers.

5

Unification

Pro-Southern men were in retreat across western Missouri. From Boonville and Lexington, the two wings of Claiborne Jackson's State Guard fell back, moving toward a central location to safely unite the columns. The conjoined segments, it was hoped, would be large enough to make a stand against Nathaniel Lyon's better equipped and trained Federals.

Could Lyon move quickly enough to trap and destroy the segments piecemeal? That thought certainly must have passed through Jackson's mind as he retreated with the Boonville wing of the State Guard. The governor commanded both pieces of the bisected army by virtue of the Military Bill, one of the last pieces of law passed by the Missouri legislature. While his family could boast of a proud military legacy dating back to the Revolutionary War, Jackson was a banker and knew little of military life. That fact became painfully apparent during the State Guard's first field encounter with the Federals. The governor had hoped to rely heavily on the military skills and charismatic persona of Sterling Price, but his untimely illness had instead left Jackson and the army in disarray just before the Boonville skirmish. Without Price's leadership the governor was forced to seek out the advice of former Mexican War officers, men who had undergone training at West Point or the Virginia Military Institute, as well as ambitious state senators who accompanied the army. Without these men Jackson's fledgling army would not receive the organization and training it so badly required.[1]

Jackson's task was a tall order. Somehow, he and his generals had to organize and train the ragtag collection of men in the midst of a retreat following a defeat in the field. Constantly on the move, there was no time to perfect the drills necessary to transform the mass of men into a respectable army. While Rains' Lexington column had not suffered a defeat, his soldiers also lacked training and firm organization. Both segments accumulated recruits during the retreat. "We broke camp and took up our line of march southward," remembered Orderly Sergeant Salem H. Ford, traveling with Rains' wing of the State Guard, "gathering some unarmed recruits along the way." Although the new recruits were welcome, the additional manpower only served to exacerbate the army's problems. Most of these new arrivals were unarmed and untrained.[2]

In the face of these seemingly insurmountable difficulties, the State Guard's upper echelon of officers went to work to whip the men into form. Former regular army officer Alexander E. Steen taught the men how to march and drill. Lewis Henry Little, a native of Maryland and veteran of the Mexican War, worked to perfect the army's organization. Although Lewis Little—who was known to his friends as Henry—walked the thin line of neutrality for a time, his meetings with Governor Jackson that May convinced him to throw his lot in with the South. The Marylander described his first service as "a kind of Nondescript Ad Genl," for Sterling Price. An appointment as colonel in the Missouri State Guard quickly followed. The Missourians, who described him as "quick and active in his speech and movements, with a look and manner somewhat French," loved him. His relationship with "Old Pap" Price never faltered. Their camaraderie would span from the first days of the war in St. Louis, when he became one of Price's favorite subordinates, until the moment he fell from his horse at Iuka with a minie ball in the forehead. Henry Little's contributions to Jackson during the retreat toward Lamar were invaluable.[3]

Others traveling with the army had some training at the West Point Military Academy. None of them (other than John Marmaduke) had graduated from the prestigious institution. The most prominent of these men was Col. Richard H. Weightman, who led

the First brigade in James Rains Division. The column also contained five graduates of the Virginia Military Institute. Together,
their training and experience went a long way toward molding the
State Guard into a cohesive fighting unit as the Missourians
tramped south. One critical fault of the State Guard at this time was
the rampant nepotism that permeated its ranks. In many situations
within the small army, family ties took precedence over military
training or competency. Sterling Price, for example, promoted his
son Edwin, who had no military experience on his resume, over
several more qualified candidates. In spite of this damaging favorit-
ism, by the end of the summer of 1861 many of the unqualified
officers were discovered and rooted out, leaving behind a State
Guard officered by a solid set of leaders.[4]

Sergeant Ford was one of those who needed the leadership and
example of an experienced officer. Ford's road to war was typical of
many of the Missourians marching into the southwestern portion of
the state that summer. Together with other men from Platte County,
Ford had traveled to Lexington, "the place of rendezvous for that part
of the State for those who wanted to join the Confederate army."
Gathered in Lexington along the banks of the Missouri River were
"about two thousand men ready to buckle on their armor in defense
of the South," wrote Ford. "Some were armed with shotguns, squirrel rifles, and the majority of them were unarmed." Needing some
type of organization, the men "organized an infantry and made Col.
John T. Hughes commander of the regiment." Ford was "appointed
orderly sergeant of the company," he boasted, although he "only
knew three or four men in the Company." He enlisted in state
service for a period of nine months, "thinking and hoping the
trouble would be over by that time, but the sequel proved our hopes
to be in vain." Ford and his company managed to tuck but one week
of drill under their belts before Jackson's defeat at Boonville forced
their retreat from Lexington.[5]

While the majority of the State Guard were inadequately or
indifferently armed and equipped, some members sported rifled
muskets obtained from the raid at the Liberty Arsenal earlier in the
year. General Rains' Lexington column of two divisions, which also
carried the spare shot and gunpowder for the army, was the benefac-
tor of the pilfered small arms. Alas, they were too few to arm even

the majority of his men, most of whom still carried all but worthless Mexican War-era smoothbore muskets, complete with woefully outdated flintlock firing mechanisms. Hundreds more sported old heavy-stock squirrel guns or shotguns. Like their indifferent armament, the State Guard also boasted a wide variety of wearing apparel. The majority of the troops marched in their daily farm clothes, a jean-like material of varying shades of brown and blue. The homespun garments were dyed in local butternut or black walnut hulls, which lent the clothes their earthy shades. The predominance of the darker brown hues earned the Southerners their first nick-name: the Butternut Boys. While less common, some of the more elite members of the army wore their Sunday best, complete with colorful coats, ruffled shirts and silk top hats. An odder looking army would have been difficult to find in any war.[6]

In an attempt to resolve ongoing supply problems, Jackson appointed state senator and former journalist, Thomas L. Snead, as his aide-de-camp for logistical matters. The inexperienced Snead quickly warmed to the thankless task and put forth a strong effort to resolve Jackson's supply difficulties. June 19 found Snead standing by the side of the rutted roadway closely observing the governor's 1,100 soldiers as they tramped by him just south of Tipton. The new staffer penned several reminiscences of the early months of the war in Missouri. "In all their motley array there was hardly a uniform to be seen," he remembered, "and then throughout all the brilliant campaign on which they were about to enter there was nothing to distinguish officers, even a general from the men in the ranks, save a bit of red flannel, or a piece of cloth fastened to the shoulder of the arm, of the former." Although poorly dressed, Snead was convinced the men were prime military material. "But for all they were the truest of the best soldiers," he wrote,

Many of them, when just emerging from boyhood, had fought under Price or [Alexander] Doniphan in Mexico; many had been across the Great Plain and were inured to the hardships of the wilderness; and many had been engaged in the hot strife which ensanguined the men, and who were not any more intelligent than the great masses of American citizens. Not one had voluntarily abandoned his home with all its tender ties, thrown away all his possessions and left father and mother, or wife and children behind enemy's lines. That he might himself stand by the south in her hour of peril, and help her defend her fields and firesides.[8]

Thomas Snead's task was a difficult one. A disturbing lack of supplies plagued both wings of the retreating State Guard. Jackson's column, for example, lost its reserve rations when it was forced from Camp Bacon at Boonville. Jackson's soldiers subsisted on small portions of cornmeal, bacon and beans. Southern sympathizers along the march donated vegetables from their summer gardens, with bread and fresh churned butter occasionally supplementing their diet. Despite orders against foraging, many Southerners slipped away from camp to raid crops of fresh greens and new potatoes. Animals, however obtained, were usually butchered on the spot and consumed immediately. George McKee, who lived near the route traversed by James Rains' column told of his four-legged "contribution" to the Southern cause. The soldiers passed his farm all night "doing us no damage, except to eat up a cow of mine."[9]

The population thinned as the column continued its journey south, making food more difficult to come by. Foraging parties were sent roaming far into the countryside to bring back what they could. As the retreat continued, politicians traveling with each column wrote out Missouri script to pay for the foodstuffs and hay the army was seizing. It was a noble gesture, but the paper and ink proved to be as worthless as Southern fortunes within the state.[10]

Jackson's column was augmented on June 19 when his withdrawal absorbed Mosby Parsons' mixed command just west of Tipton. Parsons recruited his mass of foot soldiers and cavalry, about 650 men grandly dubbed the Sixth Division, Missouri State Guard, from the state's central counties. The reinforcements, together with the precious four artillery pieces and the officer riding at their head, were a welcome sight to Jackson.[11]

Mosby Monroe Parsons, a Virginia native, had migrated to Cole County, Missouri at an early age. A thriving law practice preceded the outbreak of war with Mexico, which prompted Parsons to join the 1st Missouri Mounted Infantry. Elected captain of Company F, Parsons served with distinction during the conflict and was cited for gallantry at the little-known Battle of Sacramento on February 28, 1847. His military record and return to the legal profession served as a springboard for a successful career in politics. Parsons served from 1853 through 1857 as Missouri's Attorney General, and in the latter year took a seat as a democrat in the state senate. The Virginian-turned-Missourian was an early and strong ally of Governor Jackson's efforts to pull the state into the Confederate fold. While his support for Jackson had not waned, the governor's actions had mildly strained their friendship. Parsons, an experienced combat veteran and a solid leader, was troubled by his inability to arrive at the Boonville battlefield in time to assist his comrades.[12]

As Snead pondered the army's logistical dilemmas and Parsons stewed about Boonville, Jackson's army continued its retreat to Cole Camp, twenty-two miles southwest of Tipton. There, 350 soldiers comprising Lt. Col. Walter S. O'Kane's Battalion added their numbers to the swelling ranks of the State Guard on June 21. While camped at the small village, rumor of a Federal threat from the east reached Jackson. O'Kane's Battalion was deployed to scout and probe for the foe believed to be lurking beyond the army's vulnerable flank, but the news proved unfounded and the march southwest continued.[13]

O'Kane's men joined the State Guard at Cole Camp with a small victory tucked under their collective belts. The story of the fight, such that it was, lifted the flagging spirits of Jackson's army and reinvigorated tired legs. The inspirational affair took place on June 19 when a small German-led Home Guard regiment had failed to post a picket while sleeping in two barns. O'Kane and his men surprised the militia and, although accounts vary widely, apparently inflicted serious casualties. O'Kane's heavily exaggerated version of events places Federals losses at over 200 men, with an additional 100 captured. Other more reasonable sources claim the Federals lost, at a minimum, fifteen killed. O'Kane's casualties were light. While the skirmish at Cole Camp did not affect the development or the outcome of the campaign, O'Kane did manage to seize 362 muskets and a large quantity of bayonets, all of which went toward equipping Jackson's grateful soldiers.[14]

The fitful retreat continued another 40 miles to Warsaw, where on June 23 the 2,100-man column rested along the banks of the Osage River. The other wing of the State Guard under James Rains was at this time in the vicinity of Warrensburg. This was the first

Brig. Gen. Mosby Monroe Parsons
Missouri Historical Society

time since their flight from Boonville that the men of the State Guard could rest without imminent fear of being attacked by Nathaniel Lyon's Federals. Remarkably, neither Jackson nor his subordinates had attempted to track Lyon's movements once they started their own retreat. The state troops knew virtually nothing about Lyon's current strength or intentions and even less about the logistical difficulties under which he labored at Boonville. Jackson's desire to insert as much distance as possible between himself and the enemy—without regard to his opponent's actions—had effectively blindfolded his army. Meanwhile, the rain continued to soak the Missouri countryside.[15]

As the army rested Jackson and his staff fretted over the paucity of artillery. How could they hope to match Lyon's well-trained batteries with four small 6-lb. guns manned by an untrained crew firing largely homemade ammunition? Part of the answer was found later that afternoon when alert pickets captured two men lurking near the Southern camp. Believed to be spies, the pair were marched to the governor's headquarters in Warsaw for interrogation. The men turned out to be Capt. Henry Guibor and Lt. William P. Barlow, two militia men captured by Lyon at Camp Jackson. While both admitted to having signed paroles, neither felt obligated to obey their duress-inspired oaths. More importantly to Jackson and the Missouri State Guard, Guibor and Barlow were well-schooled in the art of artillery. Parsons, who was inexperienced in artillery tactics, welcomed the assistance, while the artillerists embraced the opportunity to create a well-trained and disciplined battery to support the governor's infantry.[16]

Henry Guibor, a native of Alsace, France, was an especially valuable acquisition. The forty-two-year old Mexican War veteran and St. Louis University graduate received his first gunnery experience in the Southwest Expedition in 1860, when he traveled with the St. Louis militia to protect the Missouri border from marauding Kansas Jayhawkers. Guibor garnered valuable additional field training on the Kansas-Missouri border during the winter of 1860, where as a lieutenant he commanded of a section of guns under the direction of Col. John Stevens Bowen. He would need to draw on all of his training and experience for the task that lay before him: the organization and training of the Missouri State Guard's artillery arm.

Capt. Henry Guibor

Missouri Historical Society

Before war's end Guibor would be widely recognized as one of the South's finest artillerists.[17]

But in June 1861, Guibor was just another Missouri officer attempting to train and equip a collection of new soldiers into battle-ready condition. The majority of his crew were exiles from all over St. Louis. A review of Guibor's roster discloses a diverse mixture of nationalities—including Irishmen, Italians, Germans, Scots, Englishmen and at least one free black. Few if any had combat experience. Two serious hurdles confronted Guibor. First, there was no official quartermaster department from which to draw supplies or equipment and as a result, the crew was forced to improvise up and down the line. Staff sponges to clean the tubes were made from thick bands of cloth wrapped around the head of a fence rail. Gunpowder—of which the South had virtually none and few avenues of obtaining sufficient quantities of the precious substance—was secured from any source possible. Quality ammunition was also difficult to come by, and before long, Guibor's men were filling their wagons with homemade artillery charges. Regulation canister—large cans filled with iron or lead balls for use against enemy personnel—was all but unobtainable, and Guibor made do by cutting iron rods into small pieces and bundling them together. The four 6-lb. iron guns were drawn not by horses but by mules, which made the trek over the muddy and rutted roads that much more difficult.[18]

The second major dilemma facing Guibor, perhaps not quite as critical as the lack of a legitimate quartermaster department, was the shortage of time in which to train his crew. The army was almost constantly on the move and Guibor was not able to drill his men on dry, open fields. While he utilized every possible moment to instruct his gunners, he knew that combat would quickly expose his battery's weaknesses. Still, he and Barlow enjoyed some success in this area. "We soon had the boys well enough instructed to do their own firing, rapidly and correctly," wrote Barlow. "By constant work and drill. . .in a week's time we gained an astonishing degree of efficiency. No one who had not witnessed it, could believe how quickly those raw country boys picked up the intricate artillery drill." The inexperienced gunners had but two things on their mind, "to kill yanks and to get something to eat." Despite Barlow's praise, Guibor knew he needed more time to drill and quality equipment. Neither was in the cards.[19]

On June 25 the Missouri state militiamen broke camp and crossed the swollen Osage River. As the retreat toward Lamar continued, so too did Claiborne Jackson's woes. The acquisition of seasoned veterans like Henry Guibor and the augmentation of the army by Walter O'Kane's Battalion were partially offset with the loss of other experienced men and officers. Hoping to secure a commission in the Confederate army, Boonville commander John S. Marmaduke departed Missouri for Arkansas, abandoning his position in the state militia. Marmaduke, who would prove himself adept as a cavalrymen, lacked confidence in the ragged Missouri army. Militia General John B. Clark, Sr. also departed, albeit temporarily, in order to return home and raise troops. Other officers left to secure weapons for the State Guard, while additional men left the ranks because of political disagreements within the army's command structure. Jackson's own controversial political positions, for example—especially his decision to support the extension of slavery, which led to a break in his alliance with former Senator Thomas Hart Benton—alienated some of the politicos traveling with the column.[20]

The hemorrhaging of officers, political dissension in the ranks and dangerous strategic situation, coupled with the army's impoverished logistical system was enough to give any commander a headache. But it was Jackson's stomach that ailed him. His abdominal difficulties may have had less to to with stress than the onset of the cancer that would combine with other ailments to take his life on December 6, 1862, in Little Rock, Arkansas. In addition to worrying about the army, a long and slow wagon train stretched out behind the marching infantry. The vehicles were filled with the state's official records as well as an assortment of clanging pots and pans and feather beds—all for the comfort of the prominent citizens of Jefferson City who had decided to evacuate the city with Jackson. The wagons slowed his march considerably, but the ailing governor did not have the heart to tell those who remained loyal to him to abandon their property by the roadside.[21]

Another difficult 25 mile march southwest from Warsaw brought Jackson's army to Osceola, where its members struggled to cross the raging tributaries of the Osage River. Although it initially appeared as though the crossing of the river would not be possible, the army and its cumbersome trains managed to ford the stream with only a minimal loss of equipment. The Boonville wing of the State Guard continued traveling southwest on well-worn road beds for another 30 miles to the small village of Montevallo, a hub for seven roads that fanned out in all directions. Jackson spent the first day of July resting his army at Montevallo while waiting for news from James Rains.

Artillerist William Barlow "witnessed a new way of giving orders" during this stage of the march. "Our division had taken the wrong road, and Gen. Parsons sent his quartermaster. . .to reverse the head of the column," explained Barlow. "The colonel galloped to the front of the leading wagon, halted, drew a navy six, cocked and pointed it at the leading driver's head and yelled, `Turn around thar, you and go back!' Our teamsters were more independent than generals, but that one `turned around' with no back talk."

While his officers used the brief respite in Montevallo to continue training the men, the governor received disappointing news from Montgomery, Alabama. Leroy P. Walker, the Confederacy's first of several Secretaries of War, replied to Jackson's earlier pleas to send regular Confederate army troops to Missouri. According to Walker, the Confederacy was "Forced to acknowledge the critical nature of her condition, environed as she is on three sides by the enemy." The Secretary went on to explain that he was denying the request. "I have not for the want of Confederate authority within your limits, been able to extend to you that measure of relief called for by your necessities." According to the governor's aide, Thomas Snead, Jackson could barely contain his anger when he read the telegram. Missouri desperately needed additional manpower and weapons. While the Richmond government's overly-technical attitude towards his state irked him, the governor understood the realities of the situation. Missouri had not officially joined the Confederacy, and thus the Missouri State Guard was being left to fight on its own hook. There would be little if any overt assistance unless or until his men were forced out of the state into Arkansas. To some it appeared as though the Davis administration either failed to grasp the emergency that confronted the retreating Southerners or did not appreciate the importance of Missouri to the Confederate cause.[22]

Not all the news that reached the army at Montevallo was bad. John Q. Burbridge, a prominent banker and farmer from Louisiana, arrived with ten men and 150 extra rifles commandeered from a Federal Home Guard unit. The 39-year-old Burbridge was a key member of the militia in northern Missouri, where he had spent time harassing local Federals attempting to capture his small force. The governor welcomed the tiny band into his army, broke camp on July 2 and continued his withdrawal toward Lamar.[23]

As Jackson and Rains guided their respective columns deeper into southwest Missouri and away from the aggressive Nathaniel Lyon, Sterling Price was riding south in his attempt to link up with Brig Gen. Ben McCulloch in northern Arkansas. "Old Pap's" journey across the rolling prairies acted like a magnet for hundreds of Missourians, who singly and in small groups joined the charismatic leader. By the time he camped at Nevada, not far from the Arkansas border, Price may have had as many as 1,200 men traveling with him. He arrived at Cowskin Prairie in early July, where he waited for the approaching McCulloch to discuss the deteriorating military situation.[24]

James Rains, meanwhile, continued to march his two-division wing of the Missouri State Guard—composed of his own Eighth Division and William Yarnel Slack's Fourth Division—toward Lamar. As far as the men of the former division were concerned, they were marching home. Their withdrawal was carrying them fitfully toward Jasper County, where the 1,800-man division had been largely raised. Rains' own home was located on a modest parcel of land in the southeast corner of the county near Sarcoxie.[25]

Colonel Richard H. Weightman
Missouri Historical Society

The infantry in Rains' Eighth Division was commanded by Col. Richard Hanson Weightman, who held the dubious distinction of being expelled from West Point for slashing a fellow cadet in a duel. It was not the only time the feisty Weightman would demonstrate a proclivity to resort to the blade. Following his dismissal Weightman worked a series of odd jobs before settling in Missouri, where he enlisted in a company of militia bound for the Mexican War. He rose to command two companies of M. L. Clark's Light Artillery, part of the famous contingent that traveled to California with Col. Alexander Doniphan. Weightman was a hard fighter who, like Mosby Parsons, had distinguished himself in the Battle of Sacramento. Colonel Doniphan, writing in his after-action report of that battle, singled out Weightman for praise: "Much has been said. . .of the gallantry of our artillery unlimbering within two hundred and fifty yards of the enemy at Palo Alto, but much more daring was the charge of Colonel Weightman when he unlimbered within fifty yards of the enemy." Weightman's bravery was well-known. During the fighting at Chapultepec, he plugged the muzzle of one of the Mexican guns with a solid shot.[26]

After the war Weightman was selected by territorial governor James C. Calhoun to represent the New Mexico territory in the United States Senate from 1851 to 1853. Shortly thereafter while running a newspaper in Santa Fe, New Mexico, Weightman printed "some slighting remarks," as one writer labeled them, about F. H. Aubrey. The alleged victim had won fame and a lucrative bet by "making a nonstop horseback ride from Santa Fe. . .to Independence, Missouri." When Aubrey learned of this, he returned to Santa Fe to garner an apology or to "keel him, by gar!" The two met in a saloon, where Weightman was sitting on the counter talking with the bartender. The unsuspecting newspaperman invited Aubrey to share a bottle of wine, even going so far as to toast him with his glass held high. An argument broke out, and Weightman dashed the contents of his glass in Aubrey's face. Although Aubrey managed to draw his pistol, Weightman seized the Frenchman's wrist with his left hand and drew a knife with his right, burying it to the hilt in Aubrey's chest. He died a short time later. After a move to Kansas in 1857, Weightman found himself in the middle of the sectional dispute raging in the state. Just prior to 1860, he relocated back to

Missouri, where he threw his support behind Sterling Price and Governor Jackson.[27]

Weightman's command was designated the First Brigade, which represented all of the infantry traveling with Rains' Division. Although organizational records are woefully deficient, it appears as though the brigade essentially formed on the march. Initially it contained only Lt. Col. Thomas H. Rosser's 400-man First Infantry, but Weightman's numbers improved as the column marched toward Lamar when additional officers and units joined the withdrawing column. Colonel Francis M. McKinney and an independent detachment of sixteen men joined early in the retreat. Colonel John R. Graves' Second Regiment added another 271 soldiers to the brigade, while Col. Edgar V. Hurst attached his 251 followers to the column by creating the Third Regiment. Hurst was an especially welcome acquisition. The farmer from Cass County and Kentucky native was a graduate of that state's Military Institute. His knowledge of military affairs improved the skills and discipline of the entire brigade. All of Weightman's subordinate officers were respected in their communities, and their decision to join the State Guard influenced others to support the Southern cause. Rains' Division continued to grow and redefine itself as it marched through the state's small towns and villages.[28]

Much like Jackson's column, Mexican War veterans were also thick within the ranks of Rains' wing. In addition to Weightman, Rains placed substantial faith in artillerist Hiram Miller Bledsoe, another veteran of the war working to develop a battery of artillery to support the division's infantry. The native Kentuckian gained his artillery experience on the famous Doniphan expedition to California. Bledsoe was living and farming in Lexington when hostilities began. He served first as a captain in a local artillery unit for the state militia before offering his services to Sterling Price. The sickly-looking officer led a ragged group of about fifty recruits, most of whom had limited or no experience with artillery. His 3-gun battery consisted of two 6-lb. brass howitzers stolen from the Lexington's Liberty Arsenal, and "Old Sacramento," Bledsoe's favorite gun from the Mexican War. According to tradition, Old Sacramento was a captured 9-lb. Mexican artillery piece partially cast from melted silver Mexican church bells. Bledsoe claimed the weapon made a dis-

Captain Hiram Bledsoe, in a postwar image.
Missouri Historical Society

tinctive ringing sound when it was discharged, noting that "sumpin always dropped on the other side." Supposedly men from both armies could recognize the sound of the unique gun, and thus know when Bledsoe's battery was on the field. Bledsoe's unique appearance made him easy to spot, even among the haphazardly attired State Guard. In addition to his cadaverous-looking face, the small-framed gunner was in the habit of wearing hats several sizes too large, which routinely slid down and rested on his ears. The gunner's odd tastes in haberdashery and unhealthy appearance belied his intense personality and tough demeanor. He instilled a strong sense of loyalty in his men and eventually established one of the premier artillery batteries in Confederate service. Unable to drill during the retreat and without proper equipment and ammunition, however, few in the early summer of 1861 would have predicted Bledsoe's success.[29]

With his infantry in Weightman's capable hands and his artillery under Bledsoe's tutelage, Rains invested his energy into organizing his cavalry. The division's largest and best equipped arm consisted of ten companies spread among three regiments, each led by an experienced officer. The 3rd Missouri Cavalry, about 115 men, was commanded by Col. Robert Yates Ludwell Peyton. Rains and Peyton knew each other from their service together in the Missouri State Senate. When the fighting erupted, Peyton rushed home to his district in Lafayette County, where he gathered whoever he could muster and attached himself to Rain's' Division. A Virginian by birth, Peyton vigorously embraced the Southern cause. His military career was destined to be brief, however, as he was elected senator in the Confederate Congress by the newly-formed Rebel state government in Neosho in the fall of 1861.[30]

The second of Rains' three cavalry regiments, the 2nd Battalion Missouri Cavalry, was led by Lt. Col. James B. McCown. Comprised of four companies, McCown's Cedar County regiment totaled 250 men. Rains' third mounted regiment was Lt. Col. Richard A. Boughan's Seventh Missouri Cavalry, about 200 men. Some sources also claim that the 200-man Fifth Missouri Cavalry, commanded by Col. Jesse L. Cravens, Rains' father-in law, was with the army at this time. While his rank and position ostensibly smacks of nepotism, Cravens possessed a stronger military background than his son-in law (he attended West Point but failed to graduate). Cravens had the reputation of a rough and tumble character and was anxious to do battle with the Federals.[31]

Also traveling with Rains was Capt. Joseph O. Shelby, a wealthy businessman from Waverly, Lafayette County, Missouri, who had witnessed Nathaniel Lyon's provocations in St. Louis. Like many of the officers riding with Rains, Shelby was also a Tennessee transplant and had substantial experience fighting Kansans during the border wars. His reputation as a respected leader was well established by the outbreak of hostilities. Shelby had personally raised and equipped his unit with the best weapons and horses, and his men responded to his hard, aggressive style of leadership. Shelby and his Lafayette County recruits impressed everyone with their tough demeanor and discipline. Rains quickly developed considerable confidence in the officer and assigned his 43 men, the Lafayette County Cavalry (also known as Shelby's Rangers) to lead the retreat through southwest Missouri.[32]

The remaining division in Rains' column was commanded by William Y. Slack. A mixture of cavalry and infantry, Slack's Fourth Division numbered some 1,200 soldiers. Both of Slack's primary subordinates were energetic leaders, although their abilities in battle were yet to be determined. When Governor Jackson appointed Slack a district brigadier general, Slack turned over leadership of his own cavalry regiment, the 1st Missouri, to Col. Benjamin Allen Rives. The cavalryman, a strong civic leader, medical doctor and large plantation owner from Ray County, stood out amongst his fellow Missourians—largely because of his aristocratic Virginia background and his medical degree from the prestigious Virginia University. The majority of Rives' 500 cavalrymen were also from Ray County, located just east of Kansas City. Many had participated in the overthrow of the Liberty Arsenal in February and arrived well armed compared to the other State Guardsmen.[33]

The 700 men that comprised Slack's infantry were divided between two units, Col. Thomas A. Hughes' 1st Missouri Infantry, which was under the immediate command of Lt. Col. James A. Pritchard, and Maj. J. C. Thornton's Battalion. Pritchard led the regiment when Hughes was bumped up to command all of Slack's infantry. Hughes had recruited hundreds of men and sent them to

Lexington before the retreat south was ordered by Price. Unlike many similar units, Hughes and his Clinton County militia group were not caught off guard by the April 1861 hostilities. He had begun organizing several companies of infantry throughout the area well before the shelling of Fort Sumter. When a rider approached his farm in May to report the outbreak of violence in St. Louis, Hughes set aside his farm implements and picked up his sword. When rounding up his militia group, the men voted to gather at Lexington and follow their local hero, Sterling Price.[34]

Bad weather and swollen rivers plagued Rains' wing of the Guard just as they did Governor Jackson's men. Retreating south from Lexington on June 19, the two small divisions struggled across the Black River and marched 20 miles to Warrensburg. The column continued south the following day and tramped another 20 miles to Clinton, just a handful of miles north of the Grand River. While camped near Clinton the town's founder, Clinton Hunter, made his appearance with a small detachment of soldiers. In addition to the thirty men who swore allegiance to the State Guard that evening, two women appeared begging to join the army. Mrs. Eliza Apperson and Mrs. Minerva Conner volunteered to donate their services as nurses. Rains personally welcomed the ladies and spoke highly of their good intentions, but explained there was no current need for their services.[35]

Thus far Rains' journey south had proved uneventful. Below Clinton, however, the treacherous Grand River crossing loomed. Traversing it proved difficult and deadly. One man drowned when he slid off one of the rafts and was swept away before he could be rescued. After struggling across, Rains ordered anything of value that could aid a Federal crossing destroyed for several miles up and down the river. Leaving little in their wake to aid the enemy, one of Rains' men remarked that "Lyon would need magic to cross the river." From Clinton the men marched over a well traveled road to the Little Osage River, which they reached on the 28th of the month. Although the waterway was still swollen from the recent rains, the two divisions successfully navigated the stream by nailing and lashing together rafts constructed from dismantled buildings. Tempers probably matched the miserable weather. "One man shot another, who was buried," a private laconically recorded in his journal. The level of communication between Rains and Jackson during this period was so poor (or nonexistent) that neither realized that a march of a day or two separated them near Osceola.[36]

Rains' Missourians continued their march through the mud and poor weather until they reached the Marmiton River on June 29. "All the carpenters were at the Marmiton making a bridge or rafts to ferry over [the column]," observed Private Cheavens, who spent the day sewing on a tent. Many of the men crossed the river that evening, swimming their horses and ferrying the wagons. "The majority [of the army] had to camp on the bank of the river in the mud," Cheavens lamented. Food was scarce and the men bedded down for the night without supper. The next morning, Cheavens poled a raft and several wagons across the river. Surprisingly, only a few minor incidents marred the all-day crossing. For Cheavens the day was but another vexing experience. After losing his Bowie knife somewhere on the march, a lens from his spectacles slipped out. He lost his glasses completely the following day, which was followed by the theft of his only blanket on the last day of the month. On July 1 fortune finally turned a kind eye in the direction of this distinctly unlucky new soldier when the quartermaster issued an assortment of new clothing items, replacing original and by now well-worn garments.[37]

On July 2 the column was on the march again, heading toward Lamar. The rigors of the journey continued to mount. "My horse was sore backed, caused by wet blankets during the rain," admitted Cheavens, who added that he himself had "Took the diarrhea from eating meat and bread without salt." Like his comrades, the ill private attempted to supplement his meager diet by foraging while on picket duty. He had some success the following morning when he managed to coax a breakfast of bread and milk from a local. His diarrhea took a turn for the better when he discussed the situation with an officer who offered the private a cure. "[He] showed me a weed to cure the flux—button head snake root," wrote Cheavens. "It cured me before night, and has everyone who used it. It grows thick on the prairies." Earlier that same day a scare had rippled through the ranks when a false alarm spread that the enemy had been spotted. The panic subsided quickly and men resumed their march.[38]

The lengthy and exhausting two-pronged retreat ended during a blinding thunderstorm on July 3 when the two wings of the Missouri State Guard united just south of Lamar. Governor Jackson camped his force on Muddy Petty Bottoms, a flat piece of ground along a bend in the North Fork of the Spring River on Roupe's Point. The long-awaited unification, despite the miserable weather, improved the morale of the army. Private Cheavens watched as Governor Jackson and some of his generals walked amongst the soldiers at the camp. "A cannon boomed upon our arrival," he exclaimed in his diary, the spirits of the men rising as the armies united. After the men settled in they began to drill in their ongoing attempt to learn the rudiments of soldiering. Frivolity also found its way into the State Guard's new camp. The men "ran some deer from the bottom," wrote a Missourian.[39]

While Jackson and his generals could justifiably congratulate themselves for bringing the wings of the badly-divided army together after a difficult and debilitating retreat, there was still little about the Missouri State Guard that bespoke organization. In actuality the army that coalesced on the third day of July was little more than two mobs of men with only a semblance of order and discipline.

With the initial formalities of uniting the military columns concluded, a council with Jackson and his four brigadier generals was held to determine a course of action. After some debate it was decided that Roupe's Point would be a good place to rest and train the army. Although Jackson had not aggressively attempted to determine exactly where and in what strength the Federals were, no reports of any close pursuit by Lyon had been received. Lamar also was a good location to await the expected return of Sterling Price, who by this time had reached northwestern Arkansas.[40]

Governor Jackson's strategic situation improved significantly with the unification of the wings of his army, but the weather did not follow suit. The torrential rains wreaked havoc with every attempt to train and drill the troops. The flooding and soggy ground created monumental problems for Henry Guibor's gunners, who found drilling especially vexing. The artillery pieces routinely sank up to their axles in the thick sticky Missouri mud, and the cannoneers spent hours pushing and pulling on ropes in attempts to free them. The heavy wagons containing the ammunition for the army

also needed regular dislodging, which added to the misery of everyone unlucky enough to be concerned with such an enterprise. To
make matters worse, most of the wagons, which were confiscated
from citizens along the march, were not equipped with canvass
awnings to protect whatever was stored in them. As a result, much
of the precious gunpowder was soaked by the rain.[41]

With his army assembled at Camp Lamar Jackson finally had an
opportunity to evaluate his men. What he beheld could not have
pleased him. Given the fluid nature of the retreat and the large
numbers of men who had drifted into and out of each column,
neither Jackson nor Rains had been in a position to accurately assess
the size of their respective commands. Each column had undertaken
its withdrawal with about 2,000 men, and each had managed to add
approximately 1,000 men along the march (or while camped along
the Spring River). Unfortunately, muster rolls and detailed reports
were not kept during this period, so it is impossible to calculate
these numbers with precision. Roughly speaking, the army that
gathered at Muddy Petty Bottoms held approximately 6,000 men, of
whom only 4,000 were armed. Few were combat ready. Equipping
these men (even those armed were poorly outfitted) and preparing
them for combat was a priority for the governor and his staff since
they would continue to eat rations and consume the State Guard's
meager resources. Until they were armed they were more of a liabil-
ity than an asset. Jackson's best hope was that Price would return
from his trip to Arkansas with weapons to place in their empty
hands.[42]

While leading a small defeated and ill-equipped army was hard
enough, the haphazard organization of the Missouri State Guard's
units probably proved as vexing to Jackson as to modern historians.
The State Guard was not completely organized until later that summer, and but few documents from its early days exist. Some units
carried the same designation, while others boasted monikers no
more formal than an officer's name. Jackson's army was a ragtag
affair, completely unlike the more precisely-defined and organized
armies forming east of the Mississippi River.[43]

Word of the growing Southern army camped near Lamar spread
throughout Missouri's southwestern counties. Local men began responding to the call for troops by the governor. George F. Ward, the

founder of the small town of Lamar, arrived in camp on the same day that Jackson's column trudged in. His presence caused other men who respected his judgment to enroll in the State Guard. The recruits elected Ward captain of their new company, which he personally presented to Jackson. The governor readily accepted the additional—and well-equipped—fighters.[44]

Another small group from the southeastern corner of Barton County led by a "Major Randall" joined the State Guard at Camp Lamar. Only a few of Randall's men arrived armed, however, and their presence merely compounded Jackson's logistical dilemma. Near sundown on July 3, George Parker arrived with another group of well-mounted local men and was assigned to serve as scouts with Jo Shelby.[45]

The camp near the North Fork of the Spring River continued to grow as more men poured into the area. The majority of these new arrivals did not report to a recruiting officer and thus were not immediately assigned to a regiment. Most simply found a place to spread their blankets and make themselves comfortable. The entire creek bottom soon resembled a disorganized series of semi-private encampments where men lounged near smoky fires, exchanged rumors and cooked rations. Many of the officers simply gave up trying to organize them. None of Jackson's subordinates had ever contended with the task of getting 6,000 civilians organized and ready for combat.[46]

As the sun rose over the Southern camp on July 4, the State Guard slowly stirred for another day of training. Jackson may have wondered why so few Missourians had heeded his call for 50,000 men to join him in overthrowing Federal authority in the state. After enduring the punishing marches to Lamar, he knew those that remained were loyal and ready to fight—but what could he reasonably accomplish with this ill-equipped mass of soldiers?[47]

And where was Nathaniel Lyon? That question added substantially to the governor's stress. Mounted scouts continued to send back reports that the Federal commander was not within striking distance. Perhaps he was struggling to cross the difficult rivers just as Jackson had a few days earlier.[48]

The hot and humid Independence Day sun brought with it a perplexing military question that Governor Jackson was not equipped to decide. Should he continue moving his army deeper into southwest Missouri, giving up more ground for security and time to train his men? Or should he choose a piece of ground and prepare to make a stand against Lyon's expected pursuit? Neither Jackson nor his brigadiers believed the State troops were ready to stand against Lyon. Boonville had been proof of that fact. New rumors confused the issue and added to Jackson's woes. The gossip, which was all that it was, held that a column of Federal soldiers under Maj. Samuel Sturgis had moved down the Missouri-Kansas border, shadowing James Rains' army to Lamar.[49]

As the governor prepared for breakfast, he would have felt considerably better had he known that Lyon had only just left Boonville. But he did not know this, and he had not taken the steps necessary to discover where his opponent was and what his intentions were. Typical of the entire campaign to date, Jackson's strategy was managed not by solid information and planning, but by instinct.[50]

Sigel's March

Thirty-six years old and involuntarily exiled from his homeland, the former German minister of war felt quite comfortable riding at the vanguard of marching soldiers. Although it had been many years since he had experienced organized warfare, Franz Sigel was once again guiding an armed force toward battle. This time his mission was not the overthrow of an established government at the head of a revolutionary army, but the interception of the withdrawing "revolutionaries" while leading a body of government troops. Instead of heading a rebellion he was attempting to thwart one. The irony was probably not lost on the career soldier.[1]

Once he arrived on the Ozark plateau, Sigel learned that Governor Jackson's army was heading south toward Lamar while and another group of Rebels (incorrectly as it turned out) was operating 65 or 70 miles southwest at Neosho. Pondering his options, Sigel decided to launch a thrust deeper into southwest Missouri to prevent the junction of these columns or prevent their escape into Arkansas. Without waiting for or receiving additional orders from Sweeny, Sigel departed Springfield on June 26. It was a fateful decision, but then the officer's past was full of such denouements.[2]

Franz Sigel's first taste of combat was during the German Revolution of 1848, when he sided with the Liberals in their attempt to overthrow Prussia's ruling elite. Influenced by his revolutionary friends, Sigel assumed command of one of the "armies" of the Liberals, which was little more than a band of 4,000 revolutionaries comprised largely of students, factory workers and artisans—with a few professional soldiers sprinkled in for good measure. Overflowing with optimism, Sigel led his men toward the enemy. The first campaign was a disaster.[3]

Sigel's ill-prepared army faced the Hessian and Baden troops at Lake Constance, in the Black Forest region near Freiburg, and again at Württemburg. He was badly defeated on each occasion. Although pursued by the enemy, Sigel managed to escape to Switzerland via France, where he spent the balance of 1848 in exile. In 1849 another revolt swept through the German states and Sigel and his ardent revolutionaries crossed back into Hesse province to plan an offensive against the government. The first real opportunity for Sigel to stand out amongst his fellow officers was during the Battle of Heppenheim, where he again led an army of some 4,000 men against the Hessians. Advancing against a superior force, Sigel's revolutionaries were thrown into disarray and driven from the field when the enemy launched a determined counter-attack. With his regiments streaming from the field, Sigel managed to rally a portion of his men and with them conducted a series of stubborn rear guard actions that saved his army from a crushing defeat. "Colonel Sigel led [the] troops personally and was at the front in every situation that called for giving orders and encouraging and inspiring his [men]," was how one source described his actions.[4]

Although his reputation suffered temporarily as a result of the setback, the determined—and slightly wounded—Sigel courted younger leaders of the movement and slowly regained favor with the newly formed Executive and State Committee. Before long he replaced army commander Alfred von Beck, who had fallen out of favor with the revolutionaries, and a few months later led the left wing of the army at the Battle of Waghäusel. Prussian reinforcements turned the tide of the desperate struggle and the center of the army broke and ran from the field. Louis Mieroslawski, the army's leader, described Sigel's conduct during the difficult withdrawal as "one of the most highly successful [and] tactical retreats" ever car-

Col. Franz Sigel
John Bradbury Collection

ried out. After the day's fighting ended Mieroslawski spoke glowingly of Sigel as a "bold and able leader."[5]

The uprising was doomed although blood would continue to be spilled. The army retreated to Rastatt, where Sigel led his old battalion from Baden in a grand but failed charge against Prussian infantry. After the Rastatt defeat Sigel and the remnants of the revolutionary army fled to Switzerland. Faced with expulsion, he chose to emigrate to the United States, where he settled in New York City along with many of his fellow "Forty-eighters," as the failed revolutionaries referred to themselves.[6]

Sigel maintained his ties to the military after he settled in his newly adopted country by joining the 5th New York, the oldest and most respected German militia unit in the country. His tactical knowledge and substantial battlefield experience, something the majority of those around him lacked, impressed his peers and earned him respect in New York's German community. He also demonstrated his abilities by becoming an instructor of local units. Although he led a comfortable life in New York, he left the city to take an assistant professorship in St. Louis when Dr. Adam Hammer of the Deutsches Instituit offered him the position. Sigel had gained a reputation among the German population as a fine teacher of mathematics at the Feldner School in New York. It was thus with some reluctance that he resigned his militia commission, turned his back on a developing political career and moved west to the Gateway City to immerse himself into academia.[7]

Once settled in St. Louis, Sigel became deeply involved in the politics of his newly-adopted city. He joined the Turner and Union Clubs and actively promoted his viewpoints through the *Westliche Post* newspaper. His passion and knowledge gained him prominence and respect among the city's ethnic community. Sigel made no attempt to cloak his partisanship toward the Republican party during the 1860 election, and he worked tirelessly to promote Lincoln's candidacy. While championing the Republican cause he received a promotion to district school superintendent of the St. Louis Public School system, a position he held in addition to his full professorship at the Deutsches Instituit.[8]

While Sigel's personal fortunes continued to rise, his adopted country's future slipped into uncertainty. Gustave Struve, one of Sigel's former military comrades from the old country, spoke for many of the Forty-eighters when he described the issue facing the country as one "between secession and Union and liberty and slavery." From Sigel's viewpoint Struve's writings accurately assessed the situation. Many people in the local German community were looking to Sigel for leadership, and the former minister of war did not hesitate to volunteer his services.[9]

One of his first goals was to make sure that Forty-eighters with military experience joined the first Home Guard units formed in the city. A series of newspaper articles began to flow from his pen and he also delivered speeches, all on the subject of retaining the Union. It came as a surprise to no one when Sigel was elected colonel to the 3rd Missouri Volunteer Infantry, a regiment composed primarily of Germans and Bohemians. Franz Sigel relished his new position. One recent biographer noted that when Sigel donned the blue coat, it "earned him the name 'Yankee Dutchman.'" The local German press had a field day with their new hero and lauded him as "a military genius, upon whose head many felt, a general's hat would fit best."[10]

It was this officer, a man with substantial field experience and a hearty following amongst the well-disciplined Germans, that was marching into southwestern Missouri to intercept the retreating State Guard. Perhaps this time around the newly-minted "military genius" would not leave defeats strewn in his wake.

At least part of Sigel's decision to leave Springfield was prompted by rumors that Sterling Price was riding south, hugging Missouri's western border. It was Price's force that was reportedly camped at Pool's Prairie, just below Neosho. After leaving Springfield on the morning of June 26 Sigel received word that the bulk of the State Guard was still somewhere north of Price, slowly following in his wake. Sigel's inability to gather reliable intelligence from the sparsely populated countryside only compounded his problems. His departure from Springfield, coupled with rumors concerning a Confederate invasion of the region from Arkansas, caused a mild panic in the town.[11]

Sigel's precipitous evacuation of Springfield did not allow time for Lt. Col. Charles Salomon's Fifth Missouri Infantry and Maj. Franz Backoff's artillery battery to arrive from Rolla. When they did straggle into town the following day, orders were waiting for them to follow Sigel southwest on the Mt. Vernon Road. Sigel's plan to interpose himself between the Confederate army in Arkansas and the retreating Missouri State Guard represented that of a confident and aggressive commander—especially when one considers that he launched his operation with only about 700 soldiers. If he believed the rumors concerning Rebel troop movements, he surely realized the danger of placing his small force squarely between two potentially larger pieces of the enemy, either one of which could crush him. The dangerous circumstance was typical of several similar situations he had experienced during the 1848 Revolution. During that war Sigel had often acted in the same manner, choosing aggressiveness over passivity. On Europe's continent, however, the former course of action had not served him well.[12]

In addition to his infantry, Sigel's column included thirty-two wagons, commandeered from Springfield area residents to carry his extra equipment and rations. Local Southern partisans derisively referred to the wagon train as Sigel's beer wagons. The train was of uneven quality and slowed substantially Sigel's journey through the rolling countryside.[13]

As the friendly town of Springfield fell away behind him, Sigel must have contemplated his tenuous situation. His march, designed to snare a retreating enemy, was carrying him deep into hostile territory between two and possibly three separate Southern forces. Worse, Sigel did not have an established supply line running back to his base. The move was certainly a bold one, although only time would tell whether it was wise or foolhardy. Perhaps a general's hat "would fit best," as a German newspaper had editorialized, but the war was young and the German exile had not yet had an opportunity to prove his worth on an American field of battle—or his ineptitude.[14]

The German troops opened this phase of the campaign with a grueling fast-paced twenty mile march southwest to Mt. Vernon, equidistant from both Lamar and Neosho. Another march of similar distance was made the following day west towards Sarcoxie. After fording the swollen Spring River and trudging past Gist's Mill and Gilbert's Post Office, Sigel's men arrived in Sarcoxie at 5:00 p.m. on June 28. Although the town appeared bereft of enemy soldiers, the Germans discovered a large Rebel flag flapping from a tall flagpole in the center of town. The sympathetic citizens had been flying the flag since well before the bombardment of Fort Sumter and considered themselves staunchly allied to the Southern cause. Sigel's solders eagerly attacked the pole with axes and cheered heartily when the staff toppled to the ground, where the fallen banner was set ablaze. Interviews of the few loyal citizens of the town confirmed rumors concerning the encampment of Sterling Price and "700 to 800 men" at Pool's Prairie. Other interesting news reached Sigel's ears in Sarcoxie. "I also received a report that Jackson's troops, Parsons in command, camped 15 miles north of Lamar, on Thursday, the 27th, and on Friday, the 28th," wrote Sigel. "They were there first informed of Government troops [Federals] being in Springfield on their march to the West." Other Southern troops were rumored to be behind Jackson by about one day's march. If Sigel's intelligence was true, the State Guard leadership now knew that a separate column was angling out of Springfield to cut them off from Arkansas. The evening passed with Sigel and his staff debating their options while the troops bivouacked on the edge of Brig. Gen. James Rains' home town. Sigel resolved to strike first against Price at Pool's Prairie, and then turn north and attack Jackson.[15]

Without a capable cavalry arm, however, the information Sigel needed was beyond his reach and the strategic situation was substantially different than he imagined it to be. By June 29 Sterling Price and his recently accumulated gathering of recruits were moving south from Pool's Prairie toward Arkansas, well beyond Sigel's reach. Governor Jackson's wing of the State Guard was approaching Montevallo, a small community fifty miles north of Sigel. The remaining segment of the State Guard, James Rains' two-division column, was marching southwest from Clinton, about fifty-five miles north and east of Jackson's wing. Worse, Nathaniel Lyon's regiments were still stranded far to the north in Boonville. If Sigel envisioned the aggressive Lyon—whom he once referred to as a "very brave and determined officer"—pressing the rear of the retreating enemy, he was sadly mistaken. The truth of the strategic situation probably would have given even Franz Sigel reason to pause, but without adequate cavalry, the configuration of troops in southwestern Missouri remained obscured.[16]

Unbeknownst to Franz Sigel, the hammer would not be striking the anvil anytime soon.

*   *   *

The elation Nathaniel Lyon experienced after his Boonville victory melted into frustration as his timetable crumbled. Although he had planned to vacate Boonville by the 26th of June, heavy rains and supply problems stalled his efforts. Reinforcements in the form of four companies of the 7th Missouri arrived the following day, as did the 1st Iowa Regiment. While the troops continued to pour in—Col. Charles Stifel's 5th Missouri Volunteers arrived on June 29—the rain continued to pour down, pushing back Lyon's departure. As a result, he was unable to begin his push against the State Guard until July 3. When he finally moved out, Lyon guided his regiments through Sedalia and Green Ridge toward Clinton, about 100 miles southwest of Boonville.[17]

*   *   *

Sigel's Third Missouri rose to an early reveille on the second to last day of June. After a quick breakfast he and his men left Sarcoxie and marched towards Neosho, about twenty miles to the southwest. His regiment had covered only a few miles when a mounted Federal patrol returned and informed Sigel that Sterling Price was no longer at Pool's Prairie. In fact, no doubt to Sigel's disgust, Price was last reported thirty miles south at Elk Mills, well out of the immediate reach of his regiment. This new information caused Sigel to rethink his strategy. Unable to trap and destroy Price, perhaps he could move against the retreating Missouri State Guard rumored to be heading south toward Lamar? "It was now my duty," he explained, "to give all my attention to the northern forces of the enemy." If he could find the State Guard and hold it in place long enough, perhaps Lyon could bore down on the Southern rear.[18]

Sigel was, metaphorically speaking, at an important crossroads in the rapidly developing campaign. His options appeared to be four-fold. He could move southwest to Neosho in an attempt to gather information; strike out north in a blind grope for the State Guard with the hope of bringing on a favorable battle that would block the retreat of the enemy; stop his advance altogether, encamp and seek definitive intelligence before determining a decisive course of action; or with his last option—probably one to which he gave little or no serious consideration—return to Springfield and obey whatever orders Sweeny chose to give him.

As it turned out, General Sweeny made the decision for him. "I issued orders to Colonel Sigel and Colonel Salomon," he penned in his after-action report, "to concentrate their forces and move in the direction of Carthage where, I was led to believe from information received, Governor Jackson's and General Rains' forces were encamped." Sending a dispatch to Colonel Salomon to meet him at Neosho with the Fifth Missouri and Backoff's artillery, Sigel put his men back on the road. He reached the town on July 1 and promptly watered his men from the town's several springs. Salomon's column joined Sigel in Neosho shortly thereafter.

The weather was beginning to change from the cool and rainy late spring Missouri had been experiencing to a more traditional hot and humid midwestern July. While at Neosho, Sigel commandeered horses from Rebel sympathizers and dispatched riders into the countryside in an attempt to gather information. The riders returned after just one day without any useful intelligence. The impact caused by a lack of seasoned cavalry for reconnaissance purposes was becoming painfully obvious to Sigel, who would have to base his next move on rumors and half-truths. Whatever he decided, he would need to use some of his infantry for reconnaissance and scouting chores, a cumbersome method of gathering information.[19]

During the march on Neosho Sigel divided his already pathetically small column and sent small contingents of men to picket the communities of Grand Falls and Cedar Creek. He also dispatched two companies of infantry and a section of artillery to reconnoiter the Military and Kansas Line Road, which stretched from Fort Scott to Fort Blair near Baxter Springs, Kansas. This road officially marked the edge of the frontier, and Sigel was concerned it was being used by the State Guard to slip out of Missouri and into northwest Arkansas. Sigel's hunch proved unfounded when Capt. John Cramer's patrol ventured into the deserted area and returned to Neosho the following day. Small groups of scouts, however, continued to range across the Missouri landscape while Sigel camped his army on Neosho's outskirts. In the face of what was almost certainly a numerically superior foe, Sigel's command was hemorrhaging bits and pieces of itself in different directions.[20]

While the citizens of Neosho had welcomed the foreigners to their town, they watched with some trepidation as the Germans drilled in the streets to the strains of foreign orders barked out by their officers. A delegation of the town's prominent elders, led by R. V. Keller, T. A. Price and A. M. Sevier, greeted the Unionists and sought protection against Rebel bushwhackers marauding throughout the area. Justifiably hesitant about assuming the additional burden, Sigel agreed to take the matter under advisement.[21]

By the morning of July 3 Sigel had determined his next course of action. Relatively solid information, garnered primarily from local citizens, placed the State Guard in camp north of Neosho at Lamar. Sigel determined to march in that direction. The small town of Carthage marked the midpoint between Neosho and Lamar. Before leaving Neosho, Sigel ordered Capt. Joseph Conrad and 94 soldiers of Rifle Company B of the Third Missouri to remain behind to garrison the town. Conrad's detachment, which amounted to nearly ten percent of Sigel's column, served a dual purpose: it provided protection for the townspeople and acted as Sigel's first line of defense against any movement of Confederate troops out of Arkansas north into Missouri. It also seriously weakened his already small force.[22]

Before he could march north Sigel had to bring his entire force together. Couriers were dispatched with orders reining in the far-flung pieces of the probing Federal regiments. Captain Jacob Hackmann, who had been left behind thirty-five miles to the east at Mt. Vernon, was directed to make a forced march to rendezvous with Sigel at Carthage, while Capt. Joseph Indest's company was ordered to march from Grand Falls and thence onto Carthage. Indest was also instructed to send a courier to Springfield to inform General Sweeny, who had just arrived that morning in the city, of the current situation at Neosho. Sigel's remaining infantry filled their canteens one last time from Neosho's springs before striking out toward Jasper's county seat.[23]

Franz Sigel was overconfident. He had marched out of Springfield without orders (or reinforcements) deep into enemy territory. If the rumors were accurate and the Missouri State Guard was camped nearby, there was little doubt that it outnumbered his 1,100 men. Being forced to utilize infantry as scouts should have alerted Sigel that he was somewhere he should not have been. What would he do if he stumbled onto the Southerners? Would he be able to disengage his regiments in the face of an aggressive enemy? If he was caught in the open by a superior force, he could easily be flanked or overwhelmed and destroyed with little or no chance of receiving assistance. But the former minister of war, was desperately seeking a battlefield victory, and his men continued their march north in search of one.

Despite the precarious strategic situation, Sigel remained upbeat and his enthusiasm proved contagious—at least initially. His men moved out smartly and for the first few miles made good time on their march to Carthage. It did not take long, however, before the poor road and stifling summer heat began to wear on the neophyte Missouri Federals, draining the energy that had initially added spring to their collective step. The heat also spoiled the water in their uncovered tin canteens, which became so hot it was almost undrinkable. The heat and humidity also wreaked havoc on their paper cartridges, which were carried in tin containers held in leather boxes. A woman who watched the long line of Germans march by her farm late that afternoon remarked to a neighbor after the campaign that "the Germans oozed beer from every pore as they marched along." While her observation might have made good small talk, it was almost certainly untrue. Franz Sigel was a stern disciplinarian and would never have allowed his men a large beer ration—especially while on a march designed to find the enemy. The remark was typical of the rampant prejudice against foreign-born soldiers.[24]

Sigel's small force covered the twenty-two miles from Neosho in approximately 12 hours and arrived on the outskirts of Carthage late on the afternoon of July 4. A campsite for the exhausted Germans was selected on the southeastern edge of town along the Sarcoxie Road next to Carter's Spring. Even though it was Independence Day, the tempo of the march had left little time for celebrating the nation's birthday. Once in camp, a few of the men managed to explode some black powder bombs, but most were too weary from the heat to engage in such activities. It did not take long before campfires dotted the generally flat and open ground. Grain was procured from local mills to feed Sigel's hungry animals and a line of pickets was posted along the Spring River and scouts were dispatched to interrogate local citizens. The soldiers ended their adopted nation's birthday by soothing their blistered feet in the cool spring water.[25]

By early evening the streets of Carthage were uncharacteristically deserted. The appearance of the Federal Dutch on the city's outskirts terrified many members of the small community. Shutters were slammed shut and windows locked in apprehension of the invaders. By late afternoon a small group of fiercely loyal, pro-Union citizens ventured into Sigel's camp. The colonel peppered the group with questions and learned a good deal of essential information from the visitors. The State Guard was definitely camped at Lamar, they informed him, just eighteen miles north of his location. Reports concerning the size of the Southern army varied from a few thousand to over 20,000. Sigel listened with particular interest to W. A. Shanks, a local cattle buyer who knew the topography and road network north of Carthage.[26]

About 6:00 p.m. Samuel B. LaForce arrived at Sigel's tent. A former county sheriff and large landowner, LaForce informed the Federal commander that loyal citizens in the area were hard to find. Information gleaned from the townspeople, he declared, should be considered suspect. The two conversed for over an hour and it was twilight before they stepped from the tent. Sigel asked the ex-sheriff if he would return in the morning to guide his regiments toward Lamar. LaForce agreed, mounting his horse to return for the night to his farm north of the Spring River.[27]

While Sigel was engaged in conversations with civilians, some of his soldiers walked up Mill Street and ventured into the courthouse square, where they encountered the teenage daughters of another ex-sheriff, Norris Hood. The girls proudly displayed an American flag stitched together from curtains that once hung in their kitchens.

The banner was mounted on a stick and attached to the white gatepost in front of the Hood residence. The soldiers crowded around the flag and serenaded the young ladies with "John Brown's Body" and "The Star Spangled Banner." Although the songs were delivered in a mixture of broken English and German that was barely intelligible to the girls, they enjoyed the unexpected attention and patriotic music. The soldiers appreciated the opportunity to spend some time with women who supported their cause, unlike those that filled the doors and windows of the farm houses they had filed past earlier in the day.[28]

Carthage was typical of the towns along Missouri's western frontier. Founded in 1842 by Able Landers and George Brown, and named after the North African city conquered by the Romans, the modest community was attempting to grow by attracting new settlers. Its business climate was surprisingly robust for a community of 400. A saloon, hotel, bakery and carpenter shop, along with three trade goods stores, dominated the local economy, which also supported farming, lead mining and milling. A new brick courthouse, which replaced an old log structure on the outskirts of town, dominated the skyline. The imposing building sat directly in the center of the town and was but one of sixty-one buildings spread across a small community that stretched but three blocks in any direction. The courthouse was built by 1852, largely from slave labor and local materials. It was a peaceful place prior to Sigel's arrival, which was preceded by lively chatter in the square about the approach of the two opposing armies. Few of Carthage citizens realized that their small town sat in the eye of a gathering storm.[29]

As Sigel's men were bedding down for the night just outside of Carthage, shots rang out near the Spring River north of the Federal camp. State Guard commissary troops led by Lt. Col. Thomas Monroe, quartermaster for Brig. Gen. Mosby Parsons' Sixth Division, were busy combing the area for supplies. As Monroe loaded his wagons, his men bumped into Sigel's pickets along the river. The exchange of a few shots evolved into a spreading engagement as both sides fed handfuls of men into the affair. Monroe dispatched a courier to Camp Lamar requesting reinforcements to continue the fight. Before the rider could reach Parsons, Monroe experienced second thoughts about fighting an enemy of unknown size along the Spring

River. Instead of continuing the skirmish, he wisely disengaged his small band of soldiers and slipped away in the deepening twilight. Casualties were light, with only State Guardsman slightly wounded in the hand and one Federal killed. The brief skirmish proved more significant than the small number of expended bullets suggests. The encounter provided the Rebels with their first solid indication that a Federal force was nearby. More importantly, the enemy was squarely across the State Guard's path of retreat.[30]

Chaos swept through much of Muddy Petty Bottoms when Lt. Col. Monroe's horseman arrived at Camp Lamar. The shouting courier rode directly to General Parsons' campsite and explained Monroe's need for more men at Carthage. Without waiting for orders from Governor Jackson, Parsons immediately issued commands and readied his division for a night march. Wagons were hastily loaded, horses were harnessed and men roused from their slumber. Captains, many just elected that morning, attempted to find and organize their companies. Shouts were heard all along the river bottom, and the confusion spread to the other divisions.[31]

The growing commotion finally reached the ear of Governor Jackson, who mounted his horse and, accompanied by James Rains, galloped to find Parsons. After assessing the situation Jackson countermanded Parsons' rash decision to engage in a night march. Order slowly flowed from the chaos and the men of the Sixth Division eventually regained their composure. Parsons had reacted hastily to the news. Perhaps his lightening response came about as a means of making up for his late arrival (through no fault of his own) at Boonville. Was Parsons seeking a vehicle to refurbish what he incorrectly believed was a tarnished reputation?[32]

The militia officers convened a meeting to discuss the stunning news that Federal troops blocked their route of retreat south. Information as to the size of the force discovered along the Spring River was sketchy. They had expected to find help from that direction in the form of Ben McCulloch's Arkansans, not a hostile enemy bent on their destruction. After a lengthy discussion Lt. Gov. Thomas C. Reynolds suggested the Federal force may have come from St. Louis through Rolla and Springfield, as indeed was the case. Regardless of where the threat came from, it needed to be addressed. The question of Nathaniel Lyon's location was also a matter for discussion. Given his past aggressive behavior, it was more likely than not that the Federal general was bearing down on the Missouri State Guard from the north.[33]

It appeared to Jackson and his fellow officers that the militia army was slowly being pinched between two strong columns. With few viable options open to him, the governor reluctantly made his decision. The army would remain in camp that night, rise early the following morning and march south to defeat the Federals.[34]

First Blood

The stunning news of a Federal army south of Camp Lamar created excitement and uneasiness throughout the Southern camp at Muddy Petty Bottoms. The majority of the men lay on thin blankets beneath a sky full of stars, contemplating their first combat of the war. The veterans of the fiasco at Boonville hoped for an opportunity to redeem themselves. Many probably prayed they would find the courage to stand and fight this time around when the Yankee artillery rained shells upon them.[1]

It was early in the morning by the time the initial excitement wore off and the men returned to sleep. The short night before reveille woke the camp was a fitful one. Just as the men were settling down a group of horses broke loose from their corral and stampeded through the camp. The thundering beasts in the dead of night caused quite a stir and nearly trampled several men. Once again the ruckus roused much of the exhausted Missouri army from its slumber, and it was not until the animals were under control that the men were able to return to their blankets.[2]

The Southern camp stirred with activity well before the first streaks of daylight broke over the horizon. "Was awaked in the morning very early with orders to get into fighting order," wrote a Missouri private, "as Sigel with his men was approaching us." According to General Rains, Jackson had sent him an order "about 1 o'clock on the morning of the 5th," advising him to begin the march south "at 4 a.m." The frenzy of preparing for battle gripped the state troops. "Hasty breakfast, horses saddled, ammunition distributed," wrote Martyn Cheavens, who rode with Ben Rives' cavalry regiment, Slack's Division.[3]

*   *   *

About eighteen miles to the south in Franz Sigel's camp, the Germans heard reveille at 4:30 a.m., shortly after the Missouri State Guard began its march. Extra rations were cooked as the soldiers of the Third and Fifth Missouri regiments prepared to break camp and march north in search of the enemy. Once the food was slipped into knapsacks the column moved out about half an hour later, tramping up the Mill Road and into the deserted Courthouse square. As the men marched through Carthage's business center, the Norris Hood girls ran from their home and gathered along a fence in front. One of them reached under her petticoats and produced the flag they had displayed for the soldiers the night before. The young girl waved the banner as the cheering men filed past the residence, their smiles fading as their feet carried them out of Carthage toward an uncertain future.[4]

Mounted on a fine horse, Sigel confidently led his men through the town. His guide for the day, Samuel B. LaForce, guided his horse next to Sigel's and fell in step with the German colonel. LaForce suggested that the Federals march toward a crossing on the Spring River about one mile northwest of town. Despite the early hour, civilians began to line the roadway. In addition to the Hood women, several young men were waiting in the streets hoping to join Sigel's ranks. One of them was 21-year-old George Knight, who received permission to join the marching column. Another eager to fight for the Union was C. B. Haywood, a former Carthage newspaper editor. He, too, was given a rifle and squeezed into the throng of marching men. Jesse Wagner rode all night from northern Barton County to meet up with Sigel's regiments, arriving in the square as the men were snaking through it. Mounted on a fine but tired horse, Wagner was placed at the head of the marching men as a scout. One of the column's occupants was Lt. Jesse Spencer, who thought enough of the small town to permanently settle in Carthage after the war long war ended.[5]

The two Union regiments picked up the pace of the march once clear of the town. After traveling a little more than a mile the soldiers reached the Spring River crossing, where the Lamar-Carthage Road bisected the stream and disappeared north into the rolling prairie. The swiftness and height of the swollen waterway caused some concern in the ranks as the infantry cautiously waded into the cold water. The men extended their weapons and cartridge boxes overhead to keep them dry. Several slipped and needed help from comrades to prevent being swept away by the fast current, but all of Sigel's troops managed to make it safely to the north bank. After the infantry struggled across, the column's wagons attempted the ford. The teamsters handling the lumbering vehicles carefully inched the front wheels of the wagons into the crossing as if to test whether or not they would be washed down river. Under the watchful eye of Lt. Sebastian Engert, all thirty-two wagons managed to roll down the steep southern embankment and lumber across to the far

The Spring River Ford. Sigel's men crossed the river at this point and marched north in search of the Missouri State Guard. *Author's Collection*

side. Once over, the wagons began the slow climb to the top of Ordnuff Hill, a small plateau that fanned out on both sides of the main road about one-half mile north of the river. The road to Ordnuff cut through open pasture dotted with a few clump of small trees.

With the Spring River behind him and the Third Missouri marching in the vanguard, Sigel moved his men north toward Lamar. The Federal commander watched his Missourians struggle up the Lamar-Carthage Road, climbing the side of Ordnuff Hill while his muleskinners checked the condition of their wagons, snapped their whips and urged the animals after the sopping infantry.[6]

Ordnuff Hill would feel the tramp of their feet again before the day was through.

*　　*　　*

As the Missouri State Guard prepared for its march, word reached James Rains' senior cavalryman, Col. Robert Peyton, that a contingent of Federals had been spotted just outside Muddy Petty Bottoms. Troopers sent to investigate soon dispelled the rumor, which only served to further delay the day's march. Peyton had his

troops prepare whatever food they had while he "ascertained the number of companies in my regiment properly armed and supplied with ammunition." To Peyton's dismay, only two companies and part of a third, about 60 men, had ammunition. Of the remaining six and one-half

Col. Robert Peyton

Missouri Historical Society

companies, "though. . . most of them had good arms," he later explained, "[they] were totally without ammunition and could obtain none." This meant that two-thirds of his regiment would not be able to participate in the upcoming fight. Those unable to procure arms or ammunition were gathered together with others similarly situated to form a "reserve corps and baggage guard." The lack of powder and small arms ammunition was not unique to Peyton's unit. In fact, many of the organizations suffered similar shortages which swelled the unarmed reserve to some 2,000 men. Given command of all of Rains' cavalry, Peyton could do nothing except assume his position in line for the beginning of the march.

The troops straggled out of the creek bottom in the black of night and began forming into a semblance of a marching column shortly before 4:00 a.m. Officers struggled to get their units into a proper road column, but the attempt to form milling and untrained (and excited) civilians into a coherent and orderly body of soldiers proved more difficult than anyone imagined. Even something as fundamental as forming for a march was perplexing for these neophyte soldiers. In spite of these problems James Rains' Eighth Division broke camp and led the march at a respectable hour, "about 4 a.m," Rains later wrote. While the head of the army marched, the tail continued to form. John Clark, whose division was third in line to march that morning, claims to have broken camp about two hours later. As Rains' Southerners picked their way over the narrow and rocky path that doubled as a road, Capt. Jo Shelby's half a hundred cavalrymen disappeared into the darkness ahead of the column. The vanguard of the militia army had already traveled some distance before the Missouri sun lifted above the horizon. It promised to be another hot day.[7]

Behind Rains marched William Slack's Division, followed by the those of John Clark and Mosby Parsons. The procession inched its way forward in fits and starts.[8] Once the army entered Lamar, Rains' First brigade under Richard Weightman turned south onto the Lamar-Carthage Road. Many of the men may have wondered why the rocky, rutted path was even dignified with a name, for it was barely suitable for animals let alone an army on the march. A command was issued to break ranks and leave the roadway, and the men gladly complied with the order. Fanning out across the prairie grass on either side of the road, Jackson's soldiers continued toward Carthage aligned eight or more abreast rather than the traditional four across.

The men passed through the small hamlet of Boston and followed the road as it curved west for a few miles before turning back to the south. Charles Harrington, an excited 8-year-old who lived on Pettis Creek, watched as the great body of men swept by him. Years later he remembered the encounter, recalling "how they moved past the creek and below the side of the hill, where the road turned South again [toward Carthage]." The difficulty of the march remained with Harrington, who commented that the soldiers struggled with the heavy brush along the creek bottom before regaining the crude roadbed.[9]

After marching about eight miles, the Southerners slowed to negotiate the banks of Coon Creek. While some of the men stopped to refill their canteens in the stream, the majority lacked that accouterment. Those bereft of the valuable container stored water in their bellies. They knelt and drank deeply from the creek, knowing full well that they might not get another opportunity any time soon. The chaos caused by hundreds of soldiers leaving the ranks, coupled with the subsequent crossing of the creek, disrupted the march. Considerable time was spent reorganizing the units. Once everyone was back in the ranks the army trudged on, skirting past the small settlement of Dublin. They had cut the distance to Carthage in half and thus far not a Federal had been spotted, despite Captain Shelby's mounted troopers scouting well in advance of the army. Many of the rank and file began to doubt that Federals were anywhere in the vicinity, but the column plodded on, making reasonably good time once it moved onto the Dry Fork Creek watershed.[10]

The ground over which the Southerners were now traveling made for easy marching. Flat to gently rolling terrain dominated the region. Most of the ground was open, under cultivation or in permanent pasture. Trees and thick brush bordered the many small creeks that cut through the plateau like thin wandering fingers. As the army pushed on it neared the geographic high point of Jasper County, and the men enjoyed a fine view of the surrounding area.

At about 7:00 a.m., "our scouts reported the enemy in force 3 miles in advance," reported James Rains. "I immediately went forward with some of my staff to reconnoiter their movements and examine the ground." Realizing that his men were marching toward elevated ground while the enemy was marching into a creek bottom, Rains "sent orders to Captain Shelby, who was in the advance, to halt and detain the whole command out of view." It was my intention, explained Rains, to "oblige them to take position in the bottom, while I drew up my force on the height commanding it." Rains waited until the Federals crossed a small creek and then ordered Shelby forward to harass the probing enemy. "I. . .directed Colonel Weightman to deploy the brigade in order of battle on the ridge of prairie overlooking the enemy."[11]

As the state troops marched up the road and neared the crest of the rise, an order came to break ranks and fall into line of battle. Surprise rippled through the army. Shelby's men, so it was said, had made contact with a Federal column of troops some distance ahead. "We came to the edge of a prairie which made a slanting hill," Cheaven's inserted in his diary, ". . .where 1 mile off we saw Sigel and his force." The Southerners scrambled to obey the shouted commands as well as untrained soldiers could. "We were soon in line a battle." Apparently their transition from column into line satisfied Rains, who commended Weightman for executing the order with "celerity and precision."[12]

It was an ironic situation. A man with no military training, leading an inexperienced and under-equipped army, was setting a trap for a veteran field commander and former German minister of war, leading two strong regiments of disciplined troops.

*   *   *

Franz Sigel's men continued to move north unaware of what was in their front. After crossing the Spring River and marching up Ordnuff Hill, the Federals struck out across the soggy prairie. They marched unopposed for about five miles. When their skirmishers clambered over to the north bank of Buck's Branch Creek, scattered shots rang out across the fields of the Vincent Gray farm. The surprised skirmishers lifted their rifles and fired back at the gray-brown figures in the distance. Unbeknownst to anyone, the first rounds of the Battle of Carthage had been fired.[13]

The outnumbered enemy slowly gave ground as Sigel's advancing infantry pushed and prodded the mounted Southerners. "I advanced slowly towards the enemy," wrote Sigel, "our skirmishers driving before them numerous squads of mounted riflemen, who were observing our march." The enemy front soon stiffened and the Federal skirmishers were unable to dislodge them. As a desultory skirmishing broke out between the antagonists, a frustrated Sigel ordered an additional company to the front, together with two pieces of artillery. The show of strength was sufficient for the task, and the enemy backed away to the north.[14]

The Federals continued to move ahead, wading across the thirty-foot wide Dry Fork Creek ford. Emerging on the far side wet to their waists, they continued up the gently sloping hillside on the northern bank, moving quickly out of the low land and again into the open prairie. The wagons followed well behind the infantry. "One piece of artillery and one company of the Third Regiment of infantry I posted behind the creek," Sigel later reported, "as a guard against movements of the cavalry toward our rear and our baggage."[15]

Once Sigel reached the top of a small rise, about a quarter mile after clearing the creek, he caught his first glimpse of the enemy. About three-quarters of a mile away a body of troops was slowly stretching out a line of battle across his line of advance. Franz Sigel had finally located the Missouri State Guard.[16]

*   *   *

Jo Shelby's rangers performed beyond expectations. After screening the army's march, Shelby had positioned his troopers to oppose the head of Sigel's column from across Buck's Branch Creek. The rattle of their small arms, fired for the first time in anger, reached the ears of the men forming into a line a battle some three miles behind them. After forcing some of the Federals to deploy into line and unlimber a pair of artillery pieces, the capable cavalryman realized that his hand was played out and withdrew north toward Dry Fork Creek.[17]

Governor Jackson and his staff arrived on the scene and watched as Sigel's men poured out of the Dry Fork Creek valley. Although Jasper County was noted for its flat terrain, Rains had managed to locate and occupy a respectable ridge. The long bump of land, one of the highest points in the county, ran perpendicular (east and west) to the Lamar-Carthage Road. Much of the surrounding ground was in pasture and newly-mown hay was being put up by its owners. A large field of corn hugged the bottom of the ridge directly in front of where Rains' men were forming. A white framed house owned by the Gresham family stood on the top of the land spine just a few hundred yards behind the center of Jackson's line and immediately east of the Lamar-Carthage Road. A second Gresham home sat directly beyond the left front of Jackson's line, while a third small house, belonging to the Widow Smith, was slightly ahead of the State Guard's left flank. Clumps of timber peppered the ridge line and its flanks. The position offered clear fields of fire in every direction. The Missouri State Guard line could not have been better chosen.[18]

*   *   *

Sigel was fortunate to have Samuel LaForce's services that morning. As the Federals marched out of the low lands surrounding Dry Fork Creek, the guide calculated the length of the Southern defensive line and analyzed various (and familiar) terrain features. After identifying the houses and other points of interest, LaForce informed Sigel that the enemy line covered a front of about one mile. This ominous news, which only confirmed what the colonel could see for himself, should have disturbed Sigel. His own estimate of the situation was remarkably accurate. "The whole force within our sight may have numbered 3,500 men, besides a strong reserve in the rear." A line stretching that long and deep could only mean one thing: the Missouri State Guard substantially outnumbered his small command. Yet, Sigel seems to have given little if any thought to pulling back. The ground between the Southern line and Sigel's position was open and generally level—perfect for using the disciplined European battlefield maneuvers Sigel preferred. Outnumbered or not, as far as he was concerned this was the place to engage the enemy.

The German commander advanced his regiments in close columns and prepared to deploy for battle. It was approximately 9:00 a.m.[19]

*   *   *

Although Claiborne Jackson presided over the opening shots of the action, he did not intend to command the army once the serious shooting began. At least that is what local legend and secondhand stories hold. If true, Jackson never publicized his reason for turning over the leadership of the army to another. Perhaps his unfortunate experience at Boonville convinced him of his shortcomings as a field commander. Possibly it was his deteriorating health. Whatever the explanation, Missouri's governor supposedly made arrangements for Brig. Gen. James Rains to take control of the battle.[20]

If Jackson turned over the command baton to Rains, his selection to head the army was a curious one. The former politico had no combat experience of any kind, while several other officers in Jackson's army had fought in the Mexican War or were at least graduates of a military academy. The thin evidence surrounding this issue hints at the possibility that the governor made the decision based on the fact that Rains led the largest contingent of men on the field and was fighting on home ground—in reality no justifiable grounds at all upon which to offer army command. The Jasper county resident was a fiery leader, and perhaps Jackson intuitively surmised the enthusiastic, albeit untried, state senator was the man for the job.

Whatever his motive, Jackson apparently supervised the placement of troops on the center and the left of the developing State Guard line while Rains worked with his infantry and cavalry on the right flank. When the time came, Jackson planned to retire to the rear and oversee the disposition of the army's wagon train and the 2,000 unarmed men that accompanied the State Guard. Unable to comfortably ride a horse, the governor was confined to a carriage which moved from place to place immediately behind the battle line. His stomach ached, as it had for the past several days.[21]

Unlike the gathering armies east of the Mississippi River, the units that made up the Missouri State Guard were haphazardly collected. The men were simply grouped together and given a desig-

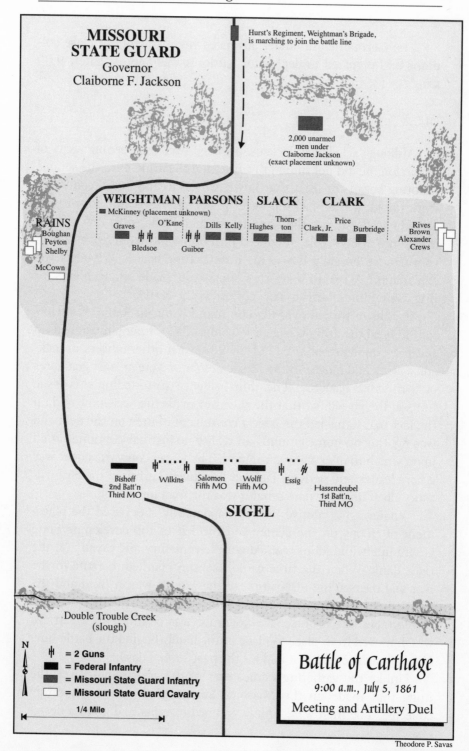

MISSOURI STATE GUARD
Governor
Claiborne F. Jackson

Hurst's Regiment, Weightman's Brigade, is marching to join the battle line

2,000 unarmed men under Claiborne Jackson (exact placement unknown)

WEIGHTMAN   **PARSONS**   **SLACK**   **CLARK**

McKinney (placement unknown)

RAINS
Boughan
Peyton
Shelby

McCown

Graves   O'Kane   Dills   Kelly   Hughes   Thornton   Clark, Jr.   Price   Burbridge   Rives
Brown
Alexander
Crews

Bledsoe   Guibor

Bishoff
2nd Batt'n
Third MO   Wilkins   Salomon
Fifth MO   Wolff
Fifth MO   Essig   Hassendeubel
1st Batt'n,
Third MO

SIGEL

Double Trouble Creek
(slough)

N

= 2 Guns
= Federal Infantry
= Missouri State Guard Infantry
= Missouri State Guard Cavalry

1/4 Mile

Battle of Carthage
9:00 a.m., July 5, 1861
Meeting and Artillery Duel

Theodore P. Savas

nation by their commanding officer. Frequently this cognomen was the officer's name (Thornton's Battalion, for example), although many units boasted numerical designations, many of them identical. With only a handful of days to organize, the soldiers were by and large allowed to remain with the men who recruited them. This unorthodox policy resulted in a confused organizational structure as well as an unusual battle line, with units fielding several hundred men aligned alongside others holding as few as sixteen.

James Rains' 1,204-man infantry brigade, capably handled by Richard Weightman, was the first to formally stake a claim on the ridge. Colonel John R. Graves' independent regiment of 271 men led the way by deploying as the far right element. As the infantry marched off the road and fanned out atop the hill, Capt. Hiram Bledsoe's 3-gun battery (one 12-pounder and two 6-pounders), rumbled and squeaked onto the grassy hillside and unlimbered on Graves' left flank, with Lt. Col. William O'Kane's 350-man battalion falling into line next to Bledsoe, extending Weightman's front east. Bledsoe's iron guns and 46 artillerists held, at least initially, the center of Weightman's developing battle line. Almost half of the

The first Southern line of Battle. The Missouri State Guard assembled for battle near the treeline in the distance about 9:00 a.m. This view, which looks north, was taken from near the base of the ridge and shows the gentle sloping terrain. *Author's Collection*

brigade, numerically speaking, was not even up. "At this time," Weightman later explained, "Colonel [Edgar V.] Hurst was 3 miles in the rear with his regiment, which, having marched since 4 o'clock in the morning without breakfast, had, with my authority and of necessity, stopped to prepare a meal." Weightman "immediately dispatched a courier to the rear for him, and directed him to come forward at speed."[22]

None of the Southern reports mention the Lamar-Carthage Road in relation to their final deployment. As this was one of the area's few landmarks of note, the omission is a curious one. The only logical reason for not mentioning it may be because the line of battle did not cross it. Contemporary maps depicting the roadbed help explain this peculiar circumstance. Just behind the modest ridge, the road—for no discernible reason—took a wide bend to the west, traveled south for some distance and then curved back east just north of Double Trouble Creek. Thus once his men were aligned, the road ran west behind Weightman's front, curving around his right flank in a giant bow-like protrusion.

"While I was deploying," explained Weightman in his battle report, Rains "with the remainder and greater portion of [his] command (composed principally of mounted men) took position on the extreme right of the Army of Missouri." Rains' decision to anchor the army's far right flank with his Eighth Division cavalry—the largest, best equipped and armed mounted force in the ranks of the State Guard—was a wise move. Its commander was Col. Robert L. Y. Peyton. Peyton was ordered by Rains just moments before the battle to take command of his own Third Cavalry, together with the battalions of Col. James McCown and Lt. Col. Richard Boughan, plus two small mounted companies. McCown's Battalion took up an advanced position 300 yards in front and to the right of Peyton's main body. Peyton's men remained mounted.

The Eighth Division's final line of battle covered something less than one-half mile of the ridge and comprised, for purposes of clarity, the "right wing" of the developing Rebel line. "The other divisions," reported Weightman, "formed [on the left] as they successively came on the ground." If Rains was elevated to command the entire State Guard, then Weightman replaced Rains in command of the division. Such an arrangement would have left the

First Brigade in the hands of Lt. Col. Thomas H. Rosser. Dressed largely in civilian clothes, Rains had tied a red sash around his waist to make him easier for his men to see in the impending fight.[23]

The development of the remaining "left wing" of the so-called "Army of Missouri" was not nearly so smooth or efficiently effected as Weightman's deployment. While the components of Weightman's division deployed together on a contiguous front, the elements comprising the next two divisions were broken up and plugged into line piecemeal.

The records of the Missouri State Guard are woefully incomplete for this period of the war. Other than official battle reports, few firsthand accounts were penned and fewer still have survived. Not surprisingly, the extant writings occasionally conflict. One of the discrepancies regards the exact alignment of the remaining divisions. The "controversy" may have begun with a lengthy account of the war in Missouri penned almost a quarter century later by aide Thomas Snead. The main discrepancy is the alignment of the divisions of Mosby Parsons and William Slack. According to Snead, Slack's command fought through the initial stages of the battle (the opening artillery duel) on Weightman's left, Parsons took position on Slack's left, and Clark's Division extended the line to the east. Other writers, apparently using Snead as a foundation, perpetuated this alignment of the Missouri State Guard divisions. A close reading of the existing battle reports, which were written within days of the events described, clarifies the issue.[24]

General Slack's Fourth Division did indeed arrive on the field after Weightman. Slack's command consisted of Col. Benjamin Allen Rives' 1st Missouri Cavalry, about 500 men, together with Col. John T. Hughes' 1st Missouri Infantry (under the command of Lt. Col. James Pritchard) and Maj. J. C. Thornton's Battalion. The latter two units were under Hughes' command and totaled 700 soldiers. Slack unwound his infantry and initially deployed it on Weightman's left, sending Rives' cavalry off to the east. "Colonel Rives' regiment of cavalry," explained Slack after the battle, "was ordered to threaten the right flank and rear of the enemy."[25]

Mosby Parsons' Sixth Division, about 650 men, was the next to reach the battlefield. "I discovered that the advanced divisions of Generals Rains [Weightman] and Slack had formed in line of battle," observed Parsons upon reaching the elevated ridge line well in advance of his own men. At this time Parsons did not know the position or the strength of the enemy. Within minutes "I discovered the enemy formed for attack at a distance of 1,000 yards," he wrote, the enemy line studded with "seven pieces of artillery." He hurried forward Henry Guibor's battery, "consisting of four brass sixes," to the front and plugged it into the line next to Weightman. Guibor's guns "unlimbered in gallant style immediately on the left of my brigade," Weightman recorded in his report. Parsons thereafter directed his infantry, Col. Joseph M. Kelly's Missouri Infantry Regiment and Col. George K. Dills' Missouri Infantry Battalion (both apparently under Kelly's leadership) into line on the left of Guibor's artillery. In a move reminiscent of Slack's earlier deployment and perhaps after consultation with that officer, Parsons dispatched Col. Benjamin Johnson Brown's First Regiment of cavalry, together with two other small obscure organizations under Captains "Crews" and "Alexander," to the east. At this point Colonel Rives' cavalry and all of Parsons' mounted men were anchoring the army's extreme left flank.[26]

Brigadier General John B. Clark, whose Third Division arrived immediately behind Parsons, witnessed that general deploying for battle. "I observed Brig. Gen. Parsons advancing with his artillery and infantry, and *seeking* to take position in line immediately on the left of Colonel Weightman [emphasis added]." Clark agreed with Parsons' decision to unlimber Guibor's pieces next to Weightman, "such position being the only available point for using successfully his battery against the enemy."[27]

Thus of the four infantry commanders, three of them agree that Parsons deployed his men and guns immediately on the left of Weightman. At first blush Slack's scanty report seems to contradict his fellow commanders by placing his division in the same spot as Parsons'. The only way to account for this is to conclude that Slack was simply in error, or else he described the initial deployment *before* Parsons reached the field. Oddly enough, Slack makes no reference to Parsons at all in his report, an unusual oversight since Parsons did indeed fight alongside Slack's command much of the day.

William Slack may have left a sizable gap between his right and Weightman's left when he initially formed on the field—and Parsons merely filled it upon his arrival with artillery and infantry. Or, Slack's men sidled to the east to make way for the additional Sixth Division troops (which is more likely, given that Clark reported that Parsons was *"seeking* to take position in line immediately on the left of Colonel Weightman. . ."] Either way, Thomas Snead is incorrect on this point, as are most other writers who have penned accounts of this battle. Parsons fought alongside Weightman during the opening round of the Carthage fight.

There is no dispute as to where John Clark's mixed cavalry and infantry command deployed. After arriving on the field, Clark consulted with Parsons and thereafter marched his men to the far left of the line. His division consisted of Col. John Q. Burbridge's small contingent of Missouri infantry, together with Lt. Col. Edwin Price and Maj. John Bullock Clark, Jr., both of whom commanded separate knots of infantry informally designated as "1st Missouri." Clark's entire Third Division totaled a mere 365 men.[28]

The officers struggled to prod their men into an organized line of battle, and there was a good deal of milling about and breaking of ranks to catch a glimpse of the Federals. Orderly Sergeant Salem Ford, who served in John T. Hughes' regiment, openly confessed ignorance when it came to military discipline. "We did not have an officer with us. . .who knew how to form a line of battle. We got together as best we could in double-rank close order." Ford, "as did all the other officers," took up a position in front of the developing line. By the time the Missouri State Guard was fully deployed for battle, it occupied a front about one mile wide, its artillery anchoring the right center and cavalry controlling both flanks. Although the command structure was ad-hock and individual regiments in many cases had been cleaved from their divisional organization, it was a solid position. Fortunately for the Southerners, they were facing a foe less than a quarter of their own strength. Once things settled down there was little for the Southerners to do but wait under the stifling July sun for the enemy to advance.[29]

And that was exactly what Franz Sigel proposed to do.

*   *   *

The information provided to the aggressive Sigel by his guide assisted him in planning the offensive battle he intended to wage. Like their confident commander, the Germans in the ranks of Sigel's two regiments expected to cover themselves in glory that July morning. How could it be otherwise? The Rebels had surrendered at Camp Jackson and deserted the field at Boonville. Surely they would not stand for long against the outstanding training and superior fire power of men fighting to secure liberty and save the Union? In addition to their drilling prowess, the rifled muskets carried by most of the Federals had an effective killing range of 800 yards, giving them a distinct advantage over their indifferently-armed opponents. Clad in their gray jackets (some trimmed with yellow piping), gray jeans pants and black shoes, Sigel's Germans offered an impressive and contrasting sight to the disheveled Rebels.[30]

Sigel had halted his small force 1,200 yards from the enemy line just north of a small spring called Double Trouble Creek. As it did near the Southern line of battle, the road jogged to the west and then north for some distance before curving back east behind the right flank of the Missouri State Guard. Sigel deployed his men northeast of the bend in the road, facing his enemy.

Major Henry Bishoff's Second Battalion, Third Missouri Infantry, formed as the leftmost element. Accompanying Bishoff was Capt. Theodore Wilkins' 4-gun battery from the Fifth Missouri. The artillerists rode roughshod over the knee-high corn and cut a line of muddy ruts through the field, eventually assuming a position on the front line on Bishoff's right flank. The center of Sigel's developing line consisted of two battalions (seven companies totaling 400 men) from the Fifth Missouri Regiment under Lt. Col. Charles Salomon and Lt. Col. Christian Wolff. These companies deployed by marching off the Lamar-Carthage Road and into the cornfield opposite the approximate center of the State Guard (across from Mosby Parsons' Division). Extending the line further east into the fields and anchoring the right flank of Sigel's command was Lt. Col. Francis Hassendeubel's 1st Battalion, Third Missouri Regiment. As Hassendeubel's soldiers marched through the corn, Lt. Christian Essig's battery (less one gun deployed behind Dry Fork Creek) was rolled into position between the battalions of the Fifth Missouri and Hassendeubel. Overall command of Sigel's artillery was in the hands of his old

Double Trouble Creek. Sigel formed his men just north of this spot early on the morning of July 5, 1861. This photo was taken during the rainy season, when this small ribbon of water has a tendency to flood well beyond its banks. *Author's Collection*

friend, Major Franz Backoff.[31] Sigel watched as his troops marched into the field and formed into line. For a reason known only to Sigel, his initial deployment divided his own Third Missouri. The seven companies of about 550 men were split into two semi-equal segments, one on each flank. It did not take long before Sigel realized that something was amiss: his right flank was overlapped by the Southern left. Sensing danger, he dispatched a courier to Hassendeubel and ordered him to extend his line to match that of the State Guard. As he watched the First Battalion slide further east, Sigel's concern graduated to outright anxiety. Both of his flanks were overlapped by Southern cavalry. To compensate Sigel formed his men into companies and moved them apart in an effort to create the illusion that he was fielding an army larger than he possessed. Out in the open with the enemy holding the high ground it was a ruse with no chance of success. With his men now deployed before a superior force, Sigel could not easily disengage. Perhaps he should have paid more attention to Samuel LaForce's earlier information about the extent of the Southern deployment.[32]

*   *   *

One man's predicament is often another's fortune, and so it was that July morning. As the Dutch troops marched through the fields at the bottom of the hill the men of the State Guard enjoyed a magnificent display of military pageantry that cheered some and disheartened others. The field of battle offered a rare opportunity for virtually everyone to see what was going on elsewhere along the front, and it did not take many of them long to realize that they outnumbered their enemy. The Southerners watched intently as the Germans executed their precise, European maneuvers in the fields below. One of the Southerners watching the maneuvers was Sergeant Ford, who admitted to some nervousness. "I must confess I felt a little shaky, it being our first encounter with the enemy." He

The terrain north of Double Trouble Creek. This is the view Sigel and his men enjoyed as they formed for the battle. The Missouri State Guard was positioned beyond the treeline in the distance. The trees were not present in 1861. *Author's Collection*

was not too nervous to be impressed with the Union men cloaked in their fine looking uniforms. "I thought that I had never seen so many men in one body, they being well drilled and armed," he later remembered. "I could not help admiring their beautiful movements in their formation of line of battle. Our side it was quite the reverse." Neither was the pageantry of the moment lost on Lt. William P. Barlow, commander of a section of guns in Guibor's Missouri State Guard battery. "I remember feeling the beauty of the scene as our mules maliciously [sic?] wheeled the pieces into battery, and we looked down from our slight ridge and saw the bright guns of the federal battery and their finely uniformed infantry deploying on the green prairie, about 800 yards distant. Both sides formed in silence looking at each other." The Southerners were confident. "I expected our side to be victorious," recalled Sergeant Ford, ". . .and thought this battle would end the war."[33]

Many noticed that the Dutch arms carried bayonets, although some of the Southerners made fun of them, perhaps to ease their own anxiety. "Look, look," yelled one, "Them Damned Dutch have lightening rods on their muskets." The Southerners were justifiably concerned since only a very few of them—John Q. Burbridge's handful of men of John Clark's Division—were armed with this particular implement of war. While the joking helped relieve tension, it was painfully obvious that the bayonets would give the Union men an advantage if the fighting should move to close quarters.[34]

When Sigel's men were finally aligned to his satisfaction, members of the State Guard defiantly raised two Confederate national flags, one on each flank of the army. Those cognizant of such things understood the significance of the act, for the army was not officially affiliated with the Confederacy. If Jackson was in a position to notice, the sight of the flags waving over the battle line must have made him smile. From the start of his gubernatorial campaign in 1860, his goal was to ally Missouri with the deep Southern states.[35]

As the two armies prepared for their bloody dance, two families living along the road were busy loading personal belongings into wagons while trying to grasp the fact that war was about to pay a visit to their land. Moses Gresham's acres were occupied by the State Guard, while Sigel's men maneuvered through cornfields and pastures owned by his brother. Although the farmers had probably heard rumors that the two armies were heading in their direction, neither expected the first large-scale battle of the Civil War to be fought on their land. Both families were Union sympathizers. By the time the battle opened they were heading in the direction of Ft. Scott, Kansas, where they remained for the duration of the war. The local hired laborers working in the Gresham fields were equally startled when the soldiers appeared. In the fields putting up hay when the armies arrived, they wisely scrambled for cover wherever they could find it. When the Gresham's returned to their homes after the war, years of looting and wanton destruction had rendered their holdings a total loss.[36]

With Rains supposedly overseeing the front line, Governor Jackson attempted to organize the rear guard of his army behind the Gresham house. He sent the army's oxen, wagons and spare horses back through the jumbled lines where they would not get in the way of the forming men and unlimbering artillery. Exactly where the 2,000 unarmed soldiers were positioned is not known.[37]

The view from the Missouri State Guard's left flank (John Clark's Division). Although the buildings are not Civil War-era structures, they were built upon the Gresham farm site. The Federal troops stationed beyond the farm belonged to Lt. Col. Francis Hassendeubel's 2nd Battalion, Third Missouri, the right flank of Sigel's battle line. *Author's Collection*

As Jackson shuffled things about behind the army, James Rains set about proving that he was unsuited for command at any level. If he was ordered to take control of the entire Missouri State Guard during the battle, Rains did little to help the confused situation and in fact made it substantially worse. In what can only be described as a serious lapse in judgment, he took up a position on the army's far right flank, where he could lead his own cavalry—and little else. Unfortunately for the State troops, although Rains had chosen his ground well (albeit largely by accident), he was unable to conceptualize battle beyond a regimental scope. On the far right he would not be in a position to make tactical decisions for his division let alone the entire army. Rains possessed "undoubted courage, patriotism and zeal," wrote a contemporary long after the war, "[but] he was profoundly ignorant of everything pertaining to military affairs." He was "so good natured that he could not say 'no' to any request, or enforce regulations that were distasteful to his men."[38]

Even as the State Guardsmen were marching to form on the ridge near the Gresham farm, many of its members refused to believe that the Federal army was in its front. One private from Clay County, James A. Broadhurst, Company H, Hughes' regiment, Slack's Division, recalled that the men thought it was simply another "Rains scare." The general had told his men on so many occasions during the long retreat that the Federals were close by that the news had lost its shock value. But Rains wasn't exaggerating on the morning of July 5, and it did not take long for his soldiers to find out firsthand. As the advance skirmishers of both armies began to settle down to their grim business, "The men started to double quick forward at Captain David Thompson's command," Broadhurst recalled. "We passed a soldier moving away from the front leaving a trail of blood. "'Go on boys,' he shouted, this is the real thing!"[39]

*　*　*

With his regiments deployed as well as his paltry numbers allowed, Sigel advanced his line several hundred yards. As if on a parade ground, the well-trained Missouri Germans moved outward with an Old World military precision that must have pleased their

Sigel's line immediately before the opening bombardment. This view, which looks south, was taken from the approximate position of Henry Guibor's Battery near the right center of the Missouri State Guard line. The Federal troops were deployed just on this side of the treeline in the distance. The open field in the center of the image was planted in corn at the time of the battle. *Author's Collection*

colonel. Despite the muddy ground and thick growing corn, there is no evidence that these impediments disrupted the inexorable advance. After a few minutes, with the opponents separated by a mere 800 yards, Sigel ordered a halt. He guided his horse amongst the men, calmly reminding them of the battles in the old country and urging them to give a good account of themselves.

By now Sigel's soldiers were spread across two cornfields at the base of the hill occupied by Governor Jackson's army. The only obstacle on the field was the white two-story Gresham home at the edge of one of the cornfields in front of the Federal right. Apparently, neither side attempted to occupy the structure, which would have served as a passable sharpshooter's nest. Odder still, the artillery on both sides remained silent despite the proximity of the combatants. Only a light smattering of small arms fire cut through the heavy morning air as the skirmishers drew beads on their counterparts and squeezed their triggers.[40]

It was between 9:30 and 10:00 a.m. Both sides were ready for what they believed would be the decisive battle for Missouri.[41]

*   *   *

Many aspects of the Carthage Campaign are either disputed, unknown, contradicted or at best, confused. The Missouri State Guard organization was informal and all but unrecorded and many of the battle reports on both sides are missing or were never filed. It thus should come as little surprise to anyone that something as simple as whose artillery opened fire first, and thus precipitated the action, is disputed by a number of credible witnesses.

"I ordered Major Backof [sic] to commence his fire with all the seven pieces against the enemy's lines," was how Sigel described the opening of the fight at Carthage in his after-action report. "The fire," remembered the German, "was answered promptly." Several Southern accounts agree with Sigel's version of events. "The action commenced by the enemy opening a heavy fire from their battery," wrote James Rains. "This was promptly responded to by the artillery of General Parsons' command, which had unlimbered on the left of my division." The engagement "was begun about 8.30 o'clock a.m. by the enemy's artillery," testified Richard Weightman, "which opened a heavy fire of round shot, shell, spherical case shot, and grape. This was promptly responded to by the artillery of General Parsons' division." According to Colonel Rives, "A brisk cannonade was opened on our lines about 10 o'clock a.m." Certainly these gentlemen were in a position to know of what they wrote, even if their recollections of the hour differed.[42]

These reports and other issues surrounding the artillery duel are contradicted by other witnesses. Who fired the first shot, the time of day of the opening rounds—regardless of who pulled the first lanyard—and how long the cannonading lasted are all in dispute. William Slack equivocated on two of these issues, claiming that "a brisk cannonading was opened from the batteries on both sides, which was kept up for fifty-five minutes." Mosby Parsons' recollection of the event sharply differed from Slack's. "I rode up to my battery and ordered Captain Guibor, its commandant, to open fire, which was done instanter. The enemy's batteries immediately responded, Colonel Weightman's battery returning the fire as promptly." John Clark's report agrees with Parsons but disagrees considerably with Slack as to the duration of the cannonade. "The enemy. . .responded to the fire of General Parsons' artillery with a brisk and continuous fire of shell, grape, and shot, lasting between twenty and thirty minutes."[43]

Regardless of who fired the first round, concussions from exploding shells heralded the onset of serious fighting. According to Southerner Archy Thomas, "When ready the order was given and off went the missles of death and destruction from the cannon's mouth with the loud roar of distant thunder in quick succession." A rolling thunder echoed across the prairie as case shot shrieked overhead and exploded in the air above the Rebels, raining a hail of iron slivers and chunks of metal into the men and horses waiting below.[44]

Henry Guibor was not one who could sit quietly under the rain of flying iron. Itching to return fire, the captain turned his horse to the east and galloped behind the lines to Mosby Parsons on the left flank of the Southern line, begging for permission to return fire. With General Rains operating on the far right of the field, each brigadier and eventually every colonel was forced to act largely on their own hook. With Parson's blessing, Guibor returned to his pieces and ordered Lieutenant Barlow to open fire with the four "brass" 6-lb. pieces. Taking a moment to carefully aim the gun unlimbered on the right front of the battery, Barlow stepped back and jerked the lanyard. "Bang she went," was his simple description, "the first shot we fired in earnest—the first gun for Missouri—went flying through the air."

Both armies were well stocked with aggressive gunners and a lively artillery duel ensued. The Federal fire from was returned with deadly accuracy. "The enemy must have fired at our smoke," explained Barlow, "for our shells barely reached them when the answering shot came roaring by, carrying off the left and right arms of [William D.] Hicks and [Thomas] Doyle, the front and rear rank men of Kelly's command."[45]

"Without any material change in position," wrote Parsons, "the batteries continued their conflict for about twenty minutes to the great disadvantage of the enemy." Clark described the duel as "brisk and continuous . . . . spiritedly replied to by the artillery from the batteries of Captain Guibor. . .Colonel Rosser . . .and Captain Bledsoe."[46] Bledsoe's unlimbered trio of guns were positioned along the right center of the line, inset behind the waiting ranks of infantry. Refusing to wait for orders to return fire, Bledsoe brought his battery to life. Southern gunners confessed to remembering little of what transpired thereafter. "It was a constant period of screaming, whizzing shot and bursting shells," was the vague description offered by one of Guibor's officers.[47]

Guibor's State Guard artillerists held up fairly well under the barrage of Federal shots, but a team of mules used to move their guns did not find the situation to their liking. After just a few rounds the beasts stampeded through the lines toward the Federals. The loss of the animals was potentially very serious. A quick-thinking officer recognized the significance of the galloping mules and raced out on horseback between the lines to intercept them before the Germans could seize or kill the animals. Somehow he managed to regain control of the frightened beasts and guided them back to the Rebel line, much to the delight of all who witnessed the event.[48]

The Federal artillery proved horrifying to man as well as animal. "I wondered how I could stand it," exclaimed one soldier on the receiving end of the German metal. "Boom! Boom! Went the enemies artillery in front of us. Smoke rose, the balls whizzed by our heads, mostly exploding in the air." Federal infantry watched as their guns ripped what appeared to them to be giant holes in the Southern lines. Sergeant Otto Lademann of the Third Missouri Infantry remembered how the inexperienced volunteers of his company reacted to the firing of the Union artillery. "We cheered every time we saw so many enemy soldiers fall down," he remembered, "but they never stayed down and [we] soon realized that we were doing little execution."

The shelling did manage substantial disruption. Many of Brig. Gen. John Clark's 365 men of his Third Division, posted on the left of the Southern line, wavered under the initial iron barrage. "The shower of grape and shell continually poured upon my forces," he wrote, "caused a momentary confusion in the line." The general himself narrowly missed being killed by one of the shells when his horse "was severely wounded in the neck by a shot from the enemy's artillery." After the first few rounds of fire Clark was able to report that his men had gathered their courage and "eventually stood firm" against Christian Essig's Missouri Battery, which was defiantly hurling iron into their ranks. "Every officer and soldier received the fire with the coolness and composure of veterans."[49]

The gunnery duel exacerbated other problems along the line that morning. Sergeant Ford, of Slack's Division, assumed control of the men near him in an effort to calm spreading panic in the ranks. The confusion worsened when his company was nearly run down by Southern cavalrymen unable to control their horses when the Federal shells began erupting about them. "The men were all lying down so close to the ground that they seemed flattened out," was how Ford remembered the scene. The terrified raw recruits were beginning to show signs of serious unease as the sharp thunder of exploding shells and the smell of the burning powder intensified around them. With the other artillery pieces far removed down the line, it was difficult for them to appreciate that their batteries were still steadily returning the fire. Would they break and run like the state troops who had faced Capt. James Totten's Federal battery at Boonville?[50]

Salem Ford hoped not. It did not take long before the Missouri militia came to realize that the bark of the guns was far worse than their bite. The fight on the prairie north of Carthage was Ford's first brush with artillery, and after the initial shock wore off he and his comrades began to speculate about stopping the solid iron shot that bounded over the cornfield. I saw a "ball coming in a direct line coming towards me, bouncing on the ground from point to point," he recalled after the war. "My first thought was to catch it, but my judgment told me to let it pass, which it did." Ford reported that Bo Roberts, lying immediately behind him, "had the ball pass between his body and left arm," leaving him disabled for six months. The shot continued on traveling up the hillside behind the group of prone Missourians.[51]

The left wing of the Rebel line attracted more than its share of Federal shells that morning. In addition to terrorizing Salem Ford's men, the second discharge from Essig's pieces killed two horses in Colonel Rives' command. "Grape shot and shell fell thick in our ranks," reported Rives, but "the officers and men remaining perfectly cool under the fire."[52]

Southern gunners, while not as well drilled as their Northern counterparts, delivered their metal to their officers' satisfaction. Unfortunately, the artillerists had nothing but solid shot to throw at their enemy, the least effective form of fixed ammunition. "Captain Bledsoe, under the direction of Colonel Weightman. . . opened a steady and well-directed fire upon the densest of the enemy's masses," wrote General Rains, "forcing them to take refuge in the depression of prairie and finally to retire some 200 yards. . ." Weightman agreed with his superior's description. "Captain Bledsoe opened upon the enemy a steady and well-directed fire, by my direction, aiming at the densest of the enemy's masses, ceasing fire whenever the enemy, driven from their ranks, took refuge in depressions on the plains so as to be out of sight." Weightman was proud of the way his battery handled itself that morning. Bledsoe reopened "upon them as they again showed themselves in masses," he boasted, "notwithstanding the fire from the enemy's artillery was rapid and well directed, and continued for forty minutes."

One Rebel private wildly exaggerated the effects of the gunfire when he recorded that "the first shot from Bledsoe's Battery killed 8, wounded 16, taking down one entire rank." The artillery's thundering ovations impressed another young warrior. "Roar followed roar from each battery," recalled militiaman Archy Thomas:

and we could see at every fire the State Battery made, a swarth open through the columns of the federal troops, and again and again discover the officer rally the men, but again and again would the State cannon belch forth death among them.[53]

One of the early losses from the duel occurred when "Major Murray, of Lieutenant-Colonel O'Kane's battalion, had his horse shot under him by grape shot." According to Weightman, however, casualties along the right wing were small "owing to the fact that our line presented no depth to them. . ." Parsons also commented on the effectiveness of the State Guard's gunners, noting that the duel continued "to the great disadvantage of the enemy." It is interesting to note that Franz Sigel did not pass any judgment on the effectiveness (or ineffectiveness) of the Southern artillery.

Federal shells also found their way into the center of the Rebel line, where there was no protection for the exposed Missourians. Parsons realized that his men could not endure such a demoralizing shelling indefinitely. "Not wishing to have my infantry any longer exposed to the enemy's batteries," wrote Parsons, "I determined to harass them with the cavalry, so as to draw their fire, at the same time sending a body of mounted riflemen to Bear Creek [Dry Fork] for the purpose of cutting the enemy's rear and to get possession of the crossing in that direction." Parsons, it must be remembered, was but one of four division commanders present that morning. Although he was thinking like an army commander, his order completely ignored military protocol, for it was made without the knowledge or authority of either Claiborne Jackson or James Rains. The fact that Parsons would even consider ordering such a move is indicative of just how chaotic the State Guard's command structure was at Carthage.[54]

Just as Mosby Parsons plotted to send his cavalry around the Federal right, James Rains was scheming to do the same thing around the enemy's opposite flank. The projected double-envelopment was apparently spontaneously conceived, for neither officer mentions discussing it with the other in their detailed after-action reports. Spotting an opportunity, Rains rode to the far right flank and sought out Colonel Peyton, who reported that Rains "took command in person of the whole [cavalry] column." "I led the cavalry on the right through the corn field with a view of our flanking the enemy," wrote Rains, "or, if the ground was suitable, of charging their battery."[55]

Shortly after Rains' cavalrymen moved out, they picked up Col. James McCown's 250 men of the First Battalion along the way several hundred yards in advance and beyond the right flank. The horsemen knocked down a fence that temporarily blocked their passage and made their way over a field of wheat and corn in the direction of a stand of timber looming up between them and Dry Fork Creek, about one mile to the south. With McCown's unit in the lead and accompanied by Rains, the troopers continued forward. "This was done under a severe and heavy fire from the cannon of the enemy," remembered Peyton. Although the colonel's Third Regiment consisted of but five dozen troopers, "both officers and privates bore themselves with calmness and gallantry. Every officer and private in the whole column, as you yourself can testify," Peyton wrote to Rains, "were ready to obey any call you might give them."[56]

Colonel Richard Boughan of the Seventh Cavalry agreed. "The men marched off in good order, and were anxious to fight." A heavy fence running parallel (north-south) to the advance, however, prevented his 200 Vernon County cavalrymen from directly galloping toward Theodore Wilkins' Federal field pieces belching flame and blue-gray smoke several hundred yards beyond. Since stopping in the open to pull it down would have entailed heavy losses, Boughan "followed in rear of Colonel Peyton's regiment through the field. . . until some confusion, occasioned by pulling down a strong fence, was discovered at the head of the column." Boughan obliqued to the right and found his horsemen "exposed to a raking fire of canister and round shot until we reached the timber." The men were "remarkably calm and cool for young soldiers," he added.[57]

While Peyton's thin command managed to avoid taking casualties while crossing the field, a few of the men under Boughan and McCown were not so fortunate. Lieutenant Francis M. Kimble of Company B, "had his leg broken and his horse killed under him by a cannon ball," reported Boughan. As Kimble and his mount rolled to the earth, Lt. Albert Badger "had his saber and scabbard broken in two by the explosion of a bomb." Four other men from Boughan's Seventh Cavalry lost their horses on the hotly contested and shelterless ground. McCown's losses were much more serious. Private George W. O'Haver's left arm was carried away by a shell that also wounded his mount. The private suffered through two days of excruciating pain before passing away. Another private, Elijah Wood, lost his left leg in the same manner, although he apparently recovered from his grievous wound. Six of McCown's horses were killed and others wounded by the Federal gunners.[58]

The brief seconds spent traversing the grain fields at Carthage were bloody ones. They could have been substantially bloodier. While some may accuse him of military ineptness, Rains knew enough not to throw his men headfirst into a pitched battle against the well-handled and supported Federal guns. Instead of attempting to bull his way through the enemy, Rains continued to move his troopers in a wide arc away from the dangerous artillery in the hope that his men would turn Sigel's line.[59]

As Rains' troopers picked their way through the shells, the cavalry on the army's opposite flank was finally preparing to move pursuant to Parsons' directive. Initially they were ordered to "take the field and house opposite to our cavalry," wrote one of Col. Ben Rives' troopers, who were the first to advance. "Reeve's [sic] regiment started; one was shot by a shell," wrote Private Cheavens. A strong fence blocked their way. "The fence was plank, and had to be broken down by the guns. We were thus in full range of the enemy in crossing the field." Once the troopers broke past the barrier and passed to the far side, "3 were shot by round shot," Cheavens recalled, "minies and grape fell short."[60]

While the small arms fire and canister may have been generally ineffective, the same can not be said for all of the artillery shells. As Cheavens and his fellow cavalrymen began their advance down the hillside, "a masked battery," as Colonel Rives described it, "discharging grape shot and shell, was opened on my regiment, by which I lost 4 brave and gallant men." One of these was the First Cavalry's Capt. John N. Stone of Company D, who was toppled from his saddle by a shell that exploded nearby. "Our captain fell," lamented Cheavens. "When we got to a clump of trees, I, with the others, volunteered to return for him." As the men rushed to his aid, a second round of exploding shells ripped through the air above them. "I found him lying in the midst of his blood in the field, with a strap bound around his wound," the private later scribbled in his journal. "A 6 lb. [fragment] had passed through, made a slight flesh wound in the right leg, and killed his horse, which lay 20 steps off." The "slight" wound was much more serious than the private initially believed. "Took a piece of flesh off the left leg immediately above the knee on the lower side, not touching the bone," he later noted. As the iron storm raged around them, the men carried the stricken captain to the nearby house. "The inhabitants had fled, leaving their breakfast on the table," Cheavens observed as they offered Stone some water while the private tightened the strap on the wounded leg in a largely vain attempt to arrest the bleeding. By the time a doctor arrived the captain had lapsed into unconsciousness. The doctor "gave him stimulants, but it was in vain. He died about 3 o'clock."[61]

As Cheavens and his comrades lingered alongside the mortally wounded officer, the artillery fire drove Rives' mounted men east of the Widow Smith house, which slowed their progress toward Sigel's right flank. The heavy shelling also forced the colonel to eventually cross Dry Fork Creek well to the east at a place where the banks were steep and difficult for his inexperienced cavalry to negotiate.[62]

Just as Rives' men took a more easterly route around Sigel's flank, so too did Col. Ben Brown's cavalrymen of Parsons' Division. "I ordered Colonel Brown's regiment of cavalry to make a demonstration on the enemy's right flank," explained Parsons, "at the same time leaving orders with my adjutant. . .for Colonel Kelly, that so soon as I could make any efficient movement with the cavalry, to advance my whole line." Brown's troopers guided their mounts due east through permanent pasture, past a few clusters of trees and eventually out of sight of the Federal artillery. They too turned south toward Dry Fork Creek.[63]

It was at this critical point in the developing battle that Governor Jackson, still well to the rear of his army, supposedly decided to move his massive unarmed reserve. "The unarmed men on horseback (about two thousand) were. . .ordered to seek shelter in the heavy timber on the right of the State troops," remembered Thomas Snead long after the war. Jackson, however, did not leave a report and no other firsthand account confirms the relocation of these men. Secondary accounts and local lore speculate that, if they were shifted, the move may have been the result of Federal artillery fire dropping into the rear area. According to these accounts, Jackson's thousands—Jo Shelby derisively called them "a line of spectators"—may unintentionally have affected the outcome of the battle.[64]

*   *   *

Franz Sigel was quite pleased with himself. His methodically-firing guns were tearing up the terrain and creating visible havoc amongst the Southerners, while his steady German infantrymen were delivering small arms fire against the enemy line, holding it in place for his guns to maul at their will. Despite being outnumbered, he had managed to seize and hold the initiative. Unfortunately for the Federals, any advantage he may have obtained proved fleeting.

A movement in the left distance caught his attention. Mounted enemy troops were moving west—well beyond the left flank of his army. Wilkin's guns were turned upon the cavalry. Shortly thereafter another mounted enemy column was seen moving east, beyond his right flank. "I observed now that the two mounted regiments of the rebel army prepared themselves to turn our right and left," wrote Sigel. "They moved by the flank, and, describing a wide circle, left great intervals between them and the center."[65]

The double flanking movement changed the complexion of the engagement entirely. Without a ready reserve to either extend his flanks or prepare a defense in depth, Sigel was unprepared to meet it. Indeed, as outnumbered as he was, his line was already extended to the breaking point. But he did have a powerful long arm to call upon. Christian Essig was ordered to train the muzzles of his guns on the Southerners riding around the right and halt the potential threat. The cannon fire found its mark but failed to stop the turning movement against the Federal right. Sigel later reported that he then "directed the whole of our artillery against the right of the enemy's center," in order to silence the Southern guns, and that "in a short time the fire of his artillery began to slacken. . ." Although the fire did lessen, it had more to do with a empty Southern limbers than effective Union counter-battery fire.[66]

Essig's shelling forced Rives' and Brown's cavalry further east in an attempt to escape the deadly Federal iron, while Wilkins' artillery fire created a similar situation with Peyton and McCown's horsemen on the opposite flank. The effective artillery fire was in one significant respect potentially disastrous for Sigel: it pushed the Rebel mounted threats deeper into his rear without inflicting serious casualties, increasing the odds that his men would be completely surrounded.

Sigel's dilemma was growing more serious by the minute, and his options were limited because of the small number of men at his disposal. He formed a chain of skirmishers between his guns and "ordered two pieces of Captain Essig's battery from the right to our left wing" to confront what he believed was the greatest threat. The

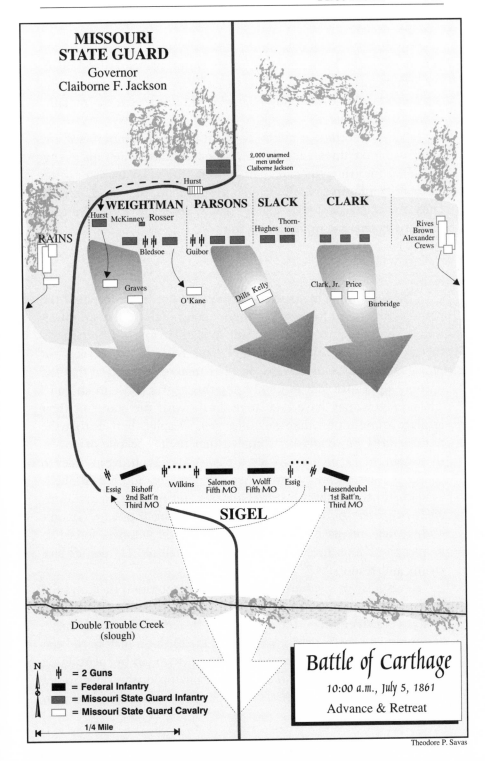

MISSOURI
STATE GUARD

Governor
Claiborne F. Jackson

2,000 unarmed
men under
Claiborne Jackson

Hurst

WEIGHTMAN   PARSONS   SLACK   CLARK

Hurst
McKinney   Rosser

RAINS

Thorn-
Hughes   ton

Rives
Brown
Alexander
Crews

Bledsoe   Guibor

Graves

O'Kane

Dills   Kelly

Clark, Jr.   Price

Burbridge

Essig   Bishoff
2nd Batt'n
Third MO

Wilkins   Salomon
Fifth MO

Wolff
Fifth MO

Essig

Hassendeubel
1st Batt'n,
Third MO

SIGEL

Double Trouble Creek
(slough)

N

╫ = 2 Guns
▬ = Federal Infantry
▮ = Missouri State Guard Infantry
▯ = Missouri State Guard Cavalry

1/4 Mile

Battle of Carthage

10:00 a.m., July 5, 1861

Advance & Retreat

Theodore P. Savas

result was that it only delayed the inevitable encirclement of Sigel's stationary army. The better trained but outnumbered Federal infantry and artillery could stand toe-to-toe with the State Guard, but Sigel was quickly discovering that he could not match the mobility of the Rebel cavalry.[67]

Sigel was nothing if not an optimist. Heavily outnumbered and with his flanks threatened, he saw an opportunity when his enemy separated into three unequal parts. Would the noisy barrage scatter the enemy infantry? He thought so. And when it did, he planned to launch a Napoleonic-style grand assault, complete with advancing artillery, against the militia in his front.[68]

*   *   *

The steady shelling, stress of battle and hot July sun paved the path to exhaustion for both Southern energy and artillery ammunition. "The excitement and the sun took their toll on the battery-men," Barlow of Guibor's Battery later reported in an account provided to a St. Louis newspaper. "The men openly prayed that the enemy would turn and run and bring this horrid battle to an end." Their prayers may have had more do do with the status of their artillery ammunition than anything else. Despite the fact that the officers knew or should have known that their stockpile of projectiles was limited, no one ordered the guns to cease firing in order to conserve their meager supply. As a result, the number of shells available in the limbers behind Guibor's and Bledsoe's guns dwindled with every pull of the lanyard. Before long the State Guard's artillery fire diminished into fitful spasms, the gunners forced to answer the Union fire with iron cut into small pieces, bits of trace chains and even rocks.[69]

Henry Guibor's battery exhausted its ammunition first, and the pieces were pulled away from the front of the line. Despite the prolonged artillery duel, the battery was in remarkably good shape, with only two men slightly wounded. One of these may have been Barlow himself, who modestly referred to his wound by mentioning his retirement to a small field hospital on top of the ridge to get "slight personal repairs." Hiram Bledsoe's battery continued firing to

keep up Southern morale more than anything, but at a much reduced rate of fire.[70]

*   *   *

The lack of a breeze that morning clogged the lowlands of the
battlefield with heavy powder smoke that hung in thick clouds near
the ground. The shroud of choking smoke made it difficult for Sigel
to judge the effects of his artillery bombardment. When should he
launch his assault? He had planned to do so when the Rebel line
began to waver under the heavy pounding of his guns and small
arms. "[I] made [it] known to the commanders and troops that it
was my intention to gain the heights by advancing with our left and
taking position on the right flank of the enemy's center," he reported
after the battle. The slackening in the return artillery fire was an
indication that he was gaining the upper hand, and the Federal
commander judged that the moment had arrived to order his two
regiments and artillery forward against the State Guard.[71]

"In this critical moment," remembered Sigel, "Captain Wilkins,
commander of one of the two batteries, declared that he was unable
to advance for want of ammunition." With his limber chests de-
pleted, the only viable way to re-supply the battery was to pull it out
of line and send it to the rear. Sigel, however, had neither the luxury
of time nor the reinforcements to plug another battery in its place,
and his wagons were two miles behind him. The dearth of ammunition forced him to rethink his tactics. He needed the weight of all of
his artillery to support his outnumbered infantry if they were to
enjoy a chance of success. "One part of the troops on the extreme
right and left were already engaged with the mounted troops," he
explained in his report, "and to advance with the rest without the
assistance of artillery seemed to me a movement which could easily
turn into a *déroute.*" At the same time his flanks were being turned
by Southern cavalry. "The moral effect of the enemy's mounted
regiments behind our lines, although the real danger was not great,"
he rationalized later, "could not be denied." The Federal wagon train
was also behind Sigel's line and completely exposed to capture. "To
lose our whole baggage was another consideration of importance."[72]

Sigel wisely weighed these factors and reached a momentous conclusion: he would abandon his original offensive plan and withdraw. "It was therefore with great mortification that I ordered one part of the troops behind Dry Fork Creek," he wrote, "whilst Lieutenant-Colonel Hassendeubel, with the First Battalion of the Third and a battalion of the Fifth Regiment, under Lieutenant-Colonel Wolff, followed by four pieces of Captain Wilkins' battery, reported to the baggage train to defend it against the projected attack."[73]

The German revolutionary's order for his army to conduct a retreat to Dry Fork Creek, about a mile to his rear, was the turning point in the Battle of Carthage. Sigel was conceding the fact that he was no longer in a position to play his cherished role as the aggressor. The best he could hope for after less than one hour of fighting was the extrication of his small force from the potentially fatal situation into which he had guided it. The initiative had passed to the Missouri State Guard.

While Sigel had substantial experience conducting retreats, the withdrawal from the plains north of Carthage offered several vexing problems. He was outnumbered, outflanked by cavalry and had almost three dozen baggage and ammunition wagons deep in his rear. With some of his men marching to turn his wagons south before the arrival of the Rebels, Sigel scribbled an order to Captain Essig, instructing him to take a section of his guns and post them overlooking the crossing at Dry Fork Creek.[74]

One must wonder whether Sigel's mind wandered back to the Revolution of 1848-49. Was the disastrous Battle of Heppenheim about to be reprised?

8

Dry Fork Creek

The rolling thunder of artillery sweeping across the prairie that morning startled the citizens of southwest Missouri. Only hours earlier young Charles Harrington had watched as the state troops marched past his home. Now he listened as the gunfire rolled and thundered miles away to the south. "There is going to be an immense amount of excitement today," he told his father. John W. Henry, standing on his farm on the outskirts of Carthage, also heard the artillery barrage. "This is it!" he exclaimed to his daughter. The roar of the artillery duel also carried 20 miles southeast to Sarcoxie, where Brig. Gen. James Rains' wife and daughter stood on their front porch with eyes glued toward the noise coming from beyond the northern skyline. Back in Camp Lamar, women who had retreated with their soldier-husbands into the southwest corner of Missouri anxiously awaited news from the front. In the small village of Fidelity, a few miles south of Carthage, 26-year-old James M. Hickey worked his muddy fields. When the sound of the guns reached his ears he he put away his tools, saddled his horse and galloped north to determine the source of the firing.[1]

The citizens of Carthage were just returning to their regular routine when the deep-throated artillery blasts reached their ears. Many hurried back into their homes and locked their doors, convinced that the soldiers would soon return. The battle was raging somewhere to the north along the road recently traveled by the Federal troops that had only vacated Carthage earlier that morning. As the sounds echoed around the square, Norris Hood remarked to his family, "Sigel and his men may get eaten up alive because of the superior numbers they face." Soon after Hood uttered his prophetic words, the last company of Union soldiers ordered by Sigel to join him near Carthage marched through the town square. Captain Joseph Indest's Rifle Company A broke into a run when it heard the sound of the guns. Sarah Ann Smith, who lived on farm north of town along the Spring River, asked her father where the thunder-like sounds were coming from. "Rains fighting the Dutch," was his terse reply.[2]

Alta Fullerton and her daughters lived along the Sarcoxie Road southeast of Carthage. The elder Fullerton realized immediately that the heavy firing involved the troops who had marched by her farm the previous day. Another civilian, Mrs. Thomas Glass, was flat on her back in bed and eight months pregnant when the firing started. The booming cannons made her fear for both the safety of the town and the security of her husband's mill along the Spring River. Although the Glass family had declared itself officially neutral in the spreading conflict, the declaration was more a ruse than the truth. The son Mrs. Glass would deliver one month after the Battle would be christened Sterling Price Glass.[3]

Others with an even more direct interest heard the gunnery duel. Twenty-five miles away at Neosho, Captain Joseph Conrad of Rifle Company B, Third Missouri, later confessed, "[he] did not know what it meant for them." Conrad, left behind on the 4th of July to garrison the small town, dispatched a courier to bring back instructions. The news was ominous. At 1:00 p.m., Conrad received a scribbled dispatch from Sigel's quartermaster, J. M. Richardson, ". . . to retreat with my command, if necessary." The stranded Missouri captain could not have been pleased with these vague and unsettling instructions.[4]

* * *

Although Franz Sigel reported after the battle that his first retreat on the morning of July 5 was predicated largely on a shortage of artillery shells, another event often overlooked may have formed the basis of his decision: the advance of the Missouri State Guard. "The enemy. . .slowly retired for about 200 yards, halted, and commenced the engagement," wrote Colonel Weightman, "when I advanced the whole line of the brigade in battle order, and reopened fire upon him by Captain Bledsoe's guns." General Parsons' artillery, he continued, "by this time retired, as I learn, for want of ammunition." The enemy, he further explained, "after cannonading us but a few minutes. . .retired under cover of the fire of his artillery." Weightman's account, which describes the action immediately following the artillery duel, is supported by other Southern witnesses. "Colonel Weightman promptly and gallantly advanced his whole brigade in battle order and reopened his fire from Captain Bledsoe's guns," explained General Rains, drawing largely from Weightman's own description of the action. By this time Rains and his cavalry had crossed the western cornfield and were in the timber beyond Sigel's left flank.[5]

Brigadier General John Clark offered a similar picture of events from his perspective on the left end of the Southern line. "After consultation with Colonel Kelly, commanding a regiment in General Parsons' division. . .I ordered an advance of my forces in the direction of the enemy." Parsons himself rode upon the scene at that moment "and gave a similar order," remembered Clark. "Our commands, together with the battalion of Colonel O'Kane, of Colonel Weightman's command, made a rapid movement in the direction of the enemy." Parsons confirms Clark's version of events, but contradicted one aspect of Weightman's report by claiming that Guibor's Battery also advanced upon the Federals. It is interesting to note that regardless of who was in command that day, Rains or Jackson, neither gave the command to advance.[6]

John Clark's description of the initial stages of the Federal retreat and Southern pursuit is the most detailed description of this phase of the battle. "After advancing some fifty yards the enemy made a retrograde movement in double-quick time over the eminence on which he had been posted into a ravine." The slight depression "effectually concealed him from our view," explained Clark, who supposed "his design by such movement was to gain a position on our left and to make an attack on our flank." Contrary to Clark's logical assumption, however, Sigel entertained no such plan, preferring instead a headlong retreat in an attempt to save his embattled regiments from the pursuing enemy.[7]

According to Clark, "the several commands changed their direction from south to east, each marching in separated columns." These "several commands" consisted of Col. Walter O'Kane's Battalion, of Weightman's Brigade, on the right end of the new line, Major Dills' and Colonel Kelly's commands extending the line north, and Clark's three small units holding the left flank. After marching in this formation for about half a mile, wrote Clark, "I discovered the enemy, who seemed to be rapidly forming into line of battle about one mile and a half from his first position, behind a cluster of trees, and upon an eminence on the south side of Bear [Dry Fork] Creek."[8]

Although Colonel O'Kane's Battalion advanced immediately with Clark and Parsons, it appears as though the balance of Weightman's line did not move out in pursuit until Col. Edgar V. Hurst's regiment formed on his right flank. "Colonel Hurst, with his regiment, came forward from the rear at double-quick time, and took the position assigned him on the right of Colonel Graves," reported Weightman. "I again advanced in battle order the whole line of the brigade."[9]

With Weightman's advance the entire state army—at least those who were armed—was on the move. Rains and his cavalrymen were driving for Dry Fork Creek beyond the Rebel right flank, the infantry was marching in pursuit, albeit slowly, across the morning battle field, and the mounted men under Cols. Rives and Brown were sweeping around the opposite flank. As General Clark's description makes clear, Sigel managed to pull his men behind the line of Dry Fork Creek and arrange them for battle before the Southerners could cut them off. The advance was not launched soon enough or pushed as vigorously as it might have been in order to cut off and destroy the Federals north of the creek. "The cavalry did not succeed in getting the position designated for them," wrote a disappointed Parsons, "in consequence of which the enemy were successful in recrossing Bear [Dry Fork] Creek and establishing themselves on a steep eminence on its southern bank." The same charge can also be leveled against the infantry.[10]

The fissured structure of the Southern high command played a role in the delay. Without one overall commander surveying the field and giving commands, Mosby Parsons, Richard Weightman, William Slack and John Clark acted independently of one another. Although there appears to have been an extraordinary amount of cooperation between several of these officers—especially Parsons and Clark—the absence of both Claiborne Jackson, who was behind the lines with the unarmed "spectators," and James Rains, who was acting like a regimental cavalry leader, made for a leaderless Missouri State Guard. The fact that the bulk of the army was lurching forward more or less at one time was in itself a significant achievement.

*   *   *

Franz Sigel decided that the best way to conduct a successful withdrawal was to divide his already small command in two sections. One would accompany the wagon train, the other defend the crossing. The first and largest of these segments consisted of Lt. Col. Francis Hassendeubel's First Battalion, Third Missouri, a battalion of the Fifth Missouri under Lt. Col. Christian Wolff and Captain Wilkins' four artillery pieces. This column crossed Dry Fork Creek—described later by one of the Confederates as "a most beautiful stream of clear and pure water"—and marched south as rapidly as possible to the trains to shepherd them out of harm's way and "defend [them] against the projected attack," explained Sigel. The smaller of the two segments, earmarked to hold the crossing and slow down enemy pursuit, consisted of three companies of the Fifth Missouri under Captains Carl Stephani (Company E), Charles E. Stark (Company G) and Charles Meissner (Company I), another two companies of the Third Missouri under Captains Adolph Dengler (Company G) and Hugo Glomer (Company F), together with Captain Essig's four artillery pieces.[11]

"Captain Essig's battery had taken up a position behind the ford," wrote Sigel, describing his defensive alignment along Dry Fork Creek. The balance of the Federal line was constructed around Essig. Captain Stephani's company deployed on the left of the guns, stretching the line west, while Dengler and Glomer formed on the right of the unlimbered artillery, extending the line eastward along the creek as far as possible to avoid being flanked by Rebels. The remaining two companies were held back as a reserve, one behind each flank.[12]

Where was Lyon? The question may well have crossed Franz Sigel's mind as the German colonel deployed his men and prepared to resist the onslaught he knew was coming. He had chosen a strong defensive position, one which presented the Missouri State Guard with several tactical dilemmas. While his initial choice of ground had proved untenable, Sigel now occupied the high ground on the southern bank of a swift-flowing creek that covered his entire front. In addition, a thin belt of timber along both edges of the creek conspired with thick undergrowth to help conceal Sigel's men from the Southerners. In order to come to grips with the Federals, Jackson's Missourians would have to cross a flat stretch of field devoid of natural protection and exposed to both artillery and rifled-musket fire. The ground was just what Sigel was looking for. Dry Fork Creek would allow him to wage a holding action long enough for his trains to withdraw out of harm's way. At least, that was how he planned it.

The key to holding the creek line was to maintain control of the ford, and that narrow avenue was dominated by Essig's artillery. The four guns were masked in heavy timber on a steep rise just a handful of yards east of the crossing. The timber helped conceal the guns, which in turn dominated the field in front of the waterway. When finally arranged, the thin Federal line stretched about one quarter of a mile long, covering the stream's crossing—and little else.[13]

Sigel's Dry Fork Creek position was well-suited to a rear guard holding action. It too, however, possessed an Achilles' Heel similar to his first battle line of the day. Despite its natural frontal strength, neither flank was firmly anchored on a strong point and thus both flanks were vulnerable to encirclement—especially by the wide-ranging and quick-riding Southern cavalry. This weakness was compounded because of Sigel's ignorance as to the current whereabouts of the Rebel horsemen. Worse, his cavalry-starved force had no ready means of locating them. While his trains rumbled south he could only hope the cavalry would find it difficult to cross the creek.[14]

While the lull in the fighting after the artillery duel may have provided some relief for the anxious citizens of southwest Missouri, it is doubtful whether Franz Sigel experienced similar feelings. The significant disparity in numbers between his small force and the Missouri State Guard army was even greater now that he had dispatched a large portion of his men south with the wagons. Within a short time after taking up his Dry Fork position an advancing line of homespun-clad infantry was spotted moving in his direction. Would his enemy launch a direct attack against such a strong position? If so, it would likely pin the thin line of defenders in place while cavalry crossed the stream and surrounded him.

*   *   *

In reality the Missouri State Guard had no plans other than general pursuit. Without a leader an overall course of action was impossible. Even without a guiding hand the divisions pushed on for Dry Fork Creek relatively intact, a testament to the leadership abilities of the army's line officers. The advance seems to have caused both confusion and a realignment in the battle line. On the east side of the Lamar-Carthage Road, Mosby Parsons' Division, with Colonel O'Kane's regiment clinging to its right, advanced south toward the creek, as did John Clark's Division further east beyond Parsons' left flank. Colonel Weightman was also moving forward on the west side of the road, probably in line of battle, with his left flank guiding on or near the road. William Slack's Division, represented at this stage of the battle by Col. John T. Hughes' regiment under Lieutenant Colonel Pritchard and Maj. J. C. Thornton's small battalion, moved into battle at some point west of the road, out of sight of Parsons and Clark and probably behind Weightman.[15]

"As I neared the timber, proceeding along the road," reported Weightman, "I discovered the enemy through the openings through which the road passed posted in force on the brow of the hill on the opposite bank of the creek." The position, "distant about 400 yards," was well masked. The only Federals visible were those "seen through the opening." Although the Rebel position was particularly exposed, Weightman "directed Lieutenant Colonel Rosser to have the artillery unlimbered and to open fire on the enemy. . . " As Rosser ordered Bledsoe's' battery forward, Weightman aligned his men and "directed the infantry on either wing of the brigade to pass

Franz Sigel's Dry Fork position. This photo looks south from the perspective of the pursuing Missouri militia. Dry Fork is marked by the treeline. Captain Essig's artillery pieces were unlimbered immediately behind the ford, which is where the road cuts through the trees. Hiram Bledsoe's Southern artillery deployed near the spot from which this picture was taken. *Author's Collection*

into and through the timber, and engage the enemy at close quarters." In other words, Weightman ordered a frontal attack without knowing where the Southern cavalry was or the strength of the enemy infantry along the creek bank.[16]

Everyone who reported on the subject was impressed with Sigel's new line. "Reconnoitering this position," wrote Parsons just five days after the battle, "I found the enemy's batteries stationed so as to completely command the crossing." The terrain "immediately in front and for some miles above him was a skirt of thick timber, through which the creek ran, and upon which his line was being formed," explained Clark. The timber, which would absorb and disrupt advancing infantry, was "about 30 yards in width to the right and left of the crossing for several miles above and below."[17]

Just getting to the timber would be difficult, thought Parsons. Directly in front of his men was "a large field, its southern boundary being on the timber north of the creek." Essig's Federal artillery, situated on the hill behind the creek "completely commanded the field." With the enemy spreading out behind the fast-flowing stream, Parsons also deemed it imperative to press the attack. "I found it absolutely necessary for the success of the day to make a rapid movement of the infantry through the field," he explained, ". . .and get possession of the timber on our side of the stream." But getting the men into the timber was just half the battle, for there were no ready crossing points except for the well-defended ford. It is more probable than not that few if any of the Southern commanders realized this.[18]

Compounding their difficulties were the weapons carried by their men. Armed largely with old flintlocks, shot guns and squirrel rifles, the Missourians would be forced to advance within a short distance of the enemy in order for them to be effective. The Federals, on the other hand, armed primarily with rifled muskets, enjoyed a substantially wider killing zone. Their defensive posture with an all but unfordable creek across their front would make the task of prying them free all the more difficult.[19]

While the Southern infantry was marching south after the artillery bombardment in search of Sigel's retreating infantry, General Rains reformed his disrupted cavalry units in a stand of timber. Captain Theodore Wilkins' Federal artillery had pounded the horsemen during their passage through the Gresham cornfields. The protection offered by the trees allowed Rains to rest and take stock of the rapidly developing situation. The sudden Federal retreat offered a number of dazzling possibilities, including the complete destruction of the enemy with his encirclement. But Rains was out of touch with the main body of the army he had been ostensibly been assigned to command, and was not aware of what was happening off to the east. Nor did he possess any information as to the location and condition of the other body of Southern horsemen who had disappeared around Sigel's eastern flank. Indeed, we do not even know if Rains realized that Colonels Rives and Brown had embarked on a mission similar to his own.[20]

After reorganizing his regiments, Rains reached a decision. The cavalry, according to Colonel Peyton, "passed through [the timber] in

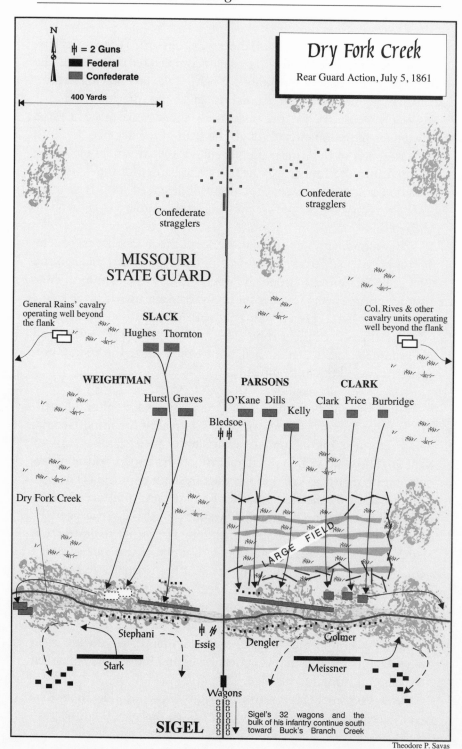

N

⫲ = 2 Guns
■ Federal
■ Confederate

400 Yards

Dry Fork Creek

Rear Guard Action, July 5, 1861

Confederate
stragglers

Confederate
stragglers

MISSOURI
STATE GUARD

General Rains' cavalry
operating well beyond
the flank

SLACK

Hughes Thornton

Col. Rives & other
cavalry units operating
well beyond the flank

WEIGHTMAN

Hurst Graves

Bledsoe
⫲ ⫲

PARSONS

O'Kane Dills

Kelly

CLARK

Clark Price Burbridge

Dry Fork Creek

LARGE FIELD

Stephani

Essig

Dengler

Colmer

Stark

Meissner

Wagons

Sigel's 32 wagons and the
bulk of his infantry continue south
toward Buck's Branch Creek

SIGEL

Theodore P. Savas

good order" and made for Dry Fork Creek. The column would continue pushing south, cross over the stream and trap the enemy.[21]

In accordance with his orders, Hiram Bledsoe unlimbered his pieces 400 yards from the ford near the Lamar-Carthage Road "amidst a storm of grape." It was approximately 1:00 p.m. Once deployed, the battery "opened a carefully-aimed fire upon the enemy." Lieutenant Colonel Thomas H. Rosser, who assisted Bledsoe, impressed his superior that morning with his coolness under fire. "With the calmness of a professor of entomology examining a rare addition to his collection," wrote Weightman, Rosser "aimed one of the guns, while the enemy's grape shot tore up the earth and disabled men and horses around him." The action was fast and deadly, and several men were wounded in the exchange of iron. Tom and Charley Young, two brothers serving in the battery, both suffered wounds while unlimbering the guns, as did Pvt. Eldrige Booten. Officers were not immune to the firing, as "the gallant" Lt. Charles Higgins discovered when a round of case shot knocked him to the ground. His wound was reported as "serious but not fatal." The fortunate officer managed to struggle to his feet and continue the fight, loading a gun "until completed, and fell exhausted under the muzzle of his piece."[22]

The losses mounted quickly. "In consequence of the number of men disabled," Captain Bledsoe, Lieutenant Wallace, and infantry captain F. M. McKinney "in person served the guns," lauded Weightman, ". . .Lieutenant Wallace remaining at his post, though twice wounded in the leg." Even Bledsoe felt the sting of Essig's metal storm when a Federal shell struck a powder keg near him. The small barrel exploded in a fireball of smoke and flames, injuring him. By the end of the fighting three officers and eight privates sustained wounds within a few yards of the battery. Remarkably, the only fatalities suffered by the artillerists were inflicted on horse flesh when three animals were wounded and four others killed.[23]

While Bledsoe's guns were taking a pounding, Parsons and Clark finalized their alignments. Parsons' troops formed immediately east of the road. Colonel Joseph Kelly's regiment advanced ahead of the rest of the line and held the far left of Parsons' Division, with "Major Dills' battalion close upon his right." Colonel William O'Kane's regiment, still separated from Weightman's First Brigade, advanced into battle holding the right flank of Parsons' divisional front, his own right hugging the roadway. John Clark's Division formed in the field immediately upon Parsons' left. "Colonel Clark, with his usual promptness," complimented Parsons, "co-operat[ed] on my extreme left." The officer and regiment to which Parsons was referring was Col. John B. Clark, Jr.'s First Regiment of Infantry, which held the right flank of his father's division. The men of Cols. John Burbridge's and Edwin Price's commands extended General Clark's line further east.[24]

With a yell the Rebels swept down into Dry Fork Creek valley in a disjointed but hearty assault. As the line moved forward, O'Kane's men rushed past Bledsoe's blazing field pieces—including "Old Sacramento." Franz Sigel's Federals gave a good account of themselves, flooding the field with shell fire in an attempt to arrest the long and serrated line of battle. "The enemy used every effort in their power

The Missouri State Guard attack at Dry Fork Creek. This image depicts the east side of the Lamar-Carthage Road. The divisions of Mosby Parsons and John B. Clark, Sr., advanced across this field and into the trees in the distance, which fringe Dry Fork Creek. The heavy growth of trees and brush helped shield the Southerners from Federal small arms fire. *Author's Collection*

to prevent the success of this movement," testified Parsons. "They fired rapid volleys of grape, shell, and round shot upon this command in its advance through the field." Unfortunately for the defenders, they did not have enough men or guns to stop the mass of gray and brown bodies from reaching the edge of the woods, just a handful of yards from the creek. "Our troops, without wavering, gallantly succeeded in gaining the south side of [the field]," exclaimed Parsons, where they "rapidly deploy[ed], [and] threw themselves over the fence and into the timber." Clark's recollections coincide with those of Parsons. "We immediately advanced to the timber on the north side of the creek and took a position near the enemy," he reported, "when a sharp and incessant fire of small-arms on either side occurred, lasting for about thirty minutes." The timber along the banks, strangely enough, assisted both sides, masking Sigel's weak rear guard while concurrently shielding the attacking state troops from small arms fire.[25]

Missouri State Guardsmen Archy Thomas remembered how "the infantry flanked around through the brush on the creek and played finely on the Federal Army with their ready and sure aim of the shot gun and rifle." Another witness testified that the Rebels "opened vigorously upon the enemy across the stream, who returned the fire with great spirit." The action raged for "the space of an hour," was how one Missourian remembered it, the firing "incessant and fierce."[26]

While the firsthand accounts of the fighting at Dry Fork Creek are remarkably consistent, Colonel Weightman maintained that Federal skirmishers were posted in the woods north of the creek and driven to the opposite side, which may well be correct. Certainly he was in a position to observe such an event. Weightman, who ordered Colonel O'Kane's 350-man battalion forward on the right flank of Mosby Parsons' Division, observed his men strike the enemy. "Lieutenant-Colonel O'Kane, with his battalion. . .advanced rapidly through a field, and on the skirt of the timber nearest to us fell in with the enemy." Acknowledging the assistance of other units deployed and advancing east of the road, Weightman reported the fighting north of the stream as brisk but relatively brief, much like his terse description of the action. O'Kane "engaged the enemy [skirmishers], and after a short conflict drove him through the timber

The Missouri State Guard attack at Dry Fork Creek. This image provides a nice view of the terrain over which two of Richard Weightman's three regiments attacked at Dry Fork Creek (Colonel O'Kane's Battalion advanced with Parsons east of the road). The creek is marked by the treeline. The Lamar-Carthage Road is immediately to the left of this photo. It is probable that William Slack's men advanced over this same ground after Weightman's infantry crossed. *Author's Collection*

across the creek back upon his main body." Weightman was more than willing to feed his brigade into the action piecemeal, as O'Kane was the only one of his units prepared for action in time to coordinate an assault with the divisions east of the road.[27]

While the attack over the field took just a few minutes, the small arms battle along the fringe of woods hugging Dry Fork Creek lasted, according to one account, about "thirty minutes." The killing zone separating the two warring factions shooting at one another across the creek was little more than one hundred feet. "The action on the enemy's right with General Clark's infantry and mine now became general," reported Parsons, "the opposing lines having arrived within 30 or 40 yards of each other." The fighting consisted of "brisk volleys. . .for nearly half an hour."[28]

Shortly after the divisions east of the road massed along the creek, Weightman had his remaining infantry on the west side, the regiments of John R. Graves and Edgar Hurst, organized and ready for action. "Responding with spirit and zeal to my order," he remembered some days after the event, "Colonels Graves and Hurst threw their regiments into the timber. . ." Given the earlier fighting and straggling suffered that day by the state army, it is reasonable to assume that the combined units did not number much more than 600 men. The officers guided their units down the gentle slope and hit the wood line some yards to the right of Essig's blazing artillery, directly in front of Capt. Carl Stephani's Company E, Fifth Missouri Regiment. The Missourians fought their way through the timber and managed to penetrate to the edge of the water, where they found the stream "impassable on the direct line of attack at which they reached it." Unable to advance any further and unwilling to stand and absorb casualties to no purpose, the colonels were, according to Weightman, "forced to seek a ford at a point below," and thus "passed through the timber" by their right flank in search of a route across Dry Fork Creek.

By this time Slack's men had also arrived on scene. Colonel Hughes guided the division's two units under Pritchard and Thornton across the same ground and struck the woods soon after Graves and Hurst had shifted to the west. Like's Weightman's men, Slack's found it impossible to ford the creek. "Colonel Hughes' command," reported General Slack, ". . .owing to the deep water in the stream failed in his effort."[29]

The fighting along Dry Fork continued on both sides of the road, with neither combatant willing to retire. Two prominent and profoundly fortunate State Guard officers had close brushes with death during the attack. "While gallantly urging and cheering forward his forces," wrote one observer, "Lieut. Col. Edwin Price had his horse killed under him." Walter O'Kane's mount suffered a similar fate, although both he and Price managed to escape serious injury. Others were not so lucky. O'Kane's Battalion suffered heavily, losing two killed and twenty wounded in the sharp action. One of the latter was company commander Capt. Leonidas Warren, who endured a severe lower leg wound when a "grape shot," as Weightman later described it, struck him near the edge of the creek.[30]

There are no firsthand Federal accounts of the important action along Dry Fork other than from Franz Sigel's pen. Unfortunately, this portion of his report is nothing more than a few perfunctory sentences describing the fight, leading one to suspect he did not remain behind to witness it. My troops "resisted the enemy's entire force for two hours," exaggerated the German colonel, "and inflicted on him the severest losses." According to Sigel, Union soldiers shot down at least one Rebel color bearer, only to see the banner rise again in the hands of another soldier. "The rebellious flag [sank] twice amidst the triumphant shouts of the United States volunteers." The German was proud of his soldiers. "Was the like never seen!" he remarked after the war. "Raw recruits not yet acquainted with war, standing their ground like veterans, hurling defiance at every discharge of the batteries against them, and cheering their own batteries whenever they discharged. Such material properly worked up, would constitute the best troops in the world," he proclaimed.[31]

If a fight was going to be waged along the creek, Sigel could not have scripted a more favorable action. Other than a passive State Guard, he could not have hoped for anything better than a frontal assault against his powerful position. Christian Essig's well-handled and timber-shielded guns had wreaked havoc with Bledsoe's lighter pieces, and had been able as well to send shells and case shot into the approaching Southern ranks. Although Essig and his comrades were unsuccessful in their attempt to break up the attack and could not drive the Southerners back once they had reached the waterway, neither could the Rebels readily cross over to the southern bank.

And so the killing continued at pointblank range while the Federal wagons rolled south out of harm's way. The climax of the Dry Fork Creek fighting was at hand.

*   *   *

While the Southern infantry pushed and probed in an effort to ford Dry Fork, James Rains continued his search for a suitable crossing for his cavalry a mile or two west of the action. His bold plan to throw his cavalry against the rear of Sigel's Dry Fork position in a coup-de-main mounted attack was unraveling. The unfamiliar, occasionally rough and unusually soggy country necessarily slowed down his column, which wandered along the swift creek. With time—and Sigel—slipping through his fingers, Rains decided to divide his command in order to improve his chances of locating a crossing. Lieutenant Colonel Richard A. Boughan's Seventh Cavalry was directed to move further west. "I was ordered to take my command down the creek and cross over at the first crossing I could find," he later reported. After Boughan trotted off with his 300 men and "Colonel Hyde's" 100-man command from St. Joseph, Missouri, which had attached itself to Boughan's regiment that day, Rains eventually stumbled onto a suitable ford. The crossing was completed without untold difficulty. None of the reports mention a word about hearing any of the fighting to the east, so it is difficult to determine exactly when the passage took place. "After crossing over on the south side of the timber and gaining the prairie the whole column was halted," reported Colonel Peyton, "and remained there for some time."[32]

A large bulk of the State Guard cavalry was finally on the southern bank. How many of the troopers wondered why James Rains had halted his command?

*   *   *

With Rains desperately seeking a ford and the Southern infantry attacking the Federals ensconced behind Dry Fork Creek, the wagon train that caused Sigel so much concern continued its journey south. It had taken some time to get the wagons facing in the opposite direction and get them moving toward Carthage. The early morning artillery fire had panicked some of the animals, and the wagons they were pulling sank in the soft ground when they left the road bed in an attempt to turn around. The arrival of Lt. Col. Francis Hassendeubel and the rest of the troops assigned to guard the precious wagons calmed the frightened teamsters and delivered some order to what had been a very chaotic and potentially disastrous situation.

As the procession of vehicles left Dry Fork behind them, the troops marching alongside surely pondered the whereabouts of the quick-riding Southern cavalry that had earlier disappeared beyond their flanks. Francis Hassendeubel may also have engaged in a bit of musing on that hot July day, for his situation was peculiarly ironic.

Lt. Col. Francis Hassendeubel
Missouri Historical Society

Fifteen years earlier, during the War With Mexico, he had served as a lieutenant of artillery under then-Brig. Gen. Sterling Price. Hassendeubel had no way of knowing that his old commander was in Arkansas seeking reinforcements, not leading the state army pounding away at his comrades holding the Dry Fork Creek line.[33]

*   *   *

The bitter exchange of firearms along the serene waters of Dry Fork Creek was reaching a crescendo. Hundreds of men from Weightman's First Brigade and Slack's Division hugged the skirt of timber west of the crossing, discharging their weapons into the woefully out-manned and thinning blue lines of Federals bravely holding firm on the opposite side. The divisions of Mosby Parsons, John Clark and Walter O'Kane's Battalion added probably another 1,000 troops east of the Lamar-Carthage Road, racheting up the pressure against Essig's gunners and the three companies led by Stephani, Dengler and Glomer. Parsons, once again thinking like an army commander, grew curious as to what was taking place west of the road. The aggressive leader spurred his horse behind the lines and rode up the hill. "Not being advised as to what was going on to the right of the road and to the right of Colonel Weightman's battery," explained Parsons, "I. . .rode up to a high point of ground which commanded a view of the enemy's position and our own lines to the right." It was approximately 1:30 p.m. The sight that greeted Parsons' tired eyes could not have been more welcome. "I. . .discovered that the whole force of the enemy were in full retreat."[34]

Exactly what touched off the sudden withdrawal is not clear. One Southern account claims that "The Missourians threw a quantity of dead timber into the stream and commenced crossing over in large numbers." The regiment or regiments responsible for the feat, however, are not named. Neither Parsons nor Clark witnessed any of their men cross the stream while the fighting was underway. William Slack's skimpy account simply states that Colonel Hughes' regiment did not cross "until the enemy had again retired in the direction of Carthage."[35]

Weightman's men, however, seem to have had more luck and may have turned the tide of the fighting along the creek. On the far right of the militia line, the regiments of Col. Edgar Hurst and Col. John Graves either found a ford beyond Carl Stephani's paper-thin Company E line or managed to cross by other means (perhaps by throwing dead timber in the water, as suggested above). However it was accomplished, the Missourians "passed through the timber on the farther bank of the creek on the enemy's left flank," reported their brigade commander after the fight, although he also added that the crossing was not effected "until he [Sigel] was in the act of retiring." Weightman's two regiments were almost certainly the first organized bodies of Southerners to reach the far bank. His carefully worded report can be read to mean that the enemy was commencing—"in the act of retiring"—to retreat in conjunction with the crossing of Graves and Hurst. General Rains' report provides a clue in this regard. With information obtained from various subordinate officers, Rains claims that O'Kane's Battalion [Weightman's First Brigade], in conjunction with Clark's Division, "repulsed the enemy from their position." When read with Weightman's account, it seems probable that Graves and Hughes effected a crossing as Sigel's line fell back under the pressure being applied from the frontal attack, triggering a complete retreat.[36]

Franz Sigel's vaunted position along Dry Fork Creek had been breached.

9

Retreat

The teamsters drove the horses and mules as quickly as they could tolerate the summer heat. The Federal wagon train had been fortunate to escape below Dry Fork, which was now about a mile and one-half behind them. Ahead about one-half mile was Buck's Branch Creek, the next obstacle on the road to Carthage. The stream cut through the roadbed, spilling out into a marshy morass on either side. Tall prairie grass, much of it head high, together with a sprinkling of trees grew along the bank of the high-running ribbon of water. Its narrow and muddy ford promised a logistical bottleneck since every one of the thirty-two wagons would have to pass across in single file. Fortunately, the determined holding action at Dry Fork Creek had slowed enemy pursuit.

Lieutenant Sebastian Engert, riding well in advance of the column, was the first to spot the trouble. As the wagons rolled south he gradually began to make out a body of troops spread across the road immediately behind the creek. The line of battle sat squarely in the path of the Federal retreat. As he rode closer he realized the men were dismounted Southern cavalry.

The Missouri State Guard had beaten Sigel to Buck's Branch Creek.[1]

* * *

It had been a frustrating day for Ben Rives. During the morning artillery duel the commander of William Slack's cavalry had attempted a ride around the enemy's right flank, only to be shelled by the enemy's guns. Forced to the east by the flying metal, his widely-drawn arc carried him away from the battlefield and away from the retreating Union infantry, which fell back just ahead of him. Instead of driving his horsemen behind the Federals, he followed a meandering route which eventually brought him up short against the flooding and difficult to cross Dry Fork Creek. After swimming his horses over the stream, Rives discovered that the enemy had only recently retreated ahead of him. Spurring on their mounts, Rives' men drove south again, well to the east of the Lamar-Carthage Road. At some point in his journey he linked up with Col. Benjamin Brown and his First Regiment of Cavalry. Brown was also determined to cut off the Federal retreat. Together they arrived at yet another stream. What they discovered there must have made them smile.[2]

Luck was finally riding with the cavalrymen. Franz Sigel's retreating regiments had not yet slipped south of the narrow water-

Buck's Branch Creek. This narrow and almost hidden stream, buried by tall and thick prairie grass, posed more of a hazard in July 1861 than it does today. At the time of the battle, Buck's Branch was flooding and its ford was narrow and muddy—and thus a serious obstacle for wagons. *Author's Collection*

way. Neither had the Federal wagon train, which was still in front of them and rolling in their direction. The opportunity Rives and Brown had been seeking for much of the morning had arrived.[3]

The troopers formed a battle line perpendicular to the Lamar-Carthage Road just south of the creek and waited for the approaching enemy.[4]

* * *

According to Franz Sigel, he was not driven from his Dry Fork position but instead chose to evacuate and fall back because of a threat in his rear. "I left the position at Dry Fork" upon learning that "two large bodies of cavalry had completely surrounded us," Sigel explained in his report. The Rebels were "posted behind a small creek. . .which we had to pass." With a large and aggressive concentration of the enemy immediately behind him, a line of the Southerners stretched across his front and other enemy horsemen maneuvering beyond his western flank, Sigel ordered his men into a variety of deployments designed to address the multi-directional threats. His tactical situation, which had looked so promising after his stout defensive stand along Dry Fork, had taken a sudden and critical turn for the worse.[5]

Understandably, a sense of panic swept through the ranks of the teamsters, who wanted to abandon their wagons and take to the high prairie grass in an effort to save themselves. The cool-headed Francis Hassendeubel, however, would have none of it. Praised in Sigel's report as an officer of "well-known ability," Hassendeubel ordered the wagoneers back onto their vehicles and deployed three companies from his 1st Battalion, Third Missouri, across the road facing south in the direction of the creek. In an attempt to protect his trains and drive away the enemy cavalry blocking the ford, Sigel also ordered two pieces of artillery deployed on either side of the road, supported by portions of the Fifth and Third Missouri regiments, which remained in column. Two guns were deployed north (behind) the wagons under Lt. Theodore Schrickel "acting as a rear guard against the main body of the enemy, moving from Dry Fork."[6]

Essentially Sigel had formed a large square around his train of wagons, which according to one account were arranged in eight rows of four wagons each. The German colonel must have pondered his chances of driving the cavalry away and clearing the ford before the aggressive Missouri State Guard fell upon him from the north.[7]

*   *   *

Colonel Rives knew he was in trouble when he saw the strength of the Federal line approaching in his direction. Although he had hundreds of men with him, his troopers were poorly armed and inexperienced. Most of his men carried short range shotguns and long-barreled single shot flintlocks, no match for the well-armed and disciplined German infantry marching toward them. The stream itself was narrow and would not pose much of a barrier to determined troops. The entire issue boiled down to one question: could the officers hold their green men in place long enough for the Southern infantry and artillery to strike the rear of the Federal column? Rives reported his precarious—and advantageous—situation by courier and requested immediate support.[8]

It was just 2:00 p.m. and it had already been a long and bloody day for the Missouri State Guard. The difficult fight for the crossing at Dry Fork Creek was finally over, and Sigel's Federals were retreating once more in the direction of Carthage. Colonel Richard Weightman's First Brigade, thoroughly exhausted and disorganized, was going into camp on the ground recently vacated by the Federals. "The entire brigade. . .had been marching since 4 o'clock a.m. (Colonel Hurst's regiment without breakfast)," Weightman later reported, "and I was proceeding to encamp the brigade upon the ground recently held by the enemy. . ." A rider galloped into camp and delivered the message that Colonel Rives' cavalry "had engaged the enemy and needed support." Without delay, "I again called upon my wearied brigade to advance, to which they promptly responded."[9]

Colonel Rives' badly-needed reinforcements were on the move, but would they arrive in time?

*   *   *

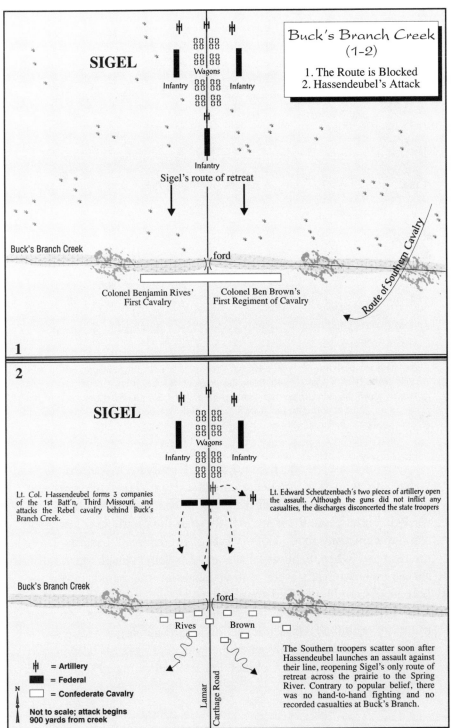

Buck's Branch Creek
(1-2)

1. The Route is Blocked
2. Hassendeubel's Attack

SIGEL

Wagons

Infantry   Infantry

Infantry

Sigel's route of retreat

Buck's Branch Creek

ford

Colonel Benjamin Rives'
First Cavalry

Colonel Ben Brown's
First Regiment of Cavalry

Route of Southern Cavalry

1

2

SIGEL

Wagons

Infantry   Infantry

Lt. Col. Hassendeubel forms 3 companies of the 1st Batt'n, Third Missouri, and attacks the Rebel cavalry behind Buck's Branch Creek.

Lt. Edward Scheutzenbach's two pieces of artillery open the assault. Although the guns did not inflict any casualties, the discharges disconcerted the state troopers

Buck's Branch Creek

ford

Rives   Brown

The Southern troopers scatter soon after Hassendeubel launches an assault against their line, reopening Sigel's only route of retreat across the prairie to the Spring River. Contrary to popular belief, there was no hand-to-hand fighting and no recorded casualties at Buck's Branch.

Lamar Carthage Road

╫ = Artillery

▮ = Federal

▭ = Confederate Cavalry

**Not to scale; attack begins
900 yards from creek**

N

Theodore P. Savas

Southern cavalry position behind Buck's Branch Creek. Colonel Ben Rives' men, to-gether with troopers from Col. Ben Brown's regiment, were stretched across the center of this photo, which looks south from the edge of Buck's Branch. The terrain has remained much the same, open and gently rolling. The brief affair here was one of the State Guard's best opportunities to slow Sigel's withdrawal and force him into a pitched fight in the open. *Author's Collection*

One of the men in Hassendeubel's Company E was Sgt. Otto Lademann, who as acting lieutenant that day had deployed with the rest of his comrades north of the creek in the attempt to clear away the Rebel horsemen. We marched "through the prairie in columns of companies within about 1,000 yards of the enemy," Lademann re-membered, "when Schuetzenbach on our left opened fire on the cavalry, whose heads were just visible over the banks of Buck's Branch." According to Lademann's recollection, which was written long after the war, when this volley did not force the Missouri militia to withdraw, Hassendeubel organized a company for a bayo-net charge. "Lieut. Col. Hassendeubel was deploying his battalion to advance in line [when] Colonel Franz Sigel galloped" upon the scene.[10]

"Colonel Hassendeubel," exclaimed Sigel, "what are you doing there?"

"I am deploying my battalion in advance in line and open fire on them," was the subordinate's reply.

According to Sergeant Lademann, this answer did not please Colonel Sigel. "For God's sake remain in column," he instructed Hassendeubel, "they are cavalry and they will cut you to pieces."

"Ah! nonsense," replied the forthright battalion commander, "those fellows haven't got any sabers. . ." Hassendeubel's admiring sergeant (and later aide-de-camp, when Hassendeubel commanded a brigade) had nothing but praise for the fiery subordinate's tactical judgment. "Lieut. Col. Hassendeubel knew what he was doing," he averred.[11]

And indeed he did. After this short verbal exchange, which amounted to a clear-cut case of insubordination in the face of the enemy, Hassendeubel turned to his battalion. "Forward! Double-quick! March!" The Federals tramped through the high prairie grass toward the dismounted cavalry. This action was "quite a novel spectacle," Lademann waxed, "and contrary to all the orthodox rules of war as known at that time. By this time the sun was high in the sky and beating down upon the men, an enemy both had to endure."[12]

And so Hassendeubel's Dutch companies marched through the grass in an effort to end the matter of the blocked ford. "After one round of our whole line," reported Sigel, "the infantry moved in double-quick time towards the enemy." It had been a long day for the Federals as well. "We ran about 500 yards when the want of breath stopped some one, and he fired his gun," Lademann recalled. "This, of course, brought on a volley." The long range discharge proved wholly ineffective if measured in blood, for not one bullet found its mark in Southern flesh. Hassendeubel's Missourians followed the smoky eruption with an impetuous assault in an effort to come to grips with the horsemen.[13]

The sight of bayonet-carrying infantry attacking in their direction, in conjunction with the sweeping (but bloodless) volley, weakened the resolve of the state troops. "In an instant the whole prairie in front of us was crowded with fugitive, mounted men, running away from us at the top of their horses speed, circling back the way they had come. . ." exclaimed Lademann. Hassendeubel's charge "routed [the enemy] completely," reported Sigel. "His flight was accompanied by tremendous hurrahs of our little army." Although Lademann later contended that one "unfortunate [Southern] captain, whose horse had been killed" was captured in the Buck's Branch skirmish, Southern reports do not confirm his claim. It is doubtful whether the Federals suffered any casualties at all in the minor affair.[14]

Once again the tactical tables had been turned to Sigel's advantage at precisely the right moment. As Weightman's infantry bore down from the north, the enemy cavalry guarding the critical ford dissolved into the prairie without the loss of a single casualty, proof that the stand made by the horsemen was in reality no stand at all. If his after-action report is any indication of what he thought of his "defensive" effort at the creek, Rives was not too proud of his performance. Instead of expounding at length on his unique opportunity and vigorous effort to stop Sigel in his tracks—the State Guard cavalry had been trying all day to obtain a position such as Rives enjoyed south of Buck's Branch—the colonel expended remarkably little ink on the affair. In his words, the action was simply "another short engagement." It was surely that and nothing more. A Federal account adds credence to Rives' unintended slight of his own defensive action by confirming both its brevity and lack of intensity. The encounter, as the soldier reported, was but "a sputtering of musketry." Rives' muddled report (perhaps intentionally) confuses the situation by claiming the enemy "retreated" when Colonel Weightman's artillery came upon the field, an assertion that is utter nonsense. The only avenue of retreat was over the ford that Colonels Rives and Brown abandoned in their wholesale effort to evacuate the position. Weightman's own report of the action states that "the enemy before our arrival had again retreated," contradicting Rives' contention.[15]

With the immediate threat to his column removed, Sigel ordered his men and wagons to continue their trek toward Carthage. "The troops and baggage train crossed the creek, and retreated unmolested. . ." was how the Federal commander described his narrow escape over the stream. But he was not out of danger. Indeed, the running engagement was entering a new phase, and the terrain below Buck's Branch posed potentially significant new problems for the Federals. The next defensive position behind which Sigel could make a stand against the pursuing enemy was the Spring River, a high and fast body of water about five miles south of Buck's Branch. The land in between, however, was essentially flat and open, ideal terrain the faster Missouri State Guard cavalry could utilize to swing ahead of Sigel and prepare for his approach—or strike his column in transit.[16]

Once the baggage wagons crossed the muddy ford in single file, Sigel re-deployed his command in order to protect his trains against an attack from any quarter. After reforming the wagons into four lines of eight vehicles, he molded his disciplined infantry around their perimeter, creating what was in essence a hollow square. When the alignment was completed to Sigel's satisfaction, he waved the train forward and the wagons rolled easily across the flat prairie toward Carthage.[17]

* * *

The Missouri State Guard discovered that crossing Dry Fork Creek quickly and without much disruption was a difficult endeavor even without vigorous enemy opposition. While at least two of Richard Weightman's First Brigade regiments (Colonels Hurst and Graves) had forded the creek west of the Lamar-Carthage Road, his other units, mixed with men from other commands, likely crowded over the main crossing. John Clark's report at least hints at such a problem when he wrote that "my forces were compelled to make a detour of half a mile up the creek before they could find a crossing." If the ford so vigorously protected by Essig's Federal guns was not jammed with militia soldiers and Rebel field pieces, Clark's regiments would not have had to seek a crossing elsewhere. After the delay occasioned by the congestion, the Southern infantry reached the far bank of the creek and reorganized for the march south.[18]

It is to their credit that the fatigued and by now sun scorched Southern soldiers managed to maintain a pursuit of the southbound Federals. With Weightman's men already on the move to support Rives and Brown, the remaining units took up the hunt. Mosby Parsons, who had watched with delight the Federal retreat from atop the hillside north of Dry Fork, demonstrated yet again the hallmark of aggressive generalship by directing an immediate pursuit. "I. . . ordered my infantry and artillery forward," was his matter-of-fact description of the event. "Colonel Kelly, Major Dills, and Captain Guibor, of the artillery, although having been engaged in a fatiguing action, promptly advanced." According to William Slack's thin account, the retiring Federals were "closely pursued by Colonel Hughes' command." After their difficult crossing of Dry Fork Creek, Clark's men also picked up the pace. "When we had effected a crossing we heard the firing of cannon in the direction of Carthage, about 1 mile in our advance," he wrote, "to which point we rapidly hurried." The enemy managed to maintain their thin margin in the race to safety, as Clark discovered upon reaching the vicinity of Buck's Branch. "We found the enemy still retreating in the direction of Carthage," he explained, "but occasionally firing his artillery to cover his retreat."[19]

With Weightman's men leading the pursuit, the State Guard closed in on the rear of Sigel's beleaguered column.

*   *   *

"The retrograde movements of our battalion continued until we had joined our train," explained Sgt. Otto Lademann. "It was followed by the rest of Colonel Sigel's troops and the whole command preceded by the train, marched back to Carthage followed by the enemy at a respectful distance." The description comprises events immediately following the brushing aside of the Southern cavalry from the Buck's Branch crossing. With nothing ahead of them but open prairie, Franz Sigel's wagons and regiments continued making good time across the flat land.[20]

*   *   *

With Rives' and Brown's troopers riding away as fast as their horses could carry them, General James Rains' cavalry was the only body of Rebels with a realistic chance of intercepting the Unionists. Inexplicably, the horsemen were marking time south of Dry Fork Creek at a critical moment in the unfolding battle. Rains ordered the halt, according to Colonel Peyton, "in order that [he] might cross over and confer with those in command of our army on the left of us." Although Rains directed his officers to remain in place until he returned or sent different orders, some of his officers decided on their own that the order was a mistake. They understood the wisdom of continuing the chase. "Before your return to my command the column was marched forward in order to intercept the enemy at or before he should march to Carthage," gently chastised Peyton, "which movement afterwards met with your approbation." Rains eventually "overtook" his leaderless units near Buck's Branch (well after Sigel had crossed), forded over to the south bank and eventually continued the pursuit.[21]

Peyton's brief narration is the only account we have of Rains' critical decision to stop his command below Dry Fork. Rains conveniently avoids discussing the issue altogether in his report. He did, however, discuss Sigel's retreat between Buck's Branch and Spring River, revealing in the process his own inability (and that of the main Southern column) to come to grips with the wagon-burdened Federals—even on the flat grassy landscape above Carthage. "Colonel Sigel again commenced a retrograde movement," Rains explained, "and retreated across a prairie 5 miles to Spring River, closely followed by the infantry and artillery."[22]

Finding himself once again behind and west of the enemy, Rains pushed his horsemen forward in an attempt to obtain a position from which to block Sigel's progress. Other than tiring his mounts and swelling his numbers with additional and unexpected reinforcements, nothing came of the movement. "The cavalry under my command," Rains later wrote, "joined by a regiment of General Slack's division, commanded by Colonel Rives, endeavored to outflank them on the right, but the retreat was so rapid as to defeat our object."[23]

And therein rests one of the several mysteries of this running engagement. How did Sigel manage to keep heavy wagons and foot soldiers well in advance of mounted cavalry while rolling and tramping along a single road? Certainly the definitive answer is not forthcoming in Rains' incomplete account of his fruitless flanking expedition. Indeed, few historians or writers of this campaign have even asked the question. Perhaps it is because additional layers of myth have been piled on top of this issue, preventing diligent inquiry.

Franz Sigel knew that he had to reach the high ground north of the Spring River and secure the fords into Carthage before Southern cavalry circled around and cut off his retreat. His quick escape at Buck's Branch had been little short of miraculous, for even a moderate delay above that stream, with the bulk of the State Guard infantry following behind, could easily have resulted in his destruction. With Buck's Branch behind him, the cross-prairie trek to Spring River posed the greatest threat to his continued existence.[24]

According to secondary sources and local lore, the crafty German employed his artillery pieces and columns of infantry in a unique manner to routinely repulse probing enemy cavalry as it harassed his flanks across the prairie, seeking a weak spot to strike. According to these accounts, Sigel deployed three field guns at the rear of the column, one on or near the road and one on each flank. After the artillery piece on the right flank fired, providing cover for that sector, its crew limbered the piece and withdrew toward the main column to prepare and fire again. Meanwhile, the middle piece fired at whatever enemy, if any, was visible in the distance and also withdrew, leaving the third weapon on the left flank to fire and fall back in the same manner. By the time the third gun was pulling back, the first piece was unlimbering and preparing to repeat the process. In this manner Sigel maintained a slow but rhythmic fire, thereby providing the appearance of strength and discipline. Sigel's artillery did occasionally unlimber and discharge shells at the distant infantry and cavalry of the Missouri State Guard. Sigel, however, does not mention the leap-frogging maneuver in his detailed and self-congratulatory report penned just six days after the fight.[25]

Ultimately Sigel's efforts, whatever they entailed, were little more than wasted energy. Despite stories to the contrary, Southern cavalry never seriously challenged the Federal column during this segment of the withdrawal. Some attribute this to Sigel's clever tactics. The truth is far more simple and obvious: none of the Southern horsemen were ever in a position to attack or even seriously threaten him. Rebel commanders even admitted as much. Not one of the cavalry reports filed within days of the action even mention Sigel's supposed "artillery" maneuver or the discharging of his retreating guns during this phase of his withdrawal. Certainly the hop-skotched handling of the Federal artillery pieces on wide-open (and thus clearly visible) terrain would have been reported if such an unusual military tactic had been witnessed. This is especially so if these same guns were the reason for the failure of the State Guard horsemen to accomplish anything of substance. Yet, no one breathed so much as a word about it.[26]

On the contrary, Rains claims "the [Federal] retreat was so rapid" he could not get ahead of the column, not that Sigel's artillery *prevented* him from doing so. Colonel James McCown, commander of the 1st Battalion, 2nd Cavalry, also riding with Rains' mounted wing, reported essentially the same thing, writing "[We] arrived too late, the enemy having gained the timber in their retreat before we arrived." The timber McCown mentions is the the belt of trees fringing the Spring River. Colonel Robert Peyton's after-action account parrots the preceding two accounts, adding only that Federal artillery "again opened upon us," although he is clearly referring to the guns stationed along the Spring River line on Ordnuff Hill, *not* those employed while running south across the prairie. Colonel Ben Rives' report is silent on the entire issue of the mythical running battle across the flat grassy terrain. The report of Col. Richard Boughan of the Seventh Cavalry provides insightful and damning evidence on this point. According to Boughan, after he rejoined Rains' cavalry south of Dry Fork Creek, "we were not near enough again during the day *to give or receive a shot* from the enemy [emphasis added]." Sigel's own report definitively closes the issue. After passing south of Buck's Branch Creek, "The troops and baggage train. . .retreated *unmolested* to the heights crowning the north side of Carthage [emphasis added]."[27]

Myths, especially of the military variety, die slow deaths even when evidence overwhelmingly contradicts them. It was not simply or even primarily Sigel's superb training or discipline that won the race from Buck's Branch to the Spring River, but the chronically inept handling of the Southern cavalry and the exhausted and disrupted state of the slowly pursuing Missouri State Guard infantry. Thus the Federals suffered not at all during this stage of the withdrawal.

Another added twist fuels the fire of controversy over Rains' handling of his cavalry during the pursuit between Buck's Branch and Spring River. Some of the battle's participants offered the story of how Rains' mounted command stumbled into a patch of ripe juicy blackberries. Tired and hungry, and perhaps reluctant to face enemy iron again, the Southerners reportedly stopped and gorged themselves on the fruit. The delay, so the tale goes, prevented Rains from reaching the Spring River before Sigel. Rains later contended that the blackberry story was a vicious rumor. He simply lost his way, he explained, and the pursuit was seriously hampered because of thick brambles. Unable to completely shake the gossip, Rains' horsemen were thereafter derisively labeled the "Blackberry Cavalry."[28]

After several miles the geographic prize Sigel was seeking came into view. Ordnuff Hill fanned out on both sides of the Lamar-Carthage Road about one-half mile north of the twisting and timber-lined Spring River. The site provided a ready defensive plateau and was quickly occupied by Federal infantry and artillery. The ford over the river boasted a gravel-lined bottom, which posed fewer difficulties for the cumbersome wagons than muddy Buck's Branch. East of Ordnuff Hill, the river jogged to the south for some distance before curving back east, creating a broad pocket or elbow. Below the Spring River the road angled southeast and then east about one mile to Carthage, which was seated near the bottom of the river's elbow. Because of this curious bit of geography, the heavy force of Southerners approaching Ordnuff Hill and the Spring River ford were actually farther from Carthage and Sigel's line of communications then they would have been had they moved to cross in force at some point upriver.[29]

Sigel's advanced companies were already in control of the key position by the time the main body of his column marched onto the sloping plateau. According to one account, five of Sigel's eight artillery pieces also rode up and unlimbered on Ordnuff Hill, with the western-most guns trained on Walker's Ford, about one mile down river, to prevent Southern horsemen from crossing at that point. The remaining three guns that had covered the rear of the retreat were added to those already unlimbered to create a strong defensive perimeter line. This, in turn, would allow the bulk of the infantry to

Ordnuff Hill. Sigel's artillery and infantry took position here late on the afternoon of July 5, 1861, during the retreat to Carthage. The Spring River is one-half mile behind (south) of this plateau, off the right hand side of the photo. The slope of the hill, as it drops off toward the river, is clearly visible. *Author's Collection*

escort the wagon train south across the river. Without an immediate threat from the pursuing enemy, Sigel continued his withdrawal.[30]

After some time, probably at least an hour or more, Federal troops on Ordnuff Hill made out the approaching infantry and artillery of the Missouri State Guard. Before long, enemy cavalry was also spotted in the distance, working its way toward the river beyond both flanks. The largest contingent of horsemen were coming up well to the west. "The enemy advanced slowly with his center," Sigel wrote, "while he pushed forward his cavalry to turn our right and left, and to gain the Springfield road [which ran east out of Carthage]." In order to dissuade the prodding enemy horsemen, Sigel opened fire on the mounted bodies with his artillery. [31]

The German colonel had successfully maneuvered and bluffed his way out of several tight spots that day. Would the developing engagement along the Spring River be any different?

*   *   *

If James Rains had anything to do with it, Spring River would be Franz Sigel's Waterloo. After spanning the open prairie between Buck's Branch and Ordnuff Hill, Rains and his regiments, including Colonel Rives' recently-arrived troopers, tried yet again to catch the wily German. "On nearing Spring River we attempted to intercept the enemy's crossing," Rains later explained, "but they again opened a heavy and destructive fire from their artillery, which compelled us to take a crossing higher up, and, pushing forward, endeavored to surround the town." With both sides reprising their roles performed at the outset of the day's battle, the Federal artillery fired on the flanking cavalry and the cavalry pulled back beyond the distance of the guns, sweeping westerly in a wide-ranging arc.[32]

While the Southern reports filed for the Carthage fighting often leave much to be desired, cavalry officers who prepared battle reports clearly recalled the artillery fire along the Ordnuff Hill line. "The cannon of the Federal forces [along Spring River] again opened upon us," penned Colonel Peyton. Unlike Peyton's 3rd Cavalry Regiment, however, Lt. Col. James McCown's men felt the sting of the Federal iron. "We received shots from the enemy's battery," McCown recalled, "one of which wounded Pvt. John Byler. . ." According to a modern chronicler of the campaign, Byler was wounded during a second attempt to ford the river. As the private's mount slid down the mossy bank and artillery fragments splattered the foliage, kicking up flecks of mud on the rider, a piece of iron tore into his left thigh and leg. The shot, which also wounded Byler's mount, knocked him from his saddle and into the swift creek. The wounded animal managed to right itself and reclaim the embankment, but Byler was unable to assist himself. He was saved from drowning by two fellow cavalrymen who pulled him from the water. The men carried him in a blanket to the nearby "Walker" residence, where the family bandaged and cleaned his serious wounds. The private would live to tell about his harrowing day and his thirteen scars, courtesy of Sigel's indefatigable gunners.[33]

*   *   *

Even though Sigel occupied the small plateau north of the Spring River, much still remained to be done to increase the odds of a successful defense and crossing. He issued a series of orders designed to both hold the Spring River line and keep his corridor of retreat and logistical lifeline open through Carthage, Sarcoxie and beyond. "As I thought it most necessary and important to keep open my communications," he explained, ". . .I ordered Lieutenant-Colonel Wolff, with two pieces of artillery. . .to pass Carthage, and to occupy the eastern heights on the Sarcoxie Road." After dispatching Wolff, Sigel ordered Capt. John Cramer of Company A, with Capt. Joseph Indest, Rifle Company A, and Capt. Henry Zeis of Rifle Company B, to follow Wolff across the Spring River "to guard the west side of the town against a movement of the enemy."[34]

While the remainder of his guns and a segment of his infantry held the enemy at bay, Sigel moved to safeguard his wagon train by pushing it south of the river. The wagons, as they had most of the day, presented more of a challenge than did his foot soldiers. As Southern cavalry searched for crossings up and down the river, the bulky vehicles wallowed in the stream and blocked traffic, forcing soldiers to jump into the swift river and assist in moving them on their short but difficult journey to the far bank.[35]

Once the wagons had rattled across and were again out of harm's way, Sigel withdrew his remaining guns from Ordnuff Hill one at a time, together with the the balance of his infantry. By now it was at least 6:00 p.m. and probably later, and the cloak of darkness was rapidly approaching. His unopposed withdrawal off the heights and across the stream without interference is not a testament to the leadership of the Missouri State Guard during this phase of the fighting.[36]

Sigel accompanied the column into Carthage. He was one of the first officers to re-enter the once-tranquil community. As his wagons and infantry poured through the narrow streets, Federal artillery rumbled past to take up a position beyond the town. Sigel dismounted in front of Norris Hood's home, which fronted the courthouse. Fifteen-year-old Thomas C. Hood, the ex-sheriff's son, remembered that Sigel spoke to his father that evening in a calm tone, assuring the elder Hood, "There [is] no danger."[37]

In all probability Sigel believed his words. His wagons had passed the last major obstacle, the aggressive Missouri militia was sitting relatively passively on the opposite bank of the Spring River and his army was well in hand. His regiments, however, were thoroughly exhausted and not a little disorganized. Knowing that his men still had a long march ahead of them, Sigel made arrangements to rest a large fraction of his enervated army. "Our rear guard took possession of the town to give the remainder of the troops time to rest," he explained "as they had, after a march of 22 miles on the 4th and 18 miles on the 5th, been in action the whole day since 9 o'clock in the morning, exposed to an intense heat, and almost without eating or drinking."[38]

With Carthage occupied Sigel could afford to be generous to his men. The fact that he felt comfortable enough to do so is the best evidence available that the Missouri State Guard was not pursuing the Federals at this phase of the fighting as closely as some have claimed. If his opponent was seriously testing the Spring River crossing, or if the Southern horsemen were aggressively attempting to ford the river and press into town, it is unlikely Sigel would have considered resting his badly-outnumbered command, risking much of his artillery and his entire train in the process.

The German officer had once more executed an almost flawless holding action, leaving his pursuers empty-handed yet again north of another river.

* * *

The long day, hot weather and hard marching, commingled with the periodic sharp encounters with the Federals, had taken their toll on the Missouri State Guard. The unwieldy divisional command structure had begun unraveling nine hours earlier with the discharge of the first artillery piece. James Rains' self-imposed segregation of his cavalry arm from the main body of the army further exacerbated the deteriorating situation. These factors, among others, preordained a completely unworkable command amalgam that ebbed and flowed in several different directions simultaneously throughout the day. By the time the bitter Dry Fork Creek fighting ended and the long trek over Buck's Branch to the Spring River was accomplished, the militia was on the brink of organizational meltdown. Officers had become separated from their commands, individual units had fragmented into often unidentifiable knots of tired warriors, and hundreds of men dressed in homespun were clogging the rear areas or had fallen out along the roadside. Martyn Cheavens, the cavalry private from Colonel Rives' regiment who had remained behind at the Widow Smith house to tend to the body of Captain Stone, wrote of the widespread straggling that had begun earlier that morning:

> I found very many standing idle and urged them to come on to the fight, but many seemed to think that prudence was the better part of valor. . .I found our soldiers all along the road between the two creeks. . .and many of our company, who I got to go with me.[39]

It is doubtful whether Cheavens' unit was the only Rebel organization to suffer from widespread straggling that day.

The temporary stalemate north of the Spring River provided the Southerners a couple of hours to catch their breath and press on to the river crossings. The brief lull was not enough to fully or effectively reorganize the Missourians. The lack of an overall commander's guiding hand—Jackson was nowhere near the front at any time after the opening bombardment—made it that much more difficult to pull together the far-flung units, collect the stream of stragglers leaking from the army and implement a cohesive strategy to effectuate Sigel's destruction. Instead of launching an organized offensive thrust against the Union bridgehead to hold it in place while other units crossed the river and surrounded the isolated enemy, no action of any significance was undertaken. Instead, large numbers of Southerners threaded their way to the front while those already in place warily watched as Sigel withdrew his last handful of men and guns to the safety of the distant bank. When the State Guard finally determined to cross the stream, it seeped over in organized driblets, fording the river at a number of locations without any definitive tactical plan.

It is impossible to conclusively establish the order of march and exact location of the individual components of the Missouri State Guard during this final phase of the Carthage engagement below the Spring River. It is necessary for the sake of clarity and understanding, however, to attempt to do so. The first organized infantry and artillery to cross the stream and resume the pursuit belonged to either Richard Weightman or William Slack. Parsons followed in their wake, while John Clark's Division brought up the rear. It is also impossible to determine when and where the several bodies of Southern cavalry crossed the river. Wherever they crossed, the horsemen enjoyed an easier time of it then their footsore comrades.

After Weightman's infantry and artillery splashed through the water at the main crossing, they fanned out and picked their way through the timber growing along the stream's southern bank. With nothing before him that could be construed as serious opposition, Weightman ordered his men back into column and pressed on toward Carthage. William Slack's troops, under Colonel Hughes, advanced in conjunction with Weightman. Hiram Bledsoe's three guns unlimbered a short distance below the ford on a flat rise just to the right of the road, where they acted as cover for the advancing infantry. Within a few moments Bledsoe was again in his element, sending a number of solid shots whistling through the air toward the small houses and buildings barely visible in the distance. The final attempt to nab Sigel and his Federal Dutch was underway.[40]

* * *

Private H. B. Kramer, a Federal artillerist serving in the detachment under Christian Wolff, arrived in the town square a short time after Sigel had ridden into Carthage. Craving a chew of tobacco, the private took the opportunity to dash into Dale's Store, which for a reason known only to its proprietor, was still open for business. Just as Kramer was preparing to pay for the cured weed, a 6-lb. cannon ball struck the corner of the outside wall of the establishment. With plaster and woodwork falling down around him, the private decided he did not need the plug after all. Scrambling out the front door and into the square, he climbed on top of his waiting caisson and in a short time was enjoying the bumpy ride out of town. Had Norris Hood sought the advice of Private Kramer, it is doubtful whether the enlisted man would have agreed with his colonel's earlier assessment that "there [is] no danger."[41]

Dale's Store was not the only building in Carthage to suffer the weight of Southern iron. Bledsoe had quickly found the range and was routinely dropping shot into the streets. One struck the bell tower of the Carthage Academy for Women, located in the northeast corner of the town at Second Street and Howard. The clanging of the dented bell only added to the macabre scene spreading through the town.[42]

James Hickey, who had dropped his tools to ride to Carthage, arrived in the town square late in the afternoon. There he saw a group of about twenty-five women milling about near the court-house, talking and making excited motions while glancing toward the road leading to the river. Following their gaze, Hickey watched with growing consternation as a knot of gray-clad Union soldiers struggled through one of the many groves of woods hugging the boundaries of the town. After hours of marching and fighting, the appearance of the men probably shocked the farmer. "[I] knew this was no place for [me]," he recalled, "and put off for home."[43]

The sounds of war always act like a magnet to those who do not know better, and James Hickey was not the only one attracted to the fighting. Local farmers James Whitehead and Stephan Crum, who decided to walk to Carthage and investigate the battle, were among the curious spectators. They arrived late in the afternoon in time to witness the courthouse square filling with hot and thirsty Union soldiers. The two men remembered that the courthouse windows shattered from the concussion of the artillery discharging on the outskirts of town. Seeking to assist the worn out Federals, the farm-ers drew water from the town's well and served the grateful men. The civilians enjoyed their task of mercy and took pride in the fact that they managed to serve Sigel while he stood in front of his makeshift headquarters.[44]

Sigel had to make a decision and his options were narrowly drawn. The enemy was pressing his rear once again, and if his men stayed put they would be surrounded and cut off. Alternatively, he could try to hold Carthage and keep his line of communications open as long as possible as he fell back toward Sarcoxie. If there had been any doubt in his mind as to whether he would evacuate the town, the advancing Rebels changed his mind. With little fanfare Sigel and his officers managed to maintain order and march their men, by company, through the streets and toward the southeast corner of the square, retracing steps taken only hours earlier when they had passed north out of Carthage to find the Missouri State Guard.[45]

The exhausted Federals never did receive the respite Sigel had planned for them.

*   *   *

As Weightman and Slack moved beyond the tree-lined river bank and into the open prairie in front of the town, the balance of the infantry faced the Spring River's fast flowing current. Mosby Parsons forded the river in his carriage but realized the exhausted and difficult plight of his men. "The river being deep, and the men wearied from their long exertion, I turned my carriage back to ford them over the stream." While Parsons' kindness was surely appreciated by his tired soldiers, the gesture was all but meaningless since only a few men could have ridden in the buggy on each crossing. Indeed, if his men waited to be carried across, the procedure significantly lengthened the time it took to reach the south bank and begin anew the pursuit of Sigel.[46]

*   *   *

The Rebel cannon shots punctuating the evening's solitude provided an apt accompaniment to the slow-moving Federal train of wagons struggling to clear Carthage and enter the Sarcoxie Road. The road to Sarcoxie bent southeast off Chestnut Street, and ran into the prairie beyond. At some point in the journey an unidentified group of Southern cavalry descended on the trains, adding to the misery of the frightened teamsters. Local resident George Knight recalled that "The train was extended about two blocks when it was struck." Nearby Federal soldiers rushed to its protection, forming a line on either side of the wagons and, according to Knight, "Poured fast and accurate fire into the fast moving Southerners, who were gone as fast as they came."

The wagons continued through town, navigating through the confusion that engulfed Carthage. The hit and run tactic only added to the clogged thoroughfares as the vehicles and infantry tried desperately to reach the far side of town and make good their escape before such a thing became impossible.[47]

* * *

While Parsons conducted his carriage-ferry operation, Weightman and Slack continued moving toward Carthage from the west. "The enemy from a concealed position opened upon us [with] his artillery," remembered Weightman. Not knowing the exact location of the enemy's guns, the colonel ordered up Hiram Bledsoe's artillery from its position in the rear and directed the regiments of Colonels John Graves and Edgar Hurst to "leave the road and pass through the timber and flank the enemy on his left." The Missourians deployed into line and passed through the trees growing along the roadway, moving steadily toward the town.[48]

With Weightman trying to turn Sigel's left flank, Colonel Hughes infantry of Slack's Division—Lt. Col. Pritchard's regiment and Maj. Thornton's Battalion—swept toward Carthage just north of Weightman's axis of advance. The duel move was undertaken with celerity. By the time Weightman's infantry arrived on the southwestern outskirts of the city, the rear of the enemy column could still be seen retreating through Carthage. As Weightman pressed on in search of Sigel's left Hughes, together with a small contingent of dismounted cavalry, reached a low wooded ridge west of town running parallel to Garrison Avenue, a north-south thoroughfare on the edge of town one block west of the court house.[49]

The sudden appearance of the enemy a short distance from the town's western limits confirmed Sigel's earlier decision to detach men to that sector. The Third Missouri Federals who took up residence amidst the buildings and behind fences included Capt. Henry Zeis' Rifle Company B, Capt. John Cramer's Company A, and the late-arriving Capt. Joseph Indest and his Rifle Company A. When Slack's Rebels approached within range, the defenders opened a brisk fire against them. The state militia had appeared on Carthage's western doorstep so quickly that Sigel was convinced the attack was launched by dismounted cavalry alone. Indeed, it seemed to Sigel and his men that the Rebels were suddenly everywhere.

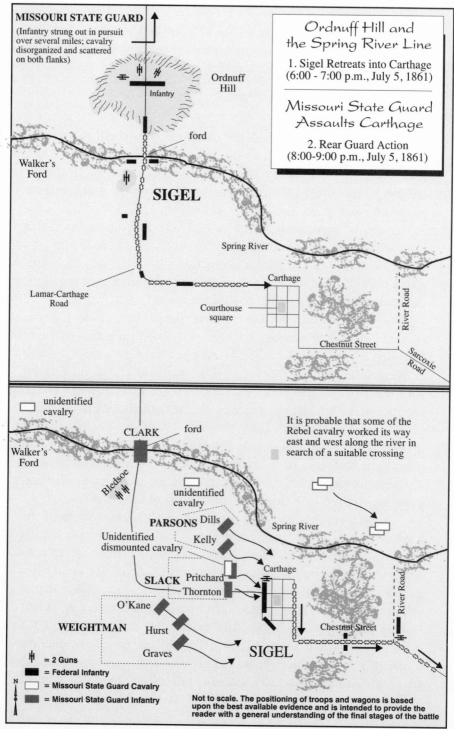

MISSOURI STATE GUARD

(Infantry strung out in pursuit over several miles; cavalry disorganized and scattered on both flanks)

Ordnuff Hill

Infantry

Walker's Ford

ford

SIGEL

Spring River

Lamar-Carthage Road

Carthage

Courthouse square

Chestnut Street

River Road

Sarcoxie Road

Ordnuff Hill and the Spring River Line

1. Sigel Retreats into Carthage (6:00 - 7:00 p.m., July 5, 1861)

Missouri State Guard Assaults Carthage

2. Rear Guard Action (8:00-9:00 p.m., July 5, 1861)

unidentified cavalry

CLARK   ford

Walker's Ford

Bledsoe

unidentified cavalry

PARSONS Dills

Unidentified dismounted cavalry

Kelly

SLACK Pritchard

Thornton

O'Kane

WEIGHTMAN Hurst

Graves

Spring River

It is probable that some of the Rebel cavalry worked its way east and west along the river in search of a suitable crossing

Carthage

Chestnut Street

River Road

SIGEL

⚑ = 2 Guns

▬ = Federal Infantry

▭ = Missouri State Guard Cavalry

▬ = Missouri State Guard Infantry

N

Not to scale. The positioning of troops and wagons is based upon the best available evidence and is intended to provide the reader with a general understanding of the final stages of the battle

Theodore P. Savas

"The enemy, taking advantage of his cavalry, forded Spring River on different points, spread through the woods, and, partly dismounted, harassed our troops from all sides."[50]

William Slack also discussed this phase of the confused early evening action. The enemy "took [their] next position, taking shelter in and behind houses, walls, and fences." Their heavy covering fire, more noisy than it was effective, included artillery. The stout defensive front impressed the division leader. "This stand of the enemy was an obstinate one, dealing shot and shell freely from their batteries into our ranks." Exactly whose field guns were pointed at Slack is difficult to determine. Most of the Federal artillery was either withdrawing from the town or already positioned about one mile further east along River Street. From that distant point they could only offer token assistance by lobbing shells into the general vicinity of the Southerners. Given the fluid nature of the fighting, it is impossible to determine whose guns were unlimbered for a short time to assist the Garrison Street defenders.

Slack's soldiers, with Hughes in command, advanced "in close proximity to the enemy's lines, when a deadly fire was opened upon them by our infantry." Although the handful of defenders fought gallantly, the remnants of the Third Missouri were no match for the masses aligned against them. The heavy firing and aggressive thrust quickly collapsed the Federal front and sent the defenders flying "in great haste," reported Slack. Hughes infantry "hotly pursued" the Federals, "a constant fire being kept up."[51]

While Slack's troops were pressing Carthage's defenders from the west, Weightman continued moving around the town's southwestern perimeter. Sigel responded to this threat by deploying another company to protect that approach. Although Weightman could make out soldiers moving to his front, the sunlight was fading away and clouds of powder smoke conspired to obscure vision. "Uncertain of his identity," wrote Weightman, "[I] did not at once open fire on him." The justly cautious but resourceful colonel immediately ordered a reconnaissance, and before long the true state of affairs was determined to his satisfaction. The combined commands of Hurst and Graves, together with Colonel Hughes' infantry—which was fighting with the three Federal companies on their left—opened what Weightman later described as "a heavy and well-directed fire upon the enemy's infantry."[52]

Colonel Hurst was attempting to move his men through the southern boundary of the town when he reported that the "effective long range musketry of the Federals stalled his attempts to gain the streets of Carthage." If Sigel's men "stalled" the enemy drive from that quarter, it was not noticed by Weightman, who reported that the combined volleys from his men threw the enemy "into confusion" and forced them to retreat "with great precipitation."[53]

While we do not know how many men he managed to ferry across the Spring River, we do know that Mosby Parsons regained his fighting edge as he neared the town. "I ordered [my men] to the front at as quick a pace as I thought they were able to march," he wrote, conscious of their weakened physical condition. "About this time I heard cannonading in Carthage, about one mile in advance," recalled the brigadier. The guns were the same pieces pounding Slack (and to a lesser degree, Weightman). Realizing that the battle was again heating up, Parsons urged his infantry to pick up the pace and ordered Henry Guibor to haul his pieces ahead and cooperate with Weightman. Guiding his men north behind Slack, the confident Parsons encountered a small and idle body of Southern cavalry, which he directed to advance to the sound of the fighting. Riding ahead, he passed around Slack's left and entered Carthage on the north side, followed by his infantry under Col. John Kelly, and shortly thereafter by his cavalry, under Captain Alexander.[54]

By this time Carthage was in utter chaos. Slack's men were reportedly the first to take control of the town's courthouse square. Weightman's infantry reached the square a few moments later, probably entering from the south. Shortly thereafter elements from Parsons' Division filtered in from the north. According to one of the Missouri Guardsmen, Federal soldiers were discovered using a wagon to loot a residence on a small side street. With a yell, the men rushed forward and chased away the thieves. Unable to capture them, they returned and examined the wagon, which contained an assortment of clothing, silverware and clocks. A closer investigation revealed, much to the delight of the discoverers, ten gallons of blackberry cordial. The thirsty men immediately began to pass around the alcohol as a reward for a hard day's work. Salem Ford of Hughes' regiment, part of the group who had liberated the intoxicating beverage, sampled the contents and proclaimed it to be "fine." In addition to capturing some badly needed weapons, Ford and his cohorts also managed to net "a jolly Dutchmen, who laughingly [asked], 'vat kind guns you shoot mit? You aim at one man before and kill tree behint.' That was our shotguns," Ford informed the Federal. Another State Guardsman spun a slightly different tale, born likely from gossip picked up in town after the fight. "The federals arrived at Carthage," wrote Archy Thomas after the fight, "and, it is said, as they were drawing water and drinking at the wells, and telling the story, that they had whipped the State [Guard] and killed from 200 to 500, the State [Guard] troops filed round on each side of town, and came in on them." We know for certain that part of Thomas' story is true. The state troops were pouring into the town from several directions and the Federals were scrambling about in an mad attempt to escape.[55]

Southern cavalry, possibly Benjamin Rives' men, rode upon another abandoned wagon and raced it through the town, creating a good deal of confusion as the jubilant horsemen fired their small arms into the air in celebration of the victorious day. Small pockets of Federals missed their chance to evacuate and were cornered by their swarming enemy. Fighting broke out in parts of the town, and in some instances the violence was delivered hand-to-hand.[56]

As the fighting swirled through the streets, those state troops retaining some semblance of organization drove east after the retreating Federals. The courthouse was turned into a hospital for the wounded from both armies, while the women of Carthage braved the flying lead and went to work offering what assistance they could to all the helpless soldiers. The Hood girls, who had flirted with the Union men earlier in the day, tried to bind bleeding wounds as the unfortunates lay on the wooden courthouse floor. With space at a premium, Southerners and Northerners were laid next to one another without regard to politics.[57]

When Mosby Parsons entered the square, he discovered that at least part of the thundering artillery fire reverberating in his ears came from his own battery under the ubiquitous Henry Guibor, who was actively ". . .engaged with the enemy at a mile distant." Under

Weightman's direction, Guibor had unlimbered his pieces near Bled-soe's smoking guns on the east side of the town square near the courthouse. From that vantage point, the seven tightly-aligned field pieces hurled their metal against the enemy's artillery, unlimbered to the east along River Road. Although the distance was too far for the light guns to be effective, there were no other suitable artillery positions from which to bombard the enemy. The Federal pieces aligned along River Road replied vigorously, arching their return fire toward the town. Although the Southerners did not suffer unduly under the ineffective counter-battery fire, the town's buildings took several direct hits. The courthouse-turned-field hospital was continually struck along the roof line even as its occupants sought comfort within.[58]

The civilians on the eastern side of town found themselves caught in a horrific crossfire. "One lady ran out when the balls were flying thick and heavy shouting, 'Hurrah for Jeff Davis, liberty and independence forever [and] down with the dutch,' cheering on the boys to brave and noble deeds," remembered one Rebel soldier. For the most part, the non-combatants remained huddled in their cellars and homes seeking shelter wherever they could find it. Mrs. D. S. Holman, the wife of the town's Methodist minister, sought cover in her bedroom. A case shot from a Federal gun exploded outside her home and bits of the shrapnel ripped through the walls and struck a pillow on her bed. A moment later an unexploded shell landed in her bedroom, rattled off the walls and came to rest in the middle of the floor. Fortunately, the Federal shell failed to explode.[59]

*   *   *

With Carthage firmly in enemy hands, Franz Sigel shepherded his men east out of town along Chestnut Street, or Mill Road, as some referred to it. About one mile from the square, Chestnut intersected River Road, which at the time of the battle was little more than a dirt path running north toward several mills near the Spring River. The intersection of the Chestnut and River roads formed the Sarcoxie Road, which angled to the southeast toward the city of the same name. Once the army passed beyond the open town square, the topography bordering the roadway, which gradually fell away to the east, changed from houses and fences to woods and underbrush. The change was a welcome one for Sigel, for it prevented the delivery of a rapid flank attack from town on the Union column. Bisecting Chestnut Street about halfway between the edge of town and River Road was a small plateau, and the keen-eyed Sigel decided to place another line of troops at this spot to further delay pursuit.[60]

Some of Sigel's infantry withdrew a short distance beyond River Road to Carter's Spring, where the Federals had camped the previous night. While the colonel personally established his final line of defense in this vicinity, probably aligned just behind the River Road, the last elements of the fighting Federal rear guard left Carthage and fell back up Chestnut Street to the small and by now occupied plateau. One of these men was the color bearer of the Third Missouri, Pvt. Owen Nichols. Refusing to show his back to the enemy for fear of taking a wound and being later labeled a coward, Nichols

Chestnut Street and Sigel's final line of defense. This modern view looks west toward Carthage from the River Road position. Sigel's artillery was placed near this spot at dusk on July 5, 1861. The terrain north (right) of Chestnut Street was rugged and wooded, which made it difficult for the Southerners to attack in this sector. Their final assault was largely delivered down both sides of this road toward the waiting guns. The Sarcoxie Road, formed by the intersection of these two roads, angled off to the southeast. It is no longer in existence. *Author's Collection*

made the trek up Chestnut while running backwards. One of the Southern guns firing in his direction blasted a load of homemade canister down the road, a piece of which struck and knocked him down. The regimental colors went flying, only to be caught by another man. Taken for dead in the confusion, his friends dragged his body out of the road and continued their hasty retreat. A short time later, State Guard troops swept past Nichols to attack Sigel's position on the River Road. Intent on attacking Sigel's line, they failed to notice Nichols' body and he remained unmolested. When he later regained consciousness, the stunned private realized that the round shot had bounced off his brass belt buckle, leaving behind a large dent and a nasty bruise beneath. Mounting a nearby horse the fortunate youth used the lengthening shadows to his benefit and slipped away in the darkness. He caught up with his regiment later the following night miles away in the small town of Aurora.[61]

*   *   *

The sun was setting by the time the Southerners were ready to test the Federal line along River Road. Although the reports that discuss this phase of the action only hint at the disorganized state of the Southern army, it would be naive to believe that the fighting at sundown was anything more systematized than a handful of dedicated officers commanding whatever men they could gather together for the assault. The best evidence suggests that three of the four Missouri State Guard division commanders—Mosby Parsons, William Slack and Richard Weightman (acting in Rains' stead)—were prepared to advance their commands or portions thereof.

After entering the town Parsons moved east beyond the square, where he discovered that the woods between the town and the Road Road were occupied by the enemy. Although he later claimed the Federals were "about 400 yards distant," their main body was much further east. The men he mistook as belonging to the main line were probably either stragglers or a small rear guard. As General Slack explained it, "the enemy. . .planted his batteries on the heights one mile east of town." The question was how best to attack them in that location.[62]

*   *   *

As the Southern officers prepared their men to move across the intervening broken ground east of Carthage, Sigel adjusted and strengthened his rear guard position along the River Road. Although his alignment remains a mystery, three artillery pieces reportedly were unlimbered along the road, while three more were set up on a slight ridge just behind overlooking Carter's Spring. George Knight, a local witness to the fight, recalled the disposition of Sigel's guns somewhat differently, claiming that "One cannon was placed north of the intersection, two in the intersection and two guns south of the road."[63]

With his wagons well away down the Sarcoxie Road, his guns unlimbered and darkness at hand, Sigel had good cause to breath easier.

*   *   *

The loosely-organized Southerners formed in the woods at the top of Chestnut Street, with Slack's infantry under Colonel Hughes on the right, near the street itself, and Parsons' infantry under Colonel Kelly and Major Dills on Hughes' left. It is difficult to determine what role if any Weightman's men played in the final attack of the day. Although the artillery eventually limbered up and followed the advancing infantry, it does not appear as though Graves, Hurst or O'Kane advanced with Slack and Parsons. It is also impossible to determine whether the final attack was coordinated, and in all likelihood it was not.

"I ordered him [Kelly] to advance immediately and take possession of the wood to my left," noted Parsons. The action was brisk and of short duration. After opening a "sharp firing the enemy was again dislodged and in full retreat across the prairie." Parsons was pleased with the result, praising two of his subordinates by name. "It is due to Major Dills. . .and to Captain Alexander. . .to say that they and their commands acted with great discretion and bravery in driving the enemy from this last position."[64]

Slack's men were more roughly handled than Parsons' soldiers. With a yell, Hughes' troops, some mounted and other on foot, swept along Chestnut Street and over the small intervening plateau that Sigel had earlier utilized as a rear guard position. If it was occupied

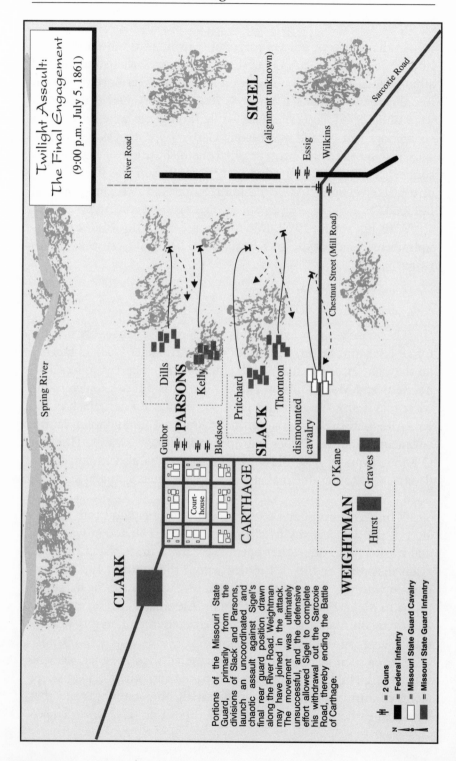

Twilight Assault:
The Final Engagement
(9:00 p.m., July 5, 1861)

Spring River

CLARK

River Road

SIGEL
(alignment unknown)

Sarcoxie Road

Essig

Wilkins

CARTHAGE

Court-
house

Guibor

PARSONS

Dills

Kelly

Bledsoe

Pritchard

SLACK

Thornton

dismounted
cavalry

Chestnut Street (Mill Road)

WEIGHTMAN

O'Kane

Graves

Hurst

Portions of the Missouri State
Guard, primarily from the
divisions of Slack and Parsons,
launch an uncoordinated and
chaotic assault against Sigel's
final rear guard position drawn
along the River Road. Weightman
may have joined in the attack.
The movement was ultimately
unsuccessful, and the defensive
effort allowed Sigel to complete
his withdrawal out the Sarcoxie
Road, thereby ending the Battle
of Carthage.

＝ 2 Guns

■ = Federal Infantry

□ = Missouri State Guard Cavalry

▨ = Missouri State Guard Infantry

N

at the time of the assault, the Southerners easily swept the thin line of men away and back onto the main line behind them on the River Road. As Hughes' men stormed toward the Federal position, the gently-sloping ground fell away into rougher terrain. "Colonel Hughes' command was pushed forward under the shelter of a skirt of woods," Slack observed in his report, "and was again brought in very close proximity in the rear of the enemy's retreating forces, and again opened a destructive fire upon their lines, the enemy still continuing to retire in rapid haste," he added with some pride.[65]

Private Martyn Cheavens, who finally caught up with some of his comrades after a lengthy hiatus with Captain Stone's corpse, struggled through the town's congested streets in his attempt to rejoin his unit. The private, who probably did not find Rives' cavalry regiment again that evening, arrived just in time for the final attack north of Chestnut Street. "We saw the enemy opposite aiming and touching off the cannon at us," he remembered. "We spurred our horses 30 or 40 yards when the balls came across where we had just left, one shell striking the fence next to which I had been standing." The ground became more difficult as the soldiers advanced. "We then passed through some ravines, joined several other companies, and came within 300 yards of his guns."[66]

The terrain over which the State Guardsmen attacked naturally funneled the men down the sloping ground toward the intersection—and into the mouths of the Union guns positioned near the bottom of the hill. By this time the commands had become inextricably intermingled and subject to the expertise of the exhausted Federal artillerists. "Just at dusk he fired two vollies at us, going over our heads, one shell bursting 20 feet above me," recalled Cheavens, adding that "These were the last cannonading of the night." General Slack appreciated that the River Road stand was nothing more than a rear guard action that protected ". . .the hasty retreat of his shattered and disorganized column."[67]

By this time darkness had set in and the battle was rapidly drawing to a close. Cheavens was not pleased with what he perceived to be a lack of leadership on the field. "As we had no general officer that night, we gave up the pursuit." The entry speaks to the confusion that permeated the ranks of the attackers. General Slack would have taken exception with the private's explanation. According to the general, exhaustion and darkness, not a command vacuum, brought the pursuit to a halt: "By this time nightfall had set in, and, owing to the exhausted condition of Colonel Hughes' command, they were called from the field."[68]

Richard Weightman also remembered the final withdrawal of Sigel's regiments. "The enemy retreated on the Sarcoxie road, and was followed for a mile or two by our indefatigable artillery and infantry," boasted the colonel. "Night put a stop to the conflict," he added, a judgment supported by Gen. John Clark's report of the end of the fighting: "[The] darkness of the night caused a cessation of the pursuit."[69]

Pried loose from the River Road line by the masses of Rebels opposing it, Sigel tried to maintain order as best as possible. He organized his remaining infantry and guns for a withdrawal into the prairie and thrust them down the Sarcoxie Road as quickly as possible. Company B of Colonel Rives' Southern cavalry, under the command of Captain McNeil, "continued in pursuit of the enemy," wrote Slack, "continuing to annoy their flank and rear until it was entirely dark, and capturing a portion of their baggage, when the chase was entirely abandoned." "During the whole of the enemy's retreat his flank was successively annoyed by Colonel Rives command," added the divisional commander in something of an exaggeration.[70]

While Colonel Ben Rives had certainly not "successively annoyed" Sigel during his "whole" retreat, he had experienced a full day. After his poorly-executed flanking maneuver above Dry Fork, Ruves allowed himself to be swept away from his superb blocking position at the Buck's Branch Creek ford. A long and fruitless cross-country ride followed after which he experienced "difficulty in crossing Spring River." For reasons known only to the colonel, he dismounted his command in or near Carthage. The move forfeited the two elements the Southerners so desperately needed at this late stage of the battle: speed and mobility. Rives reported that he pursued the enemy down the Sarcoxie Road "on foot until dark." In his report he explained that Captain McNeil and Company B had become separated from his command (perhaps because McNeil had the good sense to keep his men astride their horses?) and while unattached "succeeded in capturing a portion of the transportation and baggage of the enemy." If McNeil and a handful of men were able to inflict damage on the wagons, it is logical to assume that Rives' entire regiment would have been even more effective. The colonel's absurd directive to dismount was just another mistake in a long string of errors.[71]

Perhaps prompted in part by Captain McNeil's ghost-like strike, Sigel sought to protect his rear as the Federal column picked its way through the darkness towards Sarcoxie. In order to do so, he personally snatched one of Francis Hassendeubel's units, Company E, 1st Battalion, Third Missouri, out of line. The company, commanded by Capt. John E. Strodkamp, was directed to establish a defensive position on the dark road. "Captain Strodtman [sic] formed the company in column of platoons, across the Sarcoxie Road," remembered Sgt. Otto Lademann. "The sun went down; all troops to the right and left of us marched off, our company being left solitary and alone on the prairie, about 300 yards from the timber fringing the Spring River." Although Lademann underestimated the distance to the river, he fully appreciated the danger he and his comrades faced. The irony of the situation was not lost on the sergeant, who noted laconically that their new position "was where we had camped the night before."[72]

"It was nearly dark when we noticed the edge of that timber filling up with men," recalled Sergeant Lademann. A lone Southern officer was sent forward to ascertain the identity of the line of men stretching across the road. "A mounted officer riding toward us was met by our 1st Lieut. Poten," Lademann wrote long after the war. "They each asked 'what regiment do you belong to?'" When the Southern officer replied with "2nd Missouri Infantry," the Federal lieutenant drew and discharged his pistol, but the shot was well wide of its intended mark.[73]

Both the pistol shot and the galloping Rebel alerted the waiting Confederates that all was not well immediately in their front. When the horseman cleared their line, the front ranks opened fire on Sergeant Lademann's company. "We were greeted by a volley that knocked our Captain and three men down and owing to our foolish platoon formation, only our 1st platoon could return fire," he recalled with no little disgust. The volley was followed with an assault, which Lademann described as "three or four hundred of the enemy burst[ing] out of the woods rapidly advancing on us. . . ." Given the darkness and fatigue Lademann was experiencing, as well as the intervening years, it is difficult to know whether his figures reflect reality. Whether attacked by 30 men or 300, the cheering and firing infantry completely unnerved the captain-less company, which the sergeant honestly admits "skedaddled" from the field.[74]

With little else on their minds other than escape, Lademann's Company E continued down the Sarcoxie Road well to the rear of the main Federal column, occasionally "returning the fire of the enemy." The Federals, carrying their bleeding captain with them, continued fitfully for about one mile when they came upon a solitary horseman riding in their direction. Perhaps drawn by the small arms fire, Lt. Col. Francis Hassendeubel was more than a little surprised to stumble across a company from his own battalion wandering well behind the lines near the enemy. With Hassendeubel acting as a stabilizing foundation, as he had throughout most of the day, the company halted and reformed itself before continuing down the road. After marching another mile, Company E joined the rear of Sigel's command. "It was about 9:00 p.m.," explained Sergeant Lademann, "when the brigade was formed in line of battle on the edge of the timber, where the Sarcoxie road leaves the prairie."[75]

One strange mini-drama remained to be played out that evening. Sigel ordered three volleys of musketry and three salutes of artillery discharged in the direction of the Confederates. If indeed such an occurrence took place—and we have only Lademann's recollection confirming such an incident—it was probably Sigel's method of slowing pursuit by forcing the enemy to deploy for battle while he continued his retreat. Lademann could not see any use for the action, which he considered a waste of powder and shot. "Only God and Colonel Sigel know the military reason of this beautiful pyrotechnic display in the dark and silent prairie; no enemy being in sight."[76]

* * *

The fifth of July was remembered as a particularly unpleasant day by most of Sigel's men, even those who did not participate in the twelve-hour daylight withdrawal and the all-night general retreat to Sarcoxie. Captain Joseph Conrad and his Rifle Company B, Third Missouri Regiment, had been left in Neosho as a garrison on his nation's Independence Day. Camped near the courthouse in the center of town, Conrad later wrote that he "took all necessary precautions, by placing extra sentinels and sending out patrols every half hour, day and night. The Fourth passed off quietly." July 5, however, was an altogether different experience. "About 11 o'clock I heard the cannonading," he later reported, "whereon I immediately dispatched a patrol of 20 men. . .to inquire, if possible, the cause of it."[77]

The "cause of it," as he would soon discover, was Sigel's battle with the Missouri State Guard. About two hours later Conrad received orders from Sigel to retreat "if necessary." While pondering the vague and rather disturbing message, Conrad's small patrol returned from its trek north. Unfortunately, the captain had not posted pickets south or west of town, and it is from these directions that disaster struck.[78]

The isolated Federal officer never suspected that his handful of men, about 80 strong, had been left directly in the path of the relief column of Confederates heading north from Arkansas to assist the Missouri militia. Brigadier General Benjamin McCulloch had finally heeded Sterling Price's pleas. His small army of about 4,000 men had left its camp at Maysville, Arkansas, and moved north for two days searching for Governor Jackson and his Missouri State Guard. When McCulloch learned that a small force of Federals was garrisoning Neosho, he determined to bag the lot. Colonel James McIntosh was ordered to lead four companies of Col. Thomas Churchill's 1st Arkansas Mounted Rifles and Capt. C. D. Carroll's company of Arkansas state troops against Neosho from the south, while Churchill led six additional companies of his regiment from the west.[79]

"We started on different roads which entered the town—one from the west, the other from the south," explained McIntosh in his report of the affair to McCulloch, "with an arrangement to make the march of 16 miles in four hours, and upon entering the town to make a simultaneous attack." While the plan was sound, the distance traveled by McIntosh proved to be less than that covered by Churchill. "I found that the distance was not so much as stated," explained McIntosh. With his men positioned south of Neosho,

McIntosh found himself riding the uncomfortable horns of a dilemma. Should he wait for Churchill and risk discovery by the enemy, or attack immediately while he enjoyed the advantage of surprise? "Fearing that information would be carried into town to the enemy," he explained, "I determined to attack at once, and made my arrangements accordingly."[80]

McIntosh, a Floridian by birth and an 1849 alumnus of West Point (where he graduated dead last in his class) dismounted his four companies about a quarter mile south of the town. Still holding the element of surprise, the former Indian fighter and plains veteran "marched them by platoon at double-quick within 200 yards of the Court-House, where we found a company 80 strong." Captain Carroll's company of Arkansas troops were detoured to take Conrad's Federals from the rear. With his trap ready to be sprung, McIntosh sent a volunteer aide-de-camp, identified only as "Dr. Armstrong," forward with an unconditional demand that the Federals surrender. "I allowed them ten minutes to decide," McIntosh remembered. "At the end of the time the captain in command [Conrad] made an unconditional surrender of the company, laying down their arms and side-arms." The second half of the two-prong thrust arrived on scene shortly thereafter. "Colonel Churchhill came up in good time with his command, and made an imposing sight with his mounted riflemen." McIntosh's victory was complete.[81]

Captain Conrad recalled the affair in essentially the same light, although his brief report claims McIntosh's force consisted of "1,200 to 1,500 men," about three times more than the Floridian possessed. "Finding it impossible for me to hold my post with success," Conrad lamented, "after due deliberation, after due consultation with my officers and men, I concluded it would be best to make the surrender as it was required—namely, unconditionally."[82]

The capture of Conrad's force yielded a rich bounty. "We took 100 rifles with saber bayonets, a quantity of ammunition, and a train of seven wagons loaded with provisions," McIntosh boasted to McCulloch, justifiably proud of his accomplishment. He was also proud of his men. "The officers and men did everything in their power to make the movement as prompt as possible," he explained, "and they marched up to within a short distance of a force whose numbers were unknown with a step as regular and a front as unbroken as a body of veterans."[83]

After their capture Conrad's Federals were placed inside the courthouse for safekeeping while the Southerners pondered what to do with them. Their treatment at the hands of the Confederates was a mixed bag, at least according to Conrad. "I must mention here that the officers of the Arkansas Rangers, as well as of the Missouri troops, behaved themselves quietly, accommodatingly, and friendly, both towards myself and men, but their privates, on the contrary, [acted] in a most insulting and brutal manner." Since the captives were an impediment to the column, McIntosh paroled them. The event took place on Monday evening July 8, at 5:30 p.m. at the Confederate camp near Barlin's Mill. The local population sympathetic to the Southern cause threatened the unarmed parolees with physical harm, prompting McIntosh to provide the Unionists with a 30-man escort for the first four miles of their long journey to Springfield.[84]

"The people of Neosho and farmers of that vicinity. . .threatened to kill us in the streets," wrote a shocked Conrad. "After innumerable hardships and dangers, without food and water, our canteens having all been stolen from us by the Southern troops, we at last reached Springfield, my men all broken down, having traveled the distance of 85 miles in fifty hours, with hardly any food at all."[85]

The Wake

U nfortunately, the dearth of records and conflicting accounts make it impossible to determine how many men fell in the battle. According to Franz Sigel's after-action report, "The losses of all the troops under my command on this day were 13 killed and 31 wounded," a total almost certainly less than the losses actually suffered. "According to reliable information," he added, attempting to put a positive spin on a very negative result, shredding his own credibility in the process, "the enemy's losses have not been less than 350 or 400." One of the enemy artillery pieces was "dismounted and another burst," he added mistakenly.[1]

While none of the Federal officers were killed or mortally wounded, two from the Third Missouri, Capt. John E. Strodkamp (Company E) and Lt. Henry Bishoff (Company B) were wounded. The Federals also lost at least ten battery horses and one baggage wagon "for want of horses to move it," claimed Sigel. Despite the dogged persistence of local legend, Sigel did not lose any artillery pieces during the fighting. "I must say that [my men] fought with the greatest skill and bravery," wrote the Federal commander shortly after the fight. "Although more than once menaced in flank and rear by large forces of cavalry, and attacked in front by an overwhelming force, they stood like veterans, and defended one position after the other without one man leaving the ranks." While the latter few words are little more than hyperbole, Sigel had every right to be pleased with the way his men had conducted themselves—as well he should have been. In addition to saving Sigel's career, they saved themselves from the disaster that should have befallen them.[2]

For his part, Sigel displayed a wholesale lack of caution by marching his small force, sans cavalry, directly against what he knew was a superior enemy army. When the gravity of his mistake sunk in, he still remained on the field until Southern cavalry began to move around his flanks and infantry pressed his attenuated front. His strategy and field tactics suggest an arrogance born of overconfidence. But for the ill-equipped and indifferently led enemy, Sigel and his men would have suffered a resounding defeat much more painful than the relatively light spanking actually inflicted upon them.

For the most part, Colonel Sigel's lieutenants appear to have served him well at Carthage, although it is unfortunate that none of their reports, if they still survive, have been located or made public. The ablest of the bunch was Lt. Col. Francis Hassenduebel, who led his Missouri infantry with a firm and steady hand throughout the trying day. His decisive action at the Buck's Branch ford may have saved the Federal column. Sigel's long-arm also played a prominent role in holding back the repeated Southern threats, although exactly who is entitled to the lion's share of the credit is open to discussion. In his report Sigel heaped praise on his gunnery commander (and former European crony) Maj. Frank Backoff, while ignoring the stellar service rendered by Capts. Christian Essig and Theodore Wilkins. Essig especially seems to have been active and energetic in the handling of his pieces.[3]

Calculating losses for the Missouri State Guard is more problematic. No formal muster rolls or detailed organizational reports exist covering the early weeks of the war, and this lack of data seriously hampers study of the Missouri militia. Fortunately, the several battle reports, prepared primarily by the division commanders, allow for a relatively firm accounting of the size of the force Governor Jackson took into the fight. They are less precise in setting forth the number of killed and wounded.

Despite the successive attacks and offensive tactics of the Missouri State Guard, Southern casualties were remarkably (some would say impossibly) light. The prominent role rendered by Richard Weightman's First Brigade concentrated militia losses in the

Eighth Division. "The loss of this brigade [excluding the division's cavalry] is as follows: Killed, 2; wounded, 38; total casualties, 40," or 3.3% of the total infantry engaged. Despite all of the riding and skirmishing done by James Rains' cavalry, his several regiments sustained losses of but one man mortally wounded and five wounded. The cumulative divisional loss amounted to three killed and 43 wounded, or 2.5% for the entire division.[4]

William Slack's loss was also scant. His Fourth Division infantry under Col. John Hughes' command, which included Hughes own regiment and Major Thornton's Battalion, lost just two mortally wounded and six wounded, or just 1% of the 700 men engaged. Since Slack's participation at Dry Fork appears to have been minimal, almost certainly the bulk of these losses were sustained in the fighting around Carthage later in the day. Slack's mounted regiment under Col. Benjamin Rives left behind four killed and one missing ("supposed to be a prisoner,"), which also totaled just 1% of the 500-man regiment. All of Rives' losses can be accounted for during the early minutes of the battle from Federal artillery (except, perhaps, for the man "presumed missing.") His regiment did not suffer another loss for the balance of the day, which included the skirmish at Buck's Branch Creek, the Spring River crossing and the engagement with the Federals on the Sarcoxie Road. Thus William Slack's entire 1,200-man division suffered just six killed, six wounded, and one missing.[5]

Mosby Parsons lumped together his Sixth Division's casualties and reported them as one killed and seven wounded, or about 1% of the 650 men engaged. Parsons' soldiers had suffered under the early bombardment, directly assaulted Sigel's Dry Fork position (where they fought long and hard along the river's edge), and participated in the sharp attacks in and around Carthage late in the day. It is difficult to reconcile the steady fighting performed by his men with the paltry losses he reported.

John Clark's discussion of losses in his Third Division is somewhat more cryptic than his fellow commanders. The general notes with some specificity that he lost ten killed and wounded at Dry Fork Creek while engaged with "the enemy at distance of from forty to fifty yards, and in attempting to cross the creek to charge the enemy." Unfortunately the "detailed report of the surgeon" he mentions is unavailable. Since Clark's men were not engaged at either Buck's Branch, Spring River or the fighting in Carthage, it is reasonable to assume that the casualties he mentions comprise the extent of his day-long losses in his division, which equates to 2.7%. If we reasonably assume that two of Clark's ten men were killed, the Missouri State Guard losses on July 5 were (approximately) 12 killed, 64 wounded, and one missing.[6]

How do we account for such a low total? While we will never know for certain, several answers at least suggest themselves. Perhaps the fighting was perceived by the participants as more severe or intense than it actually was. Carthage was the first major land battle of the war, and the men had little in the way of experience against which to compare the fitful series of encounters. If the civilians-turned-soldiers unintentionally exaggerated the severity of the combat, they can be excused for having done so. After all, Wilson's Creek and Pea Ridge, two large-scale battles many of these same men would participate in, were still waiting to be fought.

We also do not know whether the "walking wounded" were counted, a circumstance that could well have added a substantial number of men to the casualty rolls. Finally, the relatively light losses on both sides might be partially attributable to lousy shooting and the poor quality of the ammunition expended. The state troops were insufficiently armed and their ammunition, especially for the artillery, was largely homemade. The Federals, contrarily, were well-drilled, but how well could they shoot? Like their Southern counterparts, they had never been in combat and were discharging their weapons hastily while under great pressure.

We do know that the Missouri State Guard division commanders were united in their praise of the way their men comported themselves during the exhaustingly fluid and lengthy affair. "General," wrote Weightman to James Rains following the battle, "it may be safely said that this brigade, your whole division, and the whole Army of the Missouri engaged in that day's battles have done the State some service." Weightman went on to recommend Lt. Col. Thomas Rosser, Lt. Col. William O'Kane and Capt. Hiram Bledsoe for brevet promotions. Rains, in forwarding his report up the chain of command, added Weightman's name to the list for "gallant and meritorious [conduct]."

John Clark was also pleased with the conduct of both the men in the ranks and the officers that led them. "I desire to express my thanks to M. M. Parsons, Colonels Weightman, Kelly, Rosser and O'Kane. . .with whom I was thrown during the engagement, and who, at the head of their respective forces cordially and efficiently united and acted with me in every movement of the forces under my command." William Slack's report was also laudatory. Everyone in his command "displayed all the energy and endurance of veterans, giving abundant evidence that they can be relied on in any emergency."

Mosby Parsons saved most of his gratitude for his artillery arm, which "by [its] prowess. . .won a position upon the field." After experiencing "real fighting in real battles," wrote artillerist William Barlow long after the war, "this high praise will sound ludicrous to the old soldier, but the general was in earnest, and we accepted the compliment as well earned." Barlow spoke for most of the men who had fought with the Missouri State Guard at Carthage when he noted that "[we had the] honest feeling that we had participated in a decisive engagement, with perhaps, a mental reservation that we were heroes on a small scale."[7]

*　*　*

Compared to the "real fighting in real battles" that would follow, the July 5 running series of engagements hardly amounts to a skirmish. Yet, the armed participants and citizens of southwest Missouri had nothing against which to compare the scores of casualties that now lay sprawled over miles of rolling prairie. The dead and wounded were concentrated along stream beds, the waterways doubling as giant nets snagging the flotsam of the battle. For soldiers and civilians, the fitful thunder of artillery and discomforting rattle of small arms fire that had torn apart their peaceful corner of the world was indeed a major clash of arms. Franz Sigel's Germans had been driven back to Carthage and beyond, a Southern army from Arkansas was moving into Missouri to join forces with the victorious militia, and Nathaniel Lyon's ceaseless campaign to crush Southern resistance in the state appeared, at least for the moment, dead in its tracks.

Like all battles in every age, the immediate result of the fighting was human suffering. The brick-walled Carthage courthouse was converted into a hospital, where dozens of maimed soldiers eventually sought refuge. The bleeding bodies filled the structure to capacity and then spilled outside. Interior doors were removed and used as operating tables in order to allow two local physicians, David Moss and Amos Caffee, to work alongside regimental surgeons. Those wounded unable to receive succor at the courthouse were distributed amongst the town's private residences. Even the town's hotel saw service as a house of mercy. The courthouse witnessed the first of the inevitable amputations, as doctors tossed severed arms and legs out a southwest corner window. Carthage resident Thomas C. Hood estimated that before long ". . .there was about a wagon load" of the freshly-sawn limbs piled high on the ground.[8]

Civilians and soldiers alike swarmed through the town's buildings in search of wounded relatives or friends. Many of the noncombatants, laden with bandages, rode in from surrounding communities to help tend the wounded. The flickering light of lanterns allowed the surgeons to continue working until the early hours of July 6. By the time the sun's rays broke over the eastern horizon, someone had buried the amputated limbs in a shallow trench two to three feet wide and thirty feet long, hastily dug and angled across the courthouse lawn.[9]

While the surgeons were still working, five of the Federal wounded were moved from the courthouse and placed outside on the lawn to make way for more Southern casualties. Locals gathered about the displaced prisoners, eyeing them with a mixture of disgust—they viewed the Germans as hired mercenaries of the Federal government—and curiosity. About this time a squad of Southern soldiers arrived at the Norris Hood home with orders to arrest him for his pro-Union views and earlier assistance to Sigel's Germans. Many of Carthage's citizens jeered and laughed as Hood was marched through the streets at the point of a bayonet. He was taken to the southeast corner of Fifth Street, where he found some of the State Guard's commanders gathered under a cluster of large blackjack oak trees. After an interrogation by the officers, Hood was held as a prisoner. His request to allow his family to feed and care for the wounded Federals was granted, and his daughters served three meals a day to the prisoners, a kindness that went a long way toward alleviating their suffering. Released the next afternoon when the State Guard left the area, the frightened civilian hurried home, packed his belongings and left Jasper County with his family forever. He was not alone. Many of the Union sympathizers steered their horses and mules toward Fort Scott, Kansas. Some unfortunates, like newspaper editor Charles Haywood, lacked four-legged transportation and made the sixty mile march on foot. As it to emphasize that townfolk with political leanings similar to the Hood's were not welcome, someone quietly resurrected the Southern flag that Sigel's men had removed just a little over twenty-four hours earlier. The home-made banner proudly proclaimed Carthage's allegiance.[10]

Watching their husband and father taken away against his will terrified the Hood women, who with nothing else to do walked back to the hospital and continued to tend the wounded. When they returned at 10:00 p.m., a large group of Southern officers had crowded around their home demanding supper. The exhausted women opened their doors to the famished Southerners. The Hood dinner scene was multiplied many times over across the small town, as the civilians of Carthage labored to feed the victorious state army. Those soldiers unable to scrounge up a meal in town settled down around campfires and ate what little food they had carried with them that day. Unfortunately for these men, the wagons accompanying the Missouri State Guard were empty of rations. They made do as best as they were able.[11]

The Southern camps stretched across the Carthage landscape with little thought given to the organizational distribution of the men. Before long, the talk turned to the day's events, especially the leadership of the army. By the time the fires burned low, much of the blame for Sigel's near-miraculous escape was being heaped upon the doorstep of James Rains and the cavalry. Private C. L. Smith of Col. Ben Rives' cavalry, lay beneath the starry sky that night reflecting on his first taste of combat and the fitful sleep that followed:

> I will never forget my night's sleep on the bare ground in the corporation limits of Carthage, right under our horses, and several times being stepped on. One incident I well remember being talked of next day was that had General Rains' cavalry turned their [Sigel's] left flank as we did their right, we could have captured their

whole army. It was said they lost the opportunity while eating blackberries. This is only hearsay, so I cannot vouch for it.[12]

After the attacks against Sigel's final defensive position had ended, the long-suffering Martyn Cheavens struggled back up Chestnut Street in the darkness. "We returned to a house on the edge of town and, getting a bite to eat, lay on a floor, covered with blood, dust and sweat. My feelings then were strange, yet I slept soundly." Archy Thomas of John Clark's Division found time that evening to pen a letter to his hometown newspaper in Carrolton concerning the performance of the army and the activities of the local men with whom he served. "Night coming on," he wrote, "the State troops were drawn off and some went into camp in the Court House yard and others at a spring about a mile from town." According to Thomas, the townspeople were pleased with the forced removal of Sigel's Germans. "The citizens and especially the Ladies of Carthage were very much rejoiced that the State troops had driven out the Federals," he remembered, adding that "The boys from Carroll County all acted boldly and nobly so far as I could learn. None flinched in the whole time."[13]

*   *   *

While the soldiers of the State Guard spread their bedrolls and attempted to obtain a good night's sleep, Franz Sigel's demoralized regiments continued their retreat toward Sarcoxie, twenty miles southeast of Carthage. They finally straggled into town the following morning, just as the sun was crawling above the horizon. Many of the Federals were so exhausted by the continuous marching and sporadic bouts of fighting that they dozed during the retreat, keeping a hand on the shoulder of the man in front. When the command to halt and fall out was heard, some crawled to the grassy side of the road and found comfort there, while others simply fell onto the roadway and refused to move. Wood was scavenged and small fires soon sprung up. Those knapsacks still containing rations cooked on the previous morning were quickly emptied of their contents. The small "army" certainly deserved the rest. They had tramped nearly

38 miles in less than twenty-four hours and fought a series of engagements under exceedingly difficult conditions.[14]

While Capt. Joseph Conrad's captured men of Rifle Company B were suffering through their first night of captivity in Neosho, Sigel was pondering how long to allow his men to rest. Fearing an attack by the State Guard cavalry, he rousted them from their slumber after just a couple hours repose and started them east on the Mount Vernon Road. For the next several hours the tired Federals were allowed only brief stops to massage their feet and wash the dust out of their mouths. The stifling July heat simply added to their sustained misery. After what must have seemed an interminable amount of time, the vanguard of Sigel's column stumbled into Mount Vernon in the middle of the afternoon. By this time his regiments were so strung out that the end of the column did not straggle in until after 9:00 p.m. Sergeant Otto Lademann and the rest of his Company E, Third Missouri, the column's rear guard, were the last Federals to arrive. "[I] marched a sum of eighty-five miles between the mornings of July 4 and the evening of July 6 with barely two meals," he recalled. In camp that night Lademann reported that the men "thought it to be a very good performance for raw and young troops."[15]

Rest was still not in the cards for the Federal Dutch troops. A camp-wide alarm was sounded six hours after Lademann's company marched into town. With State Guard cavalry rumored to be approaching from two directions, the men took up their weapons and fell into line. "We stood under arms from 3 to 10 a.m., when Colonel Sigel ordered us back to town. . .[The call to arms was] "one of those false alarms of our Homeguard friends, [which] got us under arms again," wrote Lademann with some disgust. The exhausted sergeant returned to camp, where he dined on "a cup of coffee and an abundance of those sole-leather flapjacks."

The campaign had worn heavily on the neophyte Federals. Sergeant Lademann complained about the lack of a spare change of clothes on the expedition. Marching in the hot July sun caused the men to perspire freely and Lademann and his companions desperately wished they could wash their clothes and change into a fresh uniform. He also remembered that one of the first things most of the men did at Mount Vernon was to "divest ourselves of every stitch of clothes and get into some creek, we washed our clothes to the best of our ability, remaining in the water until our clothes were sufficiently dry."[16]

The 6th of July was not a good day for either Sigel or his commander, Thomas Sweeny. Sigel's superior had arrived in Springfield just five days earlier on July 1, where he worked diligently to make the city his center of operations for the sustained thrust he was planning into southwest Missouri. Early on the morning of July 6, just a handful of hours after the running fight at Carthage, Sweeny received a frantic message from Sigel about his column's plight. The German's report carried enough detail to inform him that the enemy was "vastly superior in numbers" and that his troops had been "completely surrounded." The news spurred Sweeny into immediate action. "Upon receiving information of these facts," he later reported, "I hastily collected about 400 men, and within three hours after receiving the intelligence was on my way to relieve Colonel Sigel's command." Many of the 400 soldiers marching to relieve Sweeny's beleaguered subordinate were untried Home Guardsmen.[17]

Just a couple hours before dawn on July 7, Sweeny's column neared Mount Vernon. Although he did not know what to expect, he feared Sigel's thin command had been overwhelmed by an aggressive foe. The actual situation was better than anticipated. "I fell in with the retreating column at Mount Vernon," explained Sweeny, "and prepared to give the enemy battle." By virtue of rank Sweeny took command of the column and set about attempting to discover whether in fact another battle was imminent. "I learned from my scouts," the general later reported, that the Confederates were "advancing in great force."[18]

After two days at Mount Vernon Sweeny deemed it time to withdraw his men to Springfield. By now he was more concerned about an attack against Springfield than against his own force. "I took up my line of march for [Springfield]," he explained, "fearing an attack on it from the combined forces of Jackson, Rains, Price, and McCulloch, whose troops I learned were about to form a junction on the Arkansas frontier, toward which the enemy retired from Carthage." The Irish general was sure he could hold out at Springfield until reinforcements arrived. "I have an effective force of 2,600 officers and men, and feel confident in my ability to hold until joined by General Lyon, who I learn is within two or three days' march of me."[19]

*   *   *

The victorious State Guard did not stay in Carthage for long. With Nathaniel Lyon's Federals lurking somewhere to the north and Tom Sweeny and Franz Sigel still lingering to the east, the town remained a strategic trap. The Missourians had marched several miles on July 6 when word rippled through the army that Sterling Price and Benjamin McCulloch were approaching with reinforcements. The soldiers stood in line for about an hour until the officers made their appearance. The grand spectacle impressed Archy Thomas. Governor Jackson and a hatless General Price rode side by side down the lines followed by McCulloch, with Mosby Parsons' trotting at his elbow. Other generals followed in their wake. Price introduced the long-awaited McCulloch to each command before riding on to the next to repeat the process.[20]

The State Guard and McCulloch's Confederates traveled south through Neosho to McDonald County. Moderate weather had finally replaced the heavy rains and high heat, and the army made fine time over the dusty roads. At the Neosho courthouse Private Cheavens marched upon Captain Conrad's captured Federals. "I saw them sworn not to fight against us," he scribbled in his journal. "I asked some why they fought; all had the same answer: 'Nothing to do in St. Louis.'" The mixed armies arrived on July 9 at Cowskin Prairie on the Elkins River, where they stopped for some drill and fasting, wrote Salem Ford. "[We] were living frequently on a few ears of horse corn that was daily issued to us," complained Ford, who was used to a finer style of living than soldiering had to offer. Many of the men went to the river, washed their filthy clothes and sat naked in the sun until they dried. Others took bolts of cloth and made themselves new uniforms while in camp.[21]

Back with the army, Sterling Price set about training his men and stockpiling supplies for a campaign to recover Missouri, which by this time was largely under Federal control. The State Guard's reorganization at Cowskin Prairie was long overdue and Price's effort to turn farmers and storekeepers into soldiers and officers was only just beginning. At first it seemed impossible. Drilling was rigorous and from the soldiers' perspective, dull and monotonous. Private Cheavens described life along the Elkins River: "We drilled two hours before breakfast, 5 til 7, then 4 till 6 p.m." The hard work paid off and officers molded and patched the army's pieces together into a respectable force. Divisions were reorganized, men were promoted to fill vacancies and the training continued. Price and his officers, meanwhile, attempted to persuade Ben McCulloch to join them in a campaign to retake the state.[22]

In addition to the organizational problems that confronted Price, the army's logistics were in a shambles. To rectify the deteriorating situation, the corpulent ex-governor appointed Thomas Snead, Governor Jackson's aide, as the army's quartermaster. Snead tackled the job with great enthusiasm, although he admitted his knowledge of weaponry was somewhat lean. He quickly distributed captured weapons to unarmed men in camp and sought a way of scrounging up others. Lieutenant Barlow of Henry Guibor's battery was put to work by Snead to devise a way to refill the empty ammunition chests. The resourceful Barlow recounted that, "one of Sigel's wagons furnished us with a round shot while a lathe we found in Carthage supplied us with sabots." Other precious materials, including tin, flannel cloth and needles and thread, had been "donated" by the citizens of Carthage before the men had left town.[23]

Barlow, who drew deep satisfaction from his munitions experiments, described his first attempt to make a cartridge "as resembling a turnip." One soldier remembered wondering whether the deformed object would fit down the barrel of a gun. Barlow dedicated himself to his new craft and soon became skillful at manufacturing quality ammunition. He later reported that his shells ". . .worked very well in the next battle [at Wilson's Creek]."[24]

Food supplies continued to be collected from the distant countryside, while gunpowder remained plentiful due to the earlier raid on the Liberty Arsenal. The grayish powder, which was in woefully short supply across the Confederacy, needed only be repackaged to be combat ready. The lead mines at Granby, Missouri, which remained in Southern hands because of the victory at Carthage, supplied a ready source of the soft metal for the army's minie balls and round shots. The militia continued to improvise with accouterments and other items.

The army left Cowskin Prairie a few days later on a march that would eventually carry it to its fateful confrontation with Nathaniel Lyon and Franz Sigel at Wilson's Creek on August 10, 1861.

The campaign that culminated with the July 5, 1861, fight at Carthage, as well as the several weeks that followed the battle, had a significant impact on the war in Missouri and the Trans-Mississippi Theater.

The initial Southern retreat following the Battle of Boonville exposed the counties along the Missouri River to Federal occupation for the balance of the war. This region was a mainstay of pro-Southern support, and its loss critically hampered Rebel recruitment efforts. A large portion of the men who fought with the Missouri State Guard left families behind in "Little Dixie," which led to additional problems with desertion and long-term morale. The Southern war effort in Missouri never recovered from this loss.

The engagement itself bought precious time for the militia army as it marched to Cowskin Prairie and set up camp. While Governor Jackson's force was still weak, disorganized and utterly lacking in supplies, the victory temporarily boosted Southern morale across the state and provided an additional impetus for recruitment. In addition, Franz Sigel's retreat to Neosho (and eventually Springfield) opened the route south toward Arkansas, allowing the Missouri army to join with Ben McCulloch's Confederate army. The unification of these two bodies had decisive consequences for Nathaniel Lyon, both personally and professionally.

Major changes were in the wind by the time the Missouri State Guard arrived at the Elkins River/Cowskin Prairie encampment. The unwieldy system of divisions led by district commanders was finally scrapped in favor of more traditional military units. While the men drilled and reorganized, lead was extracted from the Granby mines south of Carthage. The army would not have been able to utilize this precious soft metal had Sigel been victorious on July 5.

While the Southern militia drilled, Lyon concentrated his men in Springfield. The difficulty of supplying campaigning armies was just beginning to be realized, although not in time to prevent Springfield from becoming another logistics headache for the general. Dangling at the end of a line of communications stretching two hundred miles, supplies for his regiments dwindled. It was the supply factor that effectively crippled Lyon's southwest Missouri Campaign. While Lyon was an able tactician and capable leader of men, his appreciation of campaign logistics was not well developed.

The campaign increased the suffering of the local population. Raids by Southern cavalry and guerrilla warfare exacerbated the situation and effectively depopulated much of the region. Carthage felt the sting of war again the following year when the town was partially burned during Jo Shelby's 1863 raid. Few appreciate the extent of the suffering experienced by Missouri's civilians.

Other ramifications of the small fight were felt on a different battlefield just over one month later. Following Sigel's near-debacle of July 5, Lyon was forced to abandon his immediate plan to crush Jackson's militia. He chose instead to remain in the southwest portion of the state to bolster the region's pro-Union faction. After some weeks Lyon made the decision to strike the enhanced Confederate-militia army. His planning included providing Franz Sigel with another independent command. The resultant engagement at Wilson's Creek, fought on August 10, 1861, was a disaster for the Federals. Sigel, whose objective was once again to act as a flanking and blocking force, was driven from the field, Lyon was killed and his army defeated. Sterling Price's Missourians turned in a credible performance under trying circumstances, serving notice that the weeks of training had transformed them from a semi-organized rabble to soldiers worthy of the name. The State Guard little resembled the army that had met Sigel's disciplined Dutch Federals on a slight ridge ten miles north of Carthage.

Given all of these ramifications it is surprising that more students of the Civil War are not familiar with (or in many cases, interested in) the battle. While results can be manipulated and debated, one thing remains clear: Carthage was the first true field victory for Southerners and one of their few successes in Missouri during four bloody years of military strife.

After Carthage

Franz Backoff, Sigel's old friend and former European revolutionary, returned to St. Louis after Carthage to recruit for the Federal cause.

Hiram Miller Bledsoe enjoyed a long and distinguished career after Carthage. The native Kentuckian silenced Sigel's artillery at Wilson's Creek, and his batterymen mustered into Confederate service in March 1862. He served with distinction at Pea Ridge and accompanied the army east of the Mississippi River thereafter, seeing hard service in many of the Western Theater's campaigns. Bledsoe was elected to the Missouri senate in the 1890s and died at Pleasant Hill, Missouri, on February 7, 1899.

John Bullock Clark, Sr., another Kentucky native, is often confused with his son, John Jr. After Carthage, Claiborne Jackson's rump Neosho legislature sent Clark to Richmond to serve in the Provisional Confederate Congress, and he was later elected to the senate. Missouri's Governor Thomas C. Reynolds refused to reappoint Clark because of his extracurricular activities, which included "mendacity, drunkenness, and the attempted seduction of General Albert Pike's mistress." Clark returned to Missouri after the war and practiced law until his death on October 29, 1885.

One of the unsung heroes of Carthage, artillerist **Christian Essig**, virtually disappears from the historical record after that action. He later drowned in the Mississippi River during the Vicksburg Campaign.

Daniel Frost, the New York native and early leader in the Missouri State Guard, was paroled and exchanged after the fiasco at Camp Jackson. Thereafter he accepted an appointment as a brigadier general in the Confederate army, but declined to lead a brigade at Pea Ridge. He saw service at Prairie Grove, Arkansas, on December 7, 1862, and the following year traveled to Canada after his wife was forced from St. Louis because of her Confederate sympathies. Frost returned to Missouri after the war and took up farming. He died on his farm near St. Louis on October 29, 1900.

Henry Guibor's career paralleled that of Hiram Bledsoe. After good service at Carthage, he handled his guns well at Wilson's Creek, Lexington and Pea Ridge. After transferring west of the Mississippi River, Guibor was severely wounded early in the Vicksburg Campaign. He fought through the Atlanta Campaign, Hood's Tennessee Campaign, and eventually surrendered in Meridan, Mississippi. After the war he was the superintendent of the St. Louis house of refuse, where he would don a Confederate uniform and drill the young boys, much to their delight.

Francis Hassendeubel, who fought so well at Carthage, left the Third Missouri in mid-July. He was promoted to colonel and given command of the 17th Missouri Infantry, which he led during the Vicksburg Campaign. Like Adolf Dengler (who had fought so well at Dry Fork Creek), Hassendeubel was killed during the Vicksburg siege.

Claiborne Fox Jackson, Missouri's displaced governor, formed a pro-secession legislature at Neosho, Missouri, which voted the state into the Confederacy even though Jackson and his "rump" legislators were no longer recognized as legitimate state officials. After the Southern defeat at Pea Ridge in March 1862, he traveled to Little Rock, Arkansas, where he died of complications from stomach cancer on December 6, 1862.

One of the better yet overlooked Confederate generals was **Mosby Monroe Parsons**, who continued to demonstrate great promise at Wilson's Creek and Pea Ridge. In the latter battle his brigade performed some of the finest and hardest fighting on that difficult field. Parsons was commissioned into Confederate service in November 1862 as a brigadier general and spent most of 1862-1863 engaged in the Arkansas campaigns. In 1864 he led with distinction a division in Louisiana during the Red River Campaign after he was sent to reinforce Richard Taylor's small army. After helping defeat Nathaniel Banks' Federals, the ubiquitous Parsons marched north and participated in the repulse of Frederick Steele's column in Arkansas. Later that year he served with Sterling Price on the ill-fated Missouri Raid. Like many others, Parsons traveled to Mexico after the war, where he was killed fighting imperial forces at Camargo, Mexico on August 17, 1865.

Together with Brig. Gen. Benjamin McCulloch, "Old Pap" **Sterling Price** went on and defeated Nathaniel Lyon at Wilson's Creek and later captured the Union garrison at Lexington. Victory in the field eluded Missouri's former governor once he was commissioned major general in Confederate service in March 1862. His participation at Pea Ridge ended in a stinging defeat, which was followed by his repulse at the head of the Army of the West at Iuka and Corinth, Mississippi, and Helena, Arkansas. At the head of the Army of Missouri in late 1864, Price led a disastrous raid to reclaim his home state. His exhausted army was eventually forced back into Arkansas, effectively ending his Civil War career. After spending time in Mexico, Price returned impoverished and in poor health in January 1867. He died just eight months later on September 29 in St. Louis.

Despite his unfitness for command, **James Spencer Rains** led a division of state troops at Wilson's Creek and Pea Ridge. He feuded with Maj. Gen. Earl Van Dorn after the latter battle and was temporarily arrested. Refusing to take his men east of the Mississippi River, Rains was accepted into Confederate service and given a mixed State Guard–Confederate command in Arkansas until relieved for "incompetence and insobriety." He ended the war as a recruiting officer in Missouri. Rains settled in Segoville, Texas, after the war, where he spent his last years as a prominent farmer, civic leader and lawyer until his death on May 19, 1880.

Benjamin Rives went on to serve at the Battle of Wilson's Creek and the siege of Lexington, Missouri. Despite his inept handling of his cavalry regiment at Carthage, he turned in credible performances thereafter. How far he would have progressed is unknown, for Rives was mortally wounded at Pea Ridge and eventually buried in his native Virginia.

Joseph Shelby, the Southern cavalry's rising star, fought at Wilson's Creek, Pea Ridge, Corinth, Mississippi, and other battles in the Trans-Mississippi

Theater. He did not surrender after the war, preferring instead exile in Mexico. He returned to Missouri in 1867 and was appointed U. S. Marshal of the Western District by President Grover Cleveland. Shelby served in that capacity until his death on February 13, 1897.

Franz Sigel's long-awaited promotion to brigadier general came on August 7, 1861, which preceded by just three days his poor showing at the Battle of Wilson's Creek. He turned in his best performance of the war at the March 7-8, 1862, fight at Pea Ridge. After his transfer east he led the Federal I Corps in John Pope's army at the crushing Federal defeat at Second Bull Run. His military career came to a sudden halt after he was beaten on May 15, 1864 at New Market, Virginia. He was relieved of command and later resigned his commission and returned to civilian life. The former German minister of war died in New York City on August 21, 1902.

William Yarnel Slack went on to serve with distinction at Wilson's Creek and was severely wounded. Although he did not have a Confederate commission, he led the Second Missouri Brigade at the Battle of Pea Ridge the following March, and was mortally wounded when a minie ball slammed into his hip an inch away from his Wilson's Creek wound. Slack seemed to improve, but surgeons feared he would be captured and transported him seven miles to Moore's Mill, where he died on March 21, 1862. He received a posthumous promotion to brigadier general to date from April 12, 1862.

Richard Hanson Weightman, who had served so well at Carthage, continued to demonstrate his capacity for field leadership while leading a charge up Oak "Bloody" Hill during the August 10, 1861 fight at Wilson's Creek. The promising soldier was mortally wounded in the attack and carried to the Ray House. A story with some credence holds that Weightman expired soon after learning that the cheering troops he could hear were triumphant Southerners atop the captured "Bloody" Hill.

ORDER OF BATTLE

The Battle of Carthage
July 5, 1861

FEDERALS

Col. Franz Sigel, Commanding

Third Regiment Infantry, Missouri Volunteers

Col. Franz Sigel
Lt. Col. Francis Hassendeubel, First Battalion
Lt. Col. Albert Anselm
Maj. Henry Bischoff, Second Battalion
Lt. Sebastian Engert, Quartermaster

Company A—Capt. John Fred Cramer
Rifle Company A—Capt. John Indest
Company B—Capt . Joseph Conrad (captured at Neosho, 7/5)
Rifle Company B—Capt. Henry Zeis
Company C—Capt. Jacob Hartmann
Company D—Capt. August Hackman

Company E—Capt. John E. Strodkamp*
Company F—Capt. Hugo Glomer
Company G—Capt. Adolph Dengler
Company H—Capt. George Friedlein

Fifth Regiment Infantry, Missouri Volunteers

Col. Charles E. Salomon
Lt. Col. Christian D. Wolff

(No Company A)
Company B—Capt. Louis Gottschalk
Company C—Capt. Fred Salomon
Company D—Capt. Charles Mehl
Company E—Capt. Carl Stephani
Company F—Capt. Alfred Arnaud
Company G—Capt. Charles Stark

Artillery
Maj. Franz Backoff

Capt. Christian Essig (4 guns)
Capt. Theodore Wilkins (4 guns)

Colonel Sigel's column numbered approximately 1,100 soldiers
at the Battle of Carthage

* * *

---

* Franz Sigel incorrectly spells Capt. John E. Strodkamp's name as "Strodt-mann." The muster roll spelling is correct.

THE
MISSOURI STATE GUARD*

Maj. Gen. Sterling Price**
Governor Claiborne F. Jackson***
Col. Henry Little, Adjutant General

Third Division: Brig Gen. John Bullock Clark, Sr.
(365 soldiers)

Infantry
Col. John Q. Burbridge—1st Missouri Infantry
Lt. Col. Edwin Price—1st Missouri Infantry
Maj. John B. Clark, Jr.—First Regiment, Missouri Infantry

Fourth Division—Brig Gen. William Yarnel Slack
(1,200 soldiers)

Infantry
Col. John T. Hughes
Col. John T. Hughes (Lt. Col. James Pritchard)—1st Missouri Infantry
Maj. John C. Thornton—Thornton's Battalion

Cavalry
Col. Benjamin A. Rives—First Cavalry

* The Missouri State Guard used the term "division" to recruit troops and denote the congressional district in which the troops were raised. Contrary to popular belief, the term has nothing to do with the size of the command.

** Sterling Price was traveling south to Arkansas to negotiate with Brig. Gen. Benjamin McCulloch about aiding the Missouri State Guard and was not present at Carthage.

*** Governor Jackson held command by virtue of the authority of the Military Bill, passed by the Missouri assembly prior to its adjournment.

Sixth Division—Brig. Gen. Monroe Mosby Parsons
(650 soldiers)

Infantry
Col. Joseph Kelly—Kelly's Missouri Infantry Regiment
Maj. George K. Dills—Dills' Battalion

Cavalry
Col. Ben Brown—1st Missouri Cavalry
Capt. — Alexander—Alexander's Cavalry
Capt. — Crews—Crew's Cavalry

Artillery
Guibor's Battery (4 guns)
Capt. Henry Guibor

Eighth Division—Brig. Gen. James Spencer Rains
Col. Richard Weightman*
(1,812 soldiers)

Infantry

First Brigade
Col. Richard H. Weightman
Lt. Col. Thomas H. Rosser**

Col. John R. Graves—Second Regiment
Col. Edgar V. Hurst—Third Regiment
Lt. Col. Walter S. O'Kane—O'Kane's Battalion
Capt. Francis. M. McKinney—Independent Detachment

---

* If Brig. Gen. James Spencer Rains was in charge of the army, as some allege, Col. Richard Weightman, as senior officer, would have taken command of the Eighth Division.

** If Col. Richard H. Weightman took command of the Eighth Division, Lt. Col. Rosser would have taken command of the First Brigade. Rosser's First Regiment does not appear to have participated at Carthage. The regiment may not have been armed.

Cavalry
Col. Robert Y. L. Peyton—Third Cavalry (Cos. A, B and part of H)
Col. James McCown—Second Cavalry (1st Battalion Independent)
Lt. Col. Richard A. Boughan—Boughan's Battalion, Seventh Cavalry

Several independent cavalry units were attached to Rains' Eighth Division, including the companies of Thomas E. Owens and
Capt. Joseph Shelby's Rangers

Artillery
Bledsoe's Battery (3 guns)
Capt. Hiram M. Bledsoe

The Missouri State Guard purportedly included over 2,000 unarmed soldiers who did not participate in the battle. Governor Jackson's army totaled 4,000 armed effectives at Carthage.

Engagement at Neosho, Missouri
July 5, 1861

FEDERALS

Third Regiment, Missouri Infantry
Company B—Capt. Joseph Conrad (80 men)

CONFEDERATES

McCulloch's Arkansas Brigade*
Brig. Gen. Benjamin McCulloch

Col. Thomas J. Churchill—1st Arkansas Mounted Rifles
Capt. James McIntosh (four companies of 1st Arkansas Mounted Rifles)
Capt. De Rosy [?] Carroll's Company of Infantry

*   *   *

* Listing includes only those portions of McCulloch's Brigade that participated in the Neosho engagement.

A Self-Guided Tour
of the Battle of Carthage
July 5, 1861

Almost all of the battlefield remains in private hands.
Please respect the privacy and property rights of the land owners

This instructional tour, coupled with the detailed maps within this volume, will help you locate and follow the series of engagements collectively known as the Battle of Carthage. Only brief summaries of the action are provided in this tour, which is intended as a supplement to this book. Therefore, it is strongly recommended that you read *The Battle of Carthage: Border War in Southwest Missouri* before taking the tour.

The battlefield is in remarkably pristine shape, primarily because of its distance from an urban center. Although the population of Carthage has increased to over 10,000, and some of the city buildings have encroached on portions of the terrain fought over late in the day, the majority of the remainder of the field remains in much the same condition as it did in 1861. The handful of markers you will see on the battlefield were placed there in 1899 by the Daughters of the Confederacy. Unfortunately, they do not provide any interpretation of the events they commemorate.

Given the number of miles over which this engagement was waged, it is recommended that you undertake this tour in an automobile.

Getting to Carthage

The town of Carthage, Missouri, is located in the southwestern corner of the state in Jasper County. Today, much like 1861, Carthage relies on a mixed economy of dairy farming, general farm production and grain milling. A major granite quarry operates on the edge of the city limits, and a variety of other manufacturing establishments are located in the town itself.

Most visitors will be find that Interstate 44, which runs east-west through much of the Midwest, is the most convenient route to reach Carthage. From the Interstate, take Exit 18B onto Highway 71 North. This is a four lane state road leading to Carthage. You will notice a sign about the battle one mile after turning onto this road. *Remember: the directions on this sign are different than the directions contained in this tour.*

Reset your odometer after exiting Interstate 44. Continue on Highway 71 North for 6.9 miles and turn right at the exit for South 71—State 96 East. Veer right at the exit ramp and continue bearing to your right. You are now driving east on Route 96. The local name for this road is Central Avenue. Continue east on Central Ave, driving in the right hand lane. When you come to an intersection marked 571–Garrison Avenue, turn right onto Garrison. Turn left (north) just past the next traffic light onto Fourth Street. Continue north two blocks and you will enter the Carthage town square. Traffic travels counter-clockwise around the square. [Proceed to TOUR STOP 1.]

Alternate Routes for Traveling into Carthage

From Joplin, Missouri, take 71 North into Carthage *past* the interchange where Highway 71 North turns and heads for Kansas City. Drive straight into Carthage on State Highway 96 East—known locally as Central Avenue. Stay on Central Ave to 571—Garrison Avenue. Turn right onto Garrison, and turn left (north) onto Fourth Street just past the first traffic light. Travel north two blocks and you will enter the Carthage town square. [Proceed to TOUR STOP 1.]

If you are traveling south on Highway 71, continue until you see the interchange for State Highway 96. Turn left (east) onto Highway 96—locally known as Central Avenue. Continue on Central until you reach the 571—Garrison Avenue intersection. Turn right onto Garrison and be make a left (north) onto Fourth Street just past the first traffic light. Drive two blocks north on Fourth Street and you enter the Carthage town square. [Proceed to TOUR STOP 1.]

If you are entering Carthage from the west on Highway 96 West, continue through town. This road turns into Central Avenue. Turn left at the intersection marked 571—Garrison Avenue, turn left (north) past the first traffic light onto Fourth Street, and proceed two blocks until you enter the Carthage town square. [Proceed to TOUR STOP 1.]

TOUR STOP 1

The Carthage Museum

**205 North Grant Street
Carthage, MO
417-358-6643**

The best place to begin your tour of the battle is at the Carthage Civil War Museum. Drive into the town square area and turn onto North Grant Street, a side street in the northwest corner of the square. Proceed one block on North Grant and the museum is the brick building on your left. Since parking is at a premium in this area, you may need to return to the square to find a parking space.

Inside you will find several exhibits about the battle as well as other information on Civil War events that occurred in Jasper County. The large mural immediately inside was painted for the museum by artist Andy Thomas. Take a moment to study the painting, and it will help you visualize what occurred on two of your stops in the square.

The museum provides an overview of both the fighting at Carthage and its ramifications on the war in Missouri and the Trans-Mississippi. In the rear of the museum is a diorama of the battle depicting the deployment of Col. Franz Sigel's soldiers and Claiborne F. Jackson's Missouri State Guard militia troops. The diorama highlights many of the spots you will be visiting in the later stages of the tour.

TOUR STOP 2

The Courthouse Square

Turn right when you exit the museum and walk one block toward the town's courthouse square, the scene of important action before, during and after the battle. In 1861, Carthage extended a few blocks on either side of the town square and was home to over 400 citizens. The Civil War-era courthouse burned in 1862 when Jo Shelby's Confederate raiders skirmished through the area (in what is popularly known as the Second Battle of Carthage). The present courthouse was constructed after the war and was built in an entirely different architectural style.

On the early morning of July 5, 1861, Sigel's Federals left their camp at Carter's Spring, marched into Carthage and through the square (southeast to northwest), over the Spring River and north across the prairie in search of the Missouri State Guard. Although the teen-aged girls of Carthage resident Norris Hood stood in front of their home in the northeast corner of the square waving a homemade American flag, many of the residents remained behind locked doors, fearful of the predominantly German column (the "Dutch," as they were known locally).

Return to your vehicle and check or reset your odometer for the next part of the tour. Head north on Grant Street (where the museum is located), and turn left at the first stop sign onto Central Avenue. Remain in the right hand lane on Central Avenue and proceed through the 571—Garrison Avenue inter-section. After driving eight-tenths (0.8) of a mile, turn north at the traffic light onto Francis Street (also known as Civil War Avenue). You are now heading toward the Spring River. Colonel Sigel took this route on the morning of July 5 after marching through the Carthage town square. Francis Street was referred to by a variety of names in 1861, including Lower Bridge Road and Lamar-Carthage Road.

The small plateau immediately across the Spring River is Ordnuff Hill, which played an important role during Sigel's retreat (see Tour Stop 9). The rolling prairie on either side of Civil War Avenue (historic Lamar-Carthage Road) looks much the same as it did when Sigel's Federals marched north to meet the State Guard troops. As it is today, this area was farmland in 1861.

Caution: As you drive north you will pass several crossroads and encounter several stop signs. Cross traffic does not stop. Please drive carefully.

TOUR STOP 3

The Initial Confederate line of battle

Continue driving north on Civil War Avenue for several miles until you reach a "T" intersection with county highway "M" (also known locally as Baseline Road). Pull over to the side of the road and park on Civil War Avenue. Be especially careful when crossing or walking along the county road, as traffic is often heavy and moves at a fair rate of speed.

A gray granite marker sits on the north side of County Road M near the fence line where the roads intersect. The inscription reads: "Line of Battle July 5, 1861." North of the marker, up the slight hill before you are the fields owned by the Gresham family. They owned the land in July of 1861 and descendants still own the property today. *Please respect their privacy and property rights.*

The Missouri State Guard marched south from Petty Foggy Bottom at 4:00 a.m. on the morning of July 5 and formed its battle line directly in front of you along the crest of the hill that ran perpendicular to the Lamar-Carthage Road. They began forming about 8:00 a.m. Although we do not know for sure, the line probably stretched about one mile in length. Governor Jackson and his generals were still attempting to deploy their untrained men for battle when Colonel Sigel first spotted them.

[Note: County Highway M was not in existence in 1861. The Lamar-Carthage Road followed the general direction of Civil War Avenue. In 1861 the road jogged or curved west of the Gresham house for about one-half mile before bowing back to the east, forming a roughly-shaped crescent in the process. It is also important to note that at the time of the battle, the Lamar-Carthage Road at this point (north of Dry Fork Creek), probably did not deserve the name "road." Few accounts even mention it, and none of the detailed Confederate battle reports refer to it for orientation in regards to the alignment of their men.]

Turn and face Carthage. You are standing approximately in the middle of the Southern line of battle. The State Guard (about 4,000 strong) deployed for the fight in the following order: Brig. Gen. Richard Weightman filed his Eighth Division infantry brigade, together with Hiram Bledsoe's battery of artillery, off the road and deployed facing south toward Carthage. Brigadier General James S. Rains formed his own Eighth Division cavalry beyond Weightman's flank, anchoring the army's far right. The middle of the line, where you are now standing, was occupied by Brig. Gen. Mosby Parsons' Sixth Division, which included Capt. Henry Guibor's battery of four brass 6-lb. guns. The infantry of Brig. Gen. William Y. Slack's Fourth Division extended the line east, while Brig. Gen. John B. Clark's Third Division infantry took position on Slack's left flank. The far left of the army, like the far right, was anchored by various cavalry commands, primarily Col. Benjamin A. Rives' and Col. Ben Brown's regiments. Another 2,000 unarmed men were kept out of the action and well behind the army, where Governor Jackson apparently spent most of the battle. The State Guard moved down off the ridge toward onto the flat ground where you are standing immediately prior to the beginning of the battle. [NOTE: We disagree with almost every modern description of the divisional alignment of the Confederate battle line. Our reasoning is discussed in detail in the text, and our sources are listed in the notes.]

Turn and look south back toward Carthage. The field on your left (east of you) was also owned by the Gresham family. A small farm house stood approximately where the two-story frame dwelling stands today. That house was in the line of fire between the two combatants (although, curiously, neither side mentions it in their official reports of the fighting). Sigel's Federals, about 1,100 men, were beyond the tree line to the south (which was not there in

1861), approximately 800 to 1,200 yards distant. The field across the road on your right (west) was planted in knee to waist-high corn on the day of the battle. Unseasonably heavy rains had turned much of the ground into a soggy morass.

Double-Trouble Creek and the
Union Line of Battle

Return to your vehicle, carefully turn around and proceed south toward Carthage on Civil War Avenue. Reset or check your odometer. Travel eight-tenths (0.8) of a mile and stop where a small creek bisects the road north of Pine Avenue. You may miss this small waterway if you do not use the odometer. While Double Trouble Creek does not appear to be much of an impediment, two sources of water to the east of the road feed the small creek, which tends to flood the field and road on a regular basis—hence its name. Pull your car off the road and carefully leave your vehicle. [This is a well traveled farm road, so watch out for large pieces of farm machinery and other vehicles.]

Turn and face north toward the Missouri State Guard line. You are now standing near where Sigel deployed his Federals for battle, just to the north of Double Trouble Creek. It is from this initial location that he moved forward to meet the enemy. On his far left Sigel deployed one-half of the Third Missouri Regiment under Maj. Franz Bischoff. In the center of the line stretching across the road and into the fields on both sides of you was the Fifth Missouri Regiment, led by Col. Charles Salomon. Lieutenant Colonel Francis Hassendeubel, who led the remaining one-half of the Third Missouri, anchored the right flank of the Federal force. Sigel positioned his artillery between his three infantry segments. Captain Christian Essig's three guns (one was held back at Dry Fork Creek during the advance) was deployed between Hassendeubel and Salomon, while Capt. Theodore Wilkins' four pieces were deployed between Salomon and Bishoff.

Colonel Sigel opened the battle with his artillery. The State Guard guns returned the fire, although they were very short of fixed ammunition. The shelling, while noisy and unnerving to the inexperienced troops, produced only a handful of casualties on both sides. Although Sigel planned to attack with his infantry, one of his artillerists, Captain Wilkins, informed him after about one-half hour that his battery was low on ammunition and could not support the assault. By this time Southern cavalry on both flanks was moving to sweep behind the Federals, and Sigel may also have seen the 2,000 mounted but unarmed Confederates moving behind the lines. Fearful of losing his wagon train of 32 vehicles, which was parked a couple miles behind him, and having no cavalry to counter the enemy's movement, Sigel ordered a retreat south over Dry Fork Creek toward Carthage.

Given the numbers involved, it is not difficult to understand and visualize Colonel Sigel's predicament: once the opposing forces had deployed, Sigel's men were overlapped on both flanks by the Rebel line. The 36-year-old colonel had extended his front to meet the more numerous State Guard by placing large spaces between his companies to make his force appear larger than it was, a waste of time given the completely open terrain. When he finally realized the seriousness of the situation, Sigel ordered Captain Essig's guns, which were located in the field to the right (east) of your position, withdrawn to the high ground immediately behind Dry Fork Creek, where Essig had earlier left one of his pieces. The rest of Sigel's command followed thereafter in good order.

The ill-trained Southerners, who were laboring under a very confused command structure, were somewhat disrupted by the artillery duel. As a result, their pursuit of the withdrawing Federals was not vigorously undertaken.

TOUR STOP 5

Confederate Line of Battle
and the Assault on Dry Fork Creek

Return to your vehicle. Be careful when you pull back into traffic. As you leave Double Trouble Creek, proceed south six-tenths (0.6) of a mile. NOTE: There is no room to pull completely off the road at this point. Do not slow down or pull over unless you are able to safely do so.

Look to the south. You will see a concrete bridge spanning Dry Fork Creek about 400 yards ahead of you. At about noon Sigel deployed a rear guard, consisting of Christian Essig's four guns and several companies of infantry, in a strong position south of the creek. This force was ordered to slow down the Confederate pursuit so that Sigel could save his wagon train, which continued moving south toward Carthage as fast as possible. The balance of the Federal infantry, together with Wilkins' artillery, accompanied the trains. At this point in the action Sigel was justifiably concerned that the Rebel cavalry, which he could no longer see, was riding to cut off his line of retreat.

The Confederates aligned on both sides of the road near where you are currently parked and assaulted the Federals. Weightman's Brigade deployed west of the road, while Clark, Parsons and Slack aligned their men to the east. Before the infantry attack began, Capt. Hiram Bledsoe's Battery unlimbered about 400 yards from the ford (near where you are parked) and opened on the Federals defending the crossing. Bledsoe was severely pounded by Essig's Union guns, and two of his lieutenants and several gunners were wounded in the exchange. Bledsoe was also wounded as he served his pieces. His battery withdrew and was not involved again until later in the day. The damage Bledsoe inflicted on Essig, if any, went unrecorded.

By this time the Missouri State Guard was badly disorganized and suffering from heavy straggling. It took some time for the generals to organize their men for the attack.

TOUR STOP 6

Sigel's Position at Dry Fork Creek

Return to your vehicle. Continue south toward the Dry Fork Creek Bridge. You are driving over the ground traversed by the Confederates in their attack against Sigel's rear guard. Cross over the bridge (which spans the Civil War-era ford) and proceed slowly up the incline on the southern bank. Pull over when you see another small granite marker on the left (or east side) of the road. Park your vehicle and carefully cross the road to the marker. All of the markers at Carthage are identical in size and shape as the first marker at Tour Stop 3.

When you reach the marker, face north toward the oncoming Confederate attack. You are now standing on the Federal line of battle just behind Dry Fork Creek. Christian Essig unlimbered his battery a few yards to your right. Captain Stephani's Company E, Fifth Missouri, was deployed in the underbrush along the creek to the left (west) of the ford, which is marked by the current bridge. Two additional companies from the Third Missouri, Capt. Dengler's Company G and Captain Glomer's Company F, extended the Federal line east of the bridge in the thickets hugging the stream's banks. Another two companies were used as a reserve behind the two wings.

The natural strength of the position is readily apparent, since the ground over which the Confederates were forced to attack was open prairie and swept by Federal artillery. In addition, the creek was high and difficult to ford. Sigel's flanks, however, were vulnerable to the Southern cavalrymen, who were at that time trying to find a way to get behind him and either cut off his retreat or destroy his wagon train.

As it turned out, the vigorous defense offered by the handful of defenders along the creek may have saved Sigel's column from destruction. Although the heavy Southern assaults managed to reach the bank of the stream on both sides of the road, the infantry discovered, much to their surprise and disgust, that the river was not fordable. Trapped along steep banks and swift-flowing waterway, they exchanged small arms fire from a distance of 30 to 50 yards for almost half an hour. The fighting eventually spread across a front approximately three-quarters of a mile wide and stretched the Federals to the breaking point. The small arms and artillery fire was so intense that many of the participants referred to the day's action as the Battle of Dry Fork, rather than the Battle of Carthage.

Both sides suffered the majority of their casualties along Dry Fork. Southern reports mention taking severe losses at this stage of the long day of marching and fighting. Unfortunately the only Federal report available on Carthage is Franz Sigel's, and he does not discuss the severity of his losses along the creek.

At about 1:00 p.m. or shortly thereafter, the gallant Federal defenders were either driven from or abandoned the Dry Fork position. Sigel later claimed that he learned that Confederate cavalry had slipped ahead of the column, and that he voluntarily abandoned the Dry Fork line. It is more probable that the heavily-outnumbered Federals were driven (and/or flanked) from their strong position by the aggressive tactics utilized by the Missouri State Guard.

TOUR STOP 7

Fiasco at Buck's Branch Creek

Return to your vehicle and reset or check your odometer. Carefully pull back onto Civil War Avenue and head south toward Carthage, following Sigel's route of retreat. The next stop is 2.2 miles. After covering two miles, however, slow down and pay close attention to the terrain, as Buck's Branch Creek can be difficult to locate. Two guardrails mark the location of the stream. There is no sign or marker for this stop, so be sure to check your odometer carefully. When you reach the bridge, pull off to the side of the road (but do not stop on the bridge!) Use extreme caution because traffic can be, and often is, very heavy along this road.

Exit your car and take in the surrounding terrain, which looks almost as it did in 1861. You are standing on the defensive position held by Southern cavalry. The action at Buck's Branch was one of many squandered Southern opportunities. Between 1:00 and 2:00 p.m., Sigel was rapidly moving his column south in an attempt to outpace the Southern cavalry and stay ahead of the pursuing Confederate infantry. It was Lt. Col. Francis Hassendeubel's task to turn the 32 Federal wagons around below Dry Fork Creek, where they were parked when the battle initially opened with the artillery duel, and move them south to Carthage.

On July 5, 1861, Buck's Branch was running high. The approaches over the single ford had been torn to muddy ribbons when the wagons passed through several hours earlier. The crossing was a natural bottleneck and potentially a dangerous position for the retreating Federals. As these same wagons rolled south toward the ford, which was about 800 yards away, the Federals discovered a line of dismounted Confederate cavalry stretched across the ground behind (south of) the creek. Hard riding had carried the regiments of Cols. Benjamin Rives and Ben Brown in front of Sigel, whose only route of retreat was now blocked by a substantial force. The battle had reached a critical stage.

Although the teamsters wanted to abandon the wagons and make a run for cover in the tall prairie grass, Hassendeubel would have none of it. After reestablishing order, he directed Company E, Third Missouri, to fix bayonets and prepare to charge the Southern cavalry. Two guns also unlimbered and began shelling the enemy. The subsequent Union infantry attack through the head-high prairie grass completely unnerved the Southern cavalry, which shot off one ragged volley and retreated as fast as possible, even though they had not suffered a single casualty.

The Federals successfully crossed Buck's Branch and continued their fitful journey toward Carthage. In a large open field below the creek, Sigel formed his wagons into eight lines of four wagons each, and deployed his infantry and artillery in a hollow square around the wagons. In this fashion he continued moving his column south.

TOUR STOP 8

The Retreat from
Buck's Branch to the Spring River

Return to your vehicle and continue south toward Carthage. Be careful as you pull back into traffic. This stage of the tour covers the wide open rolling prairie that Sigel's column managed to cross without much trouble. Enjoy the drive and visualize the retreating wagons and infantry rolling and marching south, pursued by the Missouri State Guard.

Luckily for Sigel, the gently rolling terrain allowed him to see that the enemy was not closely pressing his retreat. As an added measure of prudence, however, he deployed his guns as a moving rear guard just in case Southern cavalry made an unwelcome appearance. Three artillery pieces were set up behind the wagons (one on the road and another on each side) in order to fire in the direction of the approaching enemy. After one gun fired, it limbered and moved after the wagons, unlimbering a short distance later. This procedure was followed by the remaining guns as the entire column continued its withdrawal toward Spring River. [Note: Although some writers claim that Sigel was harassed and pressed closely by the Confederates during this stage of the retreat, firsthand evidence clearly contradicts this.] Continue driving south toward Spring River.

TOUR STOP 9

Ordnuff Hill and the Spring River Line

Your next turn is located in a potentially congested traffic zone and comes up quickly, so be prepared and alert. After you pass under Highway 71, slow down and take your first right turn on North Woods. Pull to the side of the road as soon as you can safely do so. Walk back to the corner where you turned onto North Woods. The third granite marker for the Battle of Carthage is located at this intersection (Civil War Avenue and North Woods). This small monument is difficult to see from your car.

Although you may not realize it, you are now standing on what was known in 1861 as Ordnuff Hill. Today, the plateau is called Quarry Hill because of a large underground granite mine. Sigel established a strong line of artillery and infantry on this spot late on the afternoon of July 5. He hoped that this force would hold his bridgehead on the north bank long enough for his wagon train, accompanied by some of the infantry, to get across Spring River, which is directly behind you.

As it turned out, he had little to worry about. The fighting at Dry Fork and the hard marching thereafter had thoroughly disorganized and exhausted the Missouri State Guard. By the time the Southern infantry and cavalry made an appearance, Sigel's wagons were over the river and his line of retreat into Carthage was all but established. The Southern infantry did not test the position, although they outnumbered the defenders by a substantial margin. Confederate horsemen, however, attempted to flank Ordnuff Hill and cross the river in the hope of gaining Sigel's rear. A few shells from the Federal artillery thwarted the half-hearted attempt and convinced the cavalry to move out of range and seek a crossing elsewhere.

Many members of the State Guard believed that James Rains' cavalry bungled a solid opportunity at the Spring River to pinch off Sigel's retreat. According to campfire gossip, at some point during the pursuit Rains allowed his men to stop and pick blackberries, thereby losing the race to the river. Although the charge was never substantiated, Rains' mounted men were thereafter derisively referred to as the "blackberry cavalry."

The Spring River Crossing

Return to your vehicle and reset or check your odometer. Your next stop is one-half (0.5) of a mile. Turn right (south) on Civil War Avenue. *Exercise caution as large trucks servicing the limestone mine operate in this area.* Drive down the hill to the Spring River, cross over to the south bank and make an immediate left into a parking area next to the river. There is no sign for the turn-off, which is at the end of the bridge on the left-hand side of the road. Once you make the hard left into the parking area, turn your vehicle north toward the river.

You are now facing the Spring River and are near the ford Sigel utilized to cross it. This was the last major obstacle confronting Sigel in his quest for safety. Despite the presence of the enemy and a river at his back, Sigel managed the withdrawal coolly and with commendable precision. Retreating in stages, he withdrew all of his men, guns and wagons without any reported loss. Once over the river, he pushed his men along the road to Carthage, more than a mile distant.

Turn and look southeast toward town and you will see that the ground rises slightly ahead of you. This is where Sigel deployed several artillery pieces as further insurance against any unwelcome incursion by the Missouri State Guard. According to local legend, Sigel was unable to get two of the guns off Ordnuff Hill and across the river. Unwilling to allow them to fall into the hands of the enemy, so the myth goes, the German officer buried them on a small island in the middle of the Spring River. As legends go it is a good one. Artillerists Christian Essig and Theodore Wilkins, however, would have found the story amusing, since they eventually arrived in Springfield with all of their well-served guns accounted for. The rumor, however, persists to this day.

The Carthage Town Square

Return to your car and continue the drive toward Carthage. Be careful pulling out into traffic, because it is difficult to see the cars and trucks coming off the bridge. Your next stop is the Carthage town square. Drive one-half (0.5) of a mile south on Civil War Avenue to Central Avenue. Turn left onto Central Avenue and head back toward Carthage. Drive in the right hand lane until you get to Garrison Avenue. Turn right at the traffic light on Garrison. Go two blocks and make a left after the first traffic light onto Fourth Street. You will see signs posted along this street indicating that this is a historic district. Stay on Fourth Street and drive into the town square.

Park in the town square and stroll along its sidewalks. After hours of fighting and marching, Sigel and the vanguard of his column entered the square early on the evening of July 5. The colonel told some of the locals that all was well and they had nothing to worry about. Within a short while, however, Rebel solid shot were landing in the square and striking the court house. The area was soon choked with retreating infantry, artillery pieces, wagons and distraught civilians. Remarkably, some of the stores remained open and continued selling goods to the soldiers.

Although Sigel had hoped to remain in the Carthage town square long enough to rest and feed his exhausted men, pressure from the approaching State Guard (and the irksome artillery shells) forced him to evacuate sooner then he intended. The Federal column marched out of Carthage the same way it had entered the town earlier that morning, out Chestnut Street and onto the Sarcoxie Road. Sigel left behind several small but well-positioned squads of men in order to slow down the Confederates and keep his line of communications open.

With darkness almost upon them, the men of the Missouri State Guard finally got their second wind. The Southerners had used the delay along the Spring River to reorganize and rest. Advancing south of the river, Richard Weightman's men, together with those of William Slack and Mosby Parsons, closed in on the town from three sides. Bits and pieces of the Southern cavalry also made an appearance, striking the wagon train and harassing the retreating Federals. The fight was conducted, according to one Confederate source, "behind houses, walls and fences." One shell struck the bell above the Female Academy, which rang forth above the general tumult that had seized the town. (The bell can be seen today in the lobby of Carthage High School.)

You may wish to conclude your tour of the square by walking to where Fourth Street leaves the square. In this vicinity Sigel stretched a single company across the road. The situation was so confused by this time due to the growing darkness and powder smoke that Colonel Weightman's attacking infantry held its fire for fear of hitting friendly soldiers. Within a short time, however, Sigel's men were driven off and retreated after their comrades. The State Guard quickly occupied the town square and established a line of artillery pieces on the open ground a block east of the courthouse. From this point, the guns engaged the Federals, who had taken up a defensive position well east of town where the Sarcoxie Road intersected Chestnut Street.

TOUR STOP 12

Sigel's Chestnut Road Defensive Line

Exit the square on East Fourth Street (straight across the square from where you entered) and turn right on Howard Street. Drive two-tenths (0.2) of a mile to Chestnut Street. When you turn left onto East Chestnut Street (or Mill Road, as it was called in 1861), you are driving the final route of Sigel's retreat out of town. Turn right (south) onto Fulton Street and pull over and park as soon as possible. Walk back to the intersection of Fulton and Chestnut. In this area Sigel established yet another thin line of defense as he pulled his main column out of town. Just before dark Sigel deployed a company of soldiers on this small rise to check the advancing State Guard. In 1861, thick woods and heavy undergrowth covered the ground north of Chestnut Street (Mill Road). The rough terrain made it difficult for the Rebels to quickly locate and flank this position. The Federals held this line for a short time before withdrawing east.

TOUR STOP 13

The River Road Defensive Line

Return to your vehicle drive and east one-half (0.5) mile to the intersection of River Street and Chestnut Street. In the northeast corner of the intersection are two stone pillars. Travel through the intersection and turn left between the two pillars. The fourth of the original granite markers is just behind the stone pillar on your left (west).

River Street, which runs north-south, marked Sigel's final defensive position. The German colonel placed four guns parallel to road and supported them with infantry. Heavy undergrowth and a thicket of trees covered the hilly ground in front of this position. Although several units of the State Guard managed to launch a disjointed and piecemeal attack, the difficult terrain slowed the assault and disoriented the Southerners. The Union defenders received help in repelling the final attacks when two pieces of artillery on a small ridge above Carter's Spring (east of River Street) joined in the fight.

TOUR STOP 14

Carter's Spring

Return to the intersection of River Street and Chestnut. Reset or check your odometer. Your next turn is two-tenths (0.2) of a mile. Turn left (east) onto Chestnut, cross over the railroad tracks and turn left where the sign directs you to the Battle of Carthage State Historic Site.

You are now at Carter's Spring, where Sigel's Germans camped the night prior to the Battle of Carthage. The Federals left this area about 5:00 a.m. on July 5, when they marched through Carthage in search of the Missouri State Guard. By nightfall they had been driven back to their campground. The spring that gives the area its name is in the northwest corner of the park. Its waters flow into the Spring River. The level ground made for an easy bivouac and the high ground nearby was well suited for defense. Sigel's chief of artillery, Franz Backoff, deployed a pair of artillery pieces on the ridge overlooking the spring. At the time of the battle little in the way of vegetation clogged the ridge. The high ground presented the gunners with a fine field of fire overlooking the Chestnut Street–River Road intersection, where the State Guard was trying to break the final Union defensive line. The artillery position also covered the Sarcoxie Road, which Sigel used to withdraw from Carthage. The Sarcoxie Road is no longer in existence, although the railroad tracks running near the historic site approximates the wartime roadbed.

The two-story James family residence stood during the battle on the hill east of Sigel's artillery. According to legend, there is a small cave beneath the property that was a stop on the underground railroad. Dr. John A. Carter purchased the property after the war and built a Victorian mansion on the foundation of the home. In 1897, Carter donated the land Carter's Spring Park occupies today. The Battle of Carthage State Historic Sight was created from Carter's Spring Park in 1989 by an act of the General Assembly. The new park was dedicated on July 5, 1990, the one hundred and twenty-ninth anniversary of the engagement.

Aftermath

Although Sigel had been soundly defeated, he managed to avoid disaster by saving his small column and wagons from capture. The lack of adequate records, however, makes it difficult to set forth casualties with any certainty, especially for the state militia army.

Federal losses were reported by Sigel as 13 killed and 31 wounded. Given the several intense engagements, these figures are surprisingly low. Muster rolls reveal a slightly higher figure. Unfortunately, not a single report from any of Sigel's subordinates has surfaced to substantiate or disprove his claim.

Losses for the Missouri State Guard are more problematic. According to published battle reports, they were approximately 12 killed, 64 wounded and one missing. Given that the State Guard was on the offensive all day, these losses seem paltry indeed. [A detailed discussion of the losses suffered by the Confederates is included in Chapter Ten of this book.]

*   *   *

Optional Tour Stops

Cedar Hill Cemetery: Turn left out of the State Historic Site and drive up the hill three-tenths (0.3) of a mile. Turn right into the Cedar Hill Cemetery. Cedar Hill is one of the oldest cemeteries in southwestern Missouri. It seems more probable than not that some Confederate casualties from the battle are buried here.

Federal Monument for the Battle of Carthage: Drive west back toward Carthage on Chestnut Street and return to the town square. Exit the square on North Grant Street and turn left on Central Avenue. Travel west on Central until you reach Baker Avenue, which crosses Central on a north-south axis. Turn left onto Baker and drive to West Budlong Street. Turn right onto Budlong, which is a dead end street. Proceed up Budlong until it dead ends, and turn right into the back portion of the Carthage cemetery, where you will find a stone monument to the Union soldiers.

This granite memorial is dedicated to the Union dead and those who served in the Union forces at Carthage. The monument, which was dedicated in 1905, was made possible by the Carthage Soldiers Memorial Association. Many veterans of the battle attended the ceremony. The marker reads as follows: "In Memory of the Brave Men Who Fell July 5, 1861, in The Battle Of Carthage." Situated at the southwestern edge of the cemetery, most people are not aware of its existence. The majority of the dead Federals from the battle were removed to the National Cemetery at Springfield, Missouri.

The Kendrick Place: Kendrick Place is north of the Spring River. The best way to get to the historic house is to drive to the intersection of Central Avenue—Garrison Avenue—Highway 571. When you reach the intersection turn north toward the Spring River on Highway 571 and proceed over the Spring River bridge. The Kendrick House is approximately one mile past the bridge at the intersection of Highways 571 and V on the right side.

The handsome two-story brick house, built in 1849-54 by slave labor, is one of the few ante-bellum homes still standing in Carthage. It was used by both sides during the Civil War for various purposes and somehow escaped the destruction that swept across Jasper County. The house and grounds were used as a hospital for the wounded Southerners in the days following the battle. On October 17, 1863, the Kendrick residence was the scene of light fighting when Col. Jo Shelby's troopers engaged in a skirmish west of the house (popularly known as the Second Battle of Carthage). The Kendrick House was purchased by Victorian Carthage, Inc. in 1989 and developed into a historical interpretive center. Guided tours of the facility and the grounds are available.

A Note for Victorian Enthusiasts: Carthage contains a magnificent collection of Victorian homes built during the mining boom. For information on a walking and driving tour of these well-maintained mansions, visit the Chamber of Commerce office, located on the town square in Carthage.

Notes

Prologue

1. William E. Parrish, *Missouri: A Turbulent Partnership*, 4 vols. (Columbia, 1973), vol. 3, p. 25.

2. Stephen D. Engle, *Yankee Dutchman: The Life of Franz Sigel* (Fayetteville, 1993), pp. 62-63. Engle's excellent book is the only recent biography of Sigel.

3. Ibid., p. 63.

4. United States War Department, *The War of the Rebellion, A Compilation of The Official Records of the Union and Confederate Armies*, 128 vols. (Washington DC, 1890-1902), series I, vol. 3, pp. 16-18, hereinafter cited as *OR*. All references are to series I.

Chapter 1: Discontent

1. William E. Parrish, Charles T. Jones, and Lawrence O. Christensen, *Missouri: The Heart of the Nation* (Columbia, 1980), pp. 50-51.

2. Ibid.

3. Floyd C. Shoemaker, *Missouri's Struggle for Statehood* (Jefferson City, 1916), pp. 56-58.

4. Parrish, *Heart of the Nation*, p. 52.

5. Ibid., pp. 136-144.

6. Ibid., pp. 142-144; Albert E. Castel, *A Frontier State at War, 1861-1865* (Lawrence, 1948), pp. 3-11; James C. Malin, "The Pro-slavery Background to the Kansas Struggle," *MVHR*, vol. 10 (1923), pp. 285-305.

7. Parrish, *Heart of the Nation*, pp. 142-144; Kenneth S. Davis, *Kansas: A Bicentennial History* (New York, 1976), pp. 62-70.

8. Ibid., pp. 99-108; Arthur R. Kirkpatrick, "Missouri on the Eve of the Civil War," *Missouri Historical Review*, vol. 55 (1961), pp. 99-108. Subsequent references to *Missouri Historical Review* articles are cited *MHR*.

9. Ibid., pp. 99; Floyd C. Shoemaker, "Missouri, Heir of Southern Tradition and Individuality," *MHR*, vol. 36 (1942), pp. 435-438.

10. Kirkpatrick, "Missouri on the Eve of the Civil War," *MHR*, vol. 55 (1961), p. 100-103.

11. Parrish, *Turbulent Partnership*, 3. pp. 2-3.

12. Ibid., p. 3.

13. Ibid., p. 3; Doris D. Wallace, "The Political Campaign of 1860 in Missouri," *MHR*, vol. 70 (1976), pp. 162-183.

14. Parrish, *Turbulent Partnership*, 3, p. 7; Kirkpatrick, "Missouri on the Eve of the Civil War," *MHR*, vol. 55 (1961), p. 98-102.

15. Duane G. Meyer, *The Heritage of Missouri* (St. Louis, 1971), pp. 352-354; Parrish, *Turbulent Partnership*, p. 7-8; Harrison A. Trexler, "Slavery in the Missouri Territory," *MHR*, vol. 3 (1909), pp. 179-198; Phillip V. Scarpino, "Slavery in Callaway County Missouri: 1845-1855," pt. 1, *MHR*, vol. 71 (1976), pp. 22-43.

16. Meyer, *The Heritage of Missouri*, p. 352-354; Kirkpatrick, "Missouri on the Eve of the Civil War," *MHR*, vol. 55 (1961), p. 106.

Chapter 2: The Germans

1. Virgil C. Blum, "The Political and Military Activities of the German Element in St. Louis 1859-1861," *MHR*, vol. 42 (1948), pp. 103-105. For a more complete discussion of the German Revolution of 1848 and Franz Sigel's role therein, see Engle, *Yankee Dutchman*, pp. 1-23.

2. Parrish, *Heart of the Nation*, pp. 225-230. Readers seeking additional information on St. Louis' population matrix and immigration issues during this period should refer to J. Thomas Scharf, *History of St. Louis City and County*, 2 vols. (Philadelphia, 1883); Parrish, *Turbulent Partnership*, p. 9;

James W. Goodrich, "Gottfried Duden: a Nineteenth Century Missouri Promoter," *MHR*, vol. 75 (1980), pp. 142-143. The German community differentiated between the Germans who arrived prior to 1848 by calling them "Grays." Those who emigrated to America after the Revolution of 1848 were referred to as "Greens." According to the 1860 Census, the population of St. Louis was 160,733. Germans comprised almost one-third of that number (50,510).

3. A. A. Dunson, "Notes on the Missouri Germans on Slavery," *MHR*, vol. 59 (1964), pp. 355-60; *Mississippi Blatter*, March 27, 1859; Perry McCandless, *A History of Missouri 1820-1860*, 2 vols., (Columbia, 1972), pp. 147-148.

4. Virgil C. Blum, "The Political and Military Activities of the German Element," *MHR*, vol. 61 (1948), p. 109; Engle, *Yankee Dutchman*, p. 39.

5. William E. Smith, *The Francis Preston Blair Family in Politics* (New York, 1933), pp. 404-406; Virgil C. Blum, "The Political and Military Activities of the German Element," *MHR*, vol. 61 (1948), p. 111.

6. Ibid., p. 112. The Wide Awakes were originally formed to provide protection for speakers promoting the Republican platform; *Anzeiger des Westens*, October 22, 1860.

7. Virgil C. Blum, "The Political and Military Activities of the German Element,"p. 112.

8. Ibid., p. 113.

9. Galusha Anderson, *The Story of a Border City During the Civil War* (Boston, 1908), pp. 22-23; Christopher Phillips, *Damned Yankee: the Life of General Nathaniel Lyon* (Columbia, 1990), pp. 137-138; William E. Reed, "Secessionist Strength in Missouri," *MHR*, vol. 72 (1977), p. 421.

10. Phillips, *Damned Yankee*, pp. 143-144.

11. Tom Dyer, The Liberty Arsenal, *The Western Campaigner: Journal of the Missouri Civil War Reenactors Association* (June 1995), p. 3. The arsenal, originally called the Missouri Depot, was built on a bluff overlooking the Missouri River just south of the small frontier community of Liberty. The depot was intended to serve as a fort to guard the frontier inhabitants from Indians, as well as serve as a repository for Federal equipment. The complex was approximately 200 feet by 200 feet with a factory, officers quarters, barracks and a two story storehouse. The arsenal was involved in the sectional conflict prior to 1861 during the sectional strife commonly known as "Bleeding Kansas," when Missourians and

Kansans battled over various slavery issues. In the 1850s Missouri citizens raided the depot and removed arms and ammunition used during illegal voting trips into Kansas. When the arsenal was sacked in 1861, Major Grant, ever the dutiful officer, kept a detailed list of the items removed. Some of the more prominent items involved: 3 six-pound brass guns, 12 six-pound iron guns, 1,000 pounds of cannon powder, 9,990 pounds of musket powder, 180,000 musket buck and ball cartridges, flint, 224 percussion rifles, brass mountings, 166 six-pound cannon balls and hundreds of cartridge boxes, belts, buckles, tools, etc. None of the items were ever recovered by the Federal government. The United States sold the arsenal in 1869. Major Grant, still in command of the facility, supervised the closing of the post.

12. James Peckham, *General Nathaniel Lyon, and Missouri in 1861* (New York, 1866), p. 28.

13. Phillips, *Damned Yankee*, pp. 134-137.

14. Winter, *The Civil War in St. Louis: A Guided Tour* (St. Louis, 1994), p. 31; *Missouri Democrat*, January 8 and 9, 1861.

15. Anderson, *A City at War*, p. 62; Winter, *The Civil War in St. Louis: A Guided Tour*, p. 31; Phillips, *Damned Yankee*, pp. 138-139.

16. Anderson, *A City at War*, pp. 62-70; Phillips, *Damned Yankee*, pp. 138-141.

17. Phillips, *Damned Yankee*, pp. 138-139. Smith, *Borderland in the Civil War*, pp. 116-122. Frost was a northerner who supported the pro-Southern position in St. Louis. He was born in New York and graduated from the U.S. Military Academy at West Point in 1844. Frost was brevetted for gallantry during the Mexican War and resigned from the army in 1853. A staunch supported of Governor Jackson, he was paroled in St. Louis after his capture at Camp Jackson. He declined a request to command a small brigade at the Battle of Elkhorn Tavern (Pea Ridge), and later served as an adjutant for Braxton Bragg and Thomas Hindman. In 1863, when his wife was banished from St. Louis because of her family's Confederate sympathies, Frost left the army (without submitting a formal resignation) and spent the remainder of the war with his family in Canada. He returned in 1865 and farmed his property outside St. Louis. He died in 1900. Patricia L. Faust, ed., *Historical Times Illustrated Encyclopedia of the Civil War* (New York, 1986), pp. 293-294.

18. Phillips, *Damned Yankee*, pp. 139-140; John McElroy, *Struggle for Missouri* (Washington DC, 1909), pp. 42-43.

19. Peckham, *Lyon and Missouri*, p. 111; Phillips, *Damned Yankee*, pp. 138-139.

20. Ibid., pp. 139-140.

21. Ibid.

22. Ibid., pp. 142-143.

23. Ibid.

24. Ibid.

25. Ibid., pp. 142-146; Peckham, *Lyon and Missouri*, p. 67; Robert J. Rombauer, *The Union Cause in St. Louis in 1861* (St. Louis, 1909), pp. 128-129; William Harney was no stranger to controversy. In 1846, he was promoted to colonel, which made him the senior cavalry officer under General Winfield Scott. Scott did not trust Harney's judgment and relieved him from command. His dismissal caused an uproar in the United States, especially in the south. Although Scott was the Army's commanding general he was overruled by President James K. Polk, who reinstated Harney. Harney went on to distinguish himself both in Mexico and in subsequent fighting on the plains against the indians. In 1858 he became involved in an anti-British movement in the Caribbean. In order to get him away from a brewing scandal, he was transferred to the Department of the West in St. Louis. Harney retired to his farm south of St. Louis. He also had an estate in Pass Christian, Mississippi.

26. McElroy, *Struggle for Missouri*, pp. 53; Phillips, *Damned Yankee*, p. 143; Rombauer, *Union Cause*, p. 100.

27. McElroy, *Struggle for Missouri*, p. 61; Phillips, *Damned Yankee*, pp. 155-156. Governor Jackson's refusal to allow the recruitment of forces for the United States led to the resignation of several officers and men from the state militia, especially those of German ancestry.

28. Winter, *Civil War in St. Louis*, p. 31; Phillips, *Damned Yankee*, p. 156; Kirkpatrick, "Missouri on the Eve of the Civil War," *MHR*, vol. 55 (1961), p. 156.

29. *Anzeiger des Westens*, April 16, 1861.

30. *The Westliche Post*, April 19, 1861; *Mississippi Blatter*, April 20, 1861; *Kansas City Business Journal*, April 15, 1861; *OR* 3, p. 669; John M. Schofield, *Forty-six Years in the Army* (New York, 1897), pp. 33-37; James Neal Primm, *Germans For A Free Missouri: Translations from the St. Louis Radical Press, 1857-1862* (Columbia, 1993), pp. 179-180; *Mississippi Blatter*, April 20, 1861.

31. Rombauer, *Union Cause*, p. 100; Engle, *Yankee Dutchman*, p. 46.

32. Phillips, *Damned Yankee*, p. 154; McElroy, *Struggle for Missouri*, pp. 59-60.

33. Ibid., pp. 88-92; Phillips, *Damned Yankee*, pp. 158-159.

34. Phillips, *Damned Yankee*, p. 151. Peckham, *Lyon and Missouri*, p. 107-109; O.D. Finley to Montgomery Blair, April 19, 1861, box 29, Library of Congress; Benjamin Farrar to Salmon P. Chase, April 20, 1861, Civil War Collection Missouri Historical Society; W. W. Greene to Edward Bates, April 22, 1861; *OR* 3, pp. 671-672. Charles Gibson to Bates, April 22, 1861 Missouri Historical Society Civil War Collection; Marvin E. Cain, *Lincoln's Attorney General: Edward Bates of Missouri* (Columbia, 1965), pp. 98-115. The term of enlistment into Federal service for units raised in May 1861 was ninety days.

35. Rombauer, *Union Cause*, pp. 188-189; Winter, *Civil War in St. Louis*, pp. 42-47; McElroy, *Struggle for Missouri*, pp. 63-64; Phillips, *Damned Yankee*, pp. 156-158. The colonel of the 4th Missouri is sometimes referred to as "Schittner." His company manufactured brick molds. Henry Boernstein, commander of the 2nd Missouri, was the powerful publisher of the German language newspaper *Anzeiger des Westens*.

36. Parrish, *Heart of the Nation*, pp. 173-174.

37. Snead, *Fight for Missouri*, p. 62. The Militia Act of 1858 allowed the governor to call out any part of the militia for one week of training per year.

38. Phillips, *Damned Yankee*, pp. 177-78. Robert E. Miller, "Daniel Marsh Frost, C.S.A.," *MHR*, vol. 85 (July 1991), pp. 385-391.

39. Peckham, *Lyon and Missouri*, p. 136; Phillips, *Damned Yankee*, pp. 179-182; *OR* 3, pp. 386-387. The crates held two 24-lb. howitzers, an 8-inch siege mortar, six cohorn mortars and 500 muskets with ammunition.

40. Ibid., pp. 183-184.

41. Ibid., pp. 186-188; Rombauer, *Union Cause*, p. 225; Anderson, *Border City at War*, pp. 94-96; Winter, *Civil War in St. Louis*, pp. 40-45. Winter's research tracks Nathaniel Lyon's movement through St. Louis, and the overlay maps that appear in his book add substantially to our understanding of this confusing event.

42. Phillips, *Damned Yankee*, pp. 190-191; Winter, *Civil War in St. Louis*, pp. 40-45; Peggy Robbins, "The Battle of Camp Jackson: Street Fighting in St. Louis," *Civil War Times Illustrated* (June 1981), p. 40.

43. Robbins, "Battle of Camp Jackson," pp. 40-45. U. S. Grant operated a business in St. Louis during this period, while William T. Sherman was president of a street car company. They were on opposite sides of the street during the affair; Winter, *Civil War in St. Louis*, pp. 44-46.

44. Ibid.; *OR* 3, pp. 5-6.

45. Phillips, *Damned Yankee*, p. 182; Winter, *Civil War in St. Louis*, pp. 40-53; Peggy Robbins, "The Battle of Camp Jackson," pp. 40-45; Harvey L. Carter and Norma L. Peterson, "William S. Stewart Letters, January 13, 1861 to December 4, 1862," *MHR*, vol. 61 (1967), p. 122.

46. *The Westliche Post*, May 15, 1861.

47. *The Missouri Republican*, May 15, 1861.

48. Thomas L. Snead, "The First Year of the War in Missouri," in Robert U. Johnson and Clarence C. Buell, eds., *Battles and Leaders of the Civil War*, 4 vols. (New York, 1884-1890), vol. 1, pp. 265-267; Phillips, *Damned Yankee*, p. 194; Albert Castel, *General Sterling Price and the Civil War in the West* (Baton Rouge, 1968), p. 14. Castel's book on Price is by far the best biography available on this enigmatic ex-governor and Southern general.

49. Peckham, *Lyon and Missouri*, p. 190; Snead, *The Fight for Missouri*, p. 56.

50. McElroy, *Struggle for Missouri*, p. 97; Robert E. Shalope, *Sterling Price: Portrait of a Southerner* (Columbia, 1971), p. 161. See also, generally, Castel, *General Sterling Price*, for a full biography and more background on Price; Logan U. Reavis, *The Life and Military Services of William Selby Harney* (St. Louis, 1878), p. 388-392; *OR* 3, p. 383; Peckham, *Lyon and Missouri*, pp. 220-221.

51. Castel, *General Sterling Price*, pp. 14-15; Phillips, *Damned Yankee*, pp. 204-205; Reavis, *Harney*, pp. 277-278.

52. Ibid., p. 381; Montgomery Blair to Frank Blair, Civil War Collection, Missouri State Historical Society; Smith, *Borderland in the Civil War*, p. 256; *OR* 3, p. 383. After his removal, Harney traveled by train to Washington D.C., to protest his dismissal, just as he had the first time earlier in his career. This time he was not as fortunate. His train was captured by Confederate forces at Harpers Ferry, Virginia, and Harney was taken to Richmond as a prisoner. He released soon thereafter. Mark Boatner, *Civil War Dictionary* (New York, 1959), p. 376, claims that General Harney was relieved on May 29, 1861. The more credible source cited here, Reavis, *Harney*, pp. 277-278, disputes Boatner. Based on this evidence, we believe May 30, 1861 is the correct date of his dismissal.

53. Peckham, *Lyon and Missouri*, pp. 220-221.

54. Phillips, *Damned Yankee*, pp. 211-214; Castel, *General Sterling Price*, p. 24; Snead, *The Fight for Missouri*, pp. 198-200; *The Missouri*

Democrat, July 2, 1861; Peckham, *Lyon and Missouri,* p. 248; Shalope, *Sterling Price,* p. 166; Winter, *Civil War in St. Louis,* p. 67.

55. Dorothy G. Holland, "The Planters House," *Bulletin of the Missouri Historical Society,* vol. 28 (January, 1972), pp. 109-117; Phillips, *Damned Yankee,* p. 215; Castel, *General Sterling Price,* p. 25; Snead, *The Fight for Missouri,* p. 200; *Missouri Democrat,* July 2, 1861; Peckham, *Lyon and Missouri,* p. 248; Shalope, *Sterling Price,* p. 167.

56. Peckham, *Lyon and Missouri,* p. 248; Shalope, *Sterling Price,* p. 168.

57. Richard C. Peterson, James E. McGhee, Kip A. Lindberg and Keith I. Daleen, *Sterling Price's Lieutenants: A Guide to Officers and Organization of the Missouri State Guard 1861-1865* (Shawnee Mission, 1995), pp. 11-12.

58. Ibid.

59. Castel, *General Sterling Price,* p. 27.

Chapter 3: Boonville

1. *OR* 53, pp. 696-698; Castel, *General Sterling Price,* pp. 25-26; Snead, *The Fight for Missouri,* pp. 210-220. An in-depth sketch of the life of John B. Clark, Sr., whose career is often confused with that of his son, John B. Clark, Jr., (who led a regiment in his division), is found in Ezra Warner and Buck Yearns, *Biographical Register of the Confederate Congress* (Baton Rouge, 1975), pp. 49-50. See also, Paul Rorvig, "The Significant Skirmish: Battle of Boonville, June 17, 1861," *MHR,* vol. 86 (1992), pp. 135-136 for information on the early movements and planning that led to the fight at Boonville. Dr. Rorvig's article is the best available scholarly study of this important early-war skirmish.

2. National Historical Company, *History of Cooper County, Missouri* (St. Louis, 1882), pp. 234-235; The Eighth Census of the United States, 1860, pp. 286-287. For a more complete discussion of the effect of slavery in Little Dixie, see generally, R. Douglas Hurt, *Agriculture and Slavery in Missouri's Little Dixie;* Castel, *General Sterling Price,* pp. 25-26; Snead, *Fight for Missouri,* p. 204; Rorvig, "Battle of Boonville," p. 137.

3. Phillips, *Damned Yankee,* p. 216; Peckham, *Lyon and Missouri,* pp. 254-255.

4. Ibid., p. 255; Snead, *Fight for Missouri,* pp. 268-269.

5. Phillips, *Damned Yankee,* p. 215; Peckham, *Lyon and Missouri,* p. 255.

6. Phillips, *Damned Yankee,* pp. 216-217; Adamson, *Rebellion in Missouri,* pp. 121-122.

7. Ibid., pp. 115-116.

8. Ezra J. Warner, *Generals in Blue* (Baton Rouge, 1964), pp. 491-492; Elmo Ingenthron, *Borderland Rebellion* (Branson, 1980), p. 62.

9. Ibid., pp. 62-63.

10. Engle, *Yankee Dutchman*, p. 61; Phillips, *Damned Yankee*, pp. 215-216.

11. Rorvig, "Battle of Boonville," p. 137. Rorvig's article is the best available scholarly study on the circumstances leading up to Boonville and the engagement itself. Rorvig, unlike other writers, appreciates the significance this early-war skirmish had on the war in Missouri. For details on Sterling Price's illness, see Jack Welsh, *Medical Histories of Confederate Generals* (Kent, 1995), p. 177.

12. Rorvig, "Battle of Boonville," p. 136; *OR* 3, pp. 13-14; Adamson, *Rebellion in Missouri*, pp. 123-124; Phillips, *Damned Yankee*, pp. 216-217.

13. Ibid., pp. 216; Adamson, *Rebellion in Missouri*, pp. 117-118, Castel, *Price*, pp. 25-26; Rorvig, "Battle of Boonville," pp. 137-138.

14. Castel, *General Sterling Price*, pp. 25-26; Phillips, *Damned Yankee*, p. 217-218; Rorvig, "Battle of Boonville," pp. 138-139.

15. Phillips, *Damned Yankee*, p. 218-220; *OR* 3, p. 13; *Missouri Democrat*, June 17, 1861; Peckham, *Lyon and Missouri*, pp. 269-270.

16. *OR* 3, p. 13; Phillips, *Damned Yankee*, p. 220. A few period maps depict the river road as the Rocheport Road. Rorvig, "Battle of Boonville," pp. 139-140.

17. *OR* 3, p. 13; Rorvig, "Battle of Boonville," pp. 140-141.

18. Ibid., p. 142.

19. *OR* 3, p. 13; Rorvig, "Battle of Boonville," p. 142. Whether or not the Missouri State Guard employed artillery at Boonville depends on the source you consult. Rorvig's is the most dependable. Snead, *Fight for Missouri*, pp. 212-213, fails to mention any artillery, while William Switzler, the reporter for the *Missouri Democrat*, refers to one six pounder. *Missouri Democrat*, June 17, 1861. Nathaniel Lyon's report, *OR* 3, p. 13, records the capture of two pieces at the armory after the battle. Newspaper accounts—there were four reporters traveling with Lyon's army—fail to mention any Southern artillery fire during the fight. The only artillery fire reported came from Totten's guns and the howitzer on the steamboat. No Confederate reports on the battle have been found. See also, *Columbia Missouri Statesman*, June 21, 1861; Thomas W. Knox, *Camp-fire and*

Cotton Field: Southern Adventure in the Time of War (Philadelphia, 1865), pp. 43-44; Adamson, *Rebellion in Missouri*, pp. 126-127.

20. Rorvig, "Battle of Boonville," p. 142.

21. *Columbia Missouri Statesman*, June 21, 1861; Thomas W. Knox, *Camp-fire and Cotton Field: Southern Adventure in the Time of War* (Philadelphia, 1865), pp. 43-44.

22. Rorvig, "Battle of Boonville," p. 142; Castel, *General Sterling Price*, p. 26; Phillips, *Damned Yankee*, p. 220.

23. Rorvig, "Battle of Boonville," p. 146; *Missouri Democrat*, June 17, 1861; *OR* 3, pp. 10-14. For additional information on Boonville, see John Barnes, "Boonville: The First Land Battle of the Civil War," *Infantry Journal*, 35 (December, 1929), pp. 601-607.

24. Snead, *Fight for Missouri*, p. 214.

Chapter 4: Advance

1. Castel, *General Sterling Price*, p. 26; *OR* 3, p. 14; Snead, *The Fight for Missouri*, pp. 210-214; Rorvig, "Battle of Boonville," p. 142.

2. Richard N. Current, ed. In Chief, *Encyclopedia of the Confederacy*, 4 vols. (New York, 1993) vol. 4, p. 1432. See also, Ezra J. Warner, *Generals in Gray* (Baton Rouge, 1959), p. 278; James A. Payne, "Fighting in Missouri," *Confederate Veteran*, 40 vols. (Nashville, 1930), vol. 38, p. 307, who fought with William Slack, described him as "an officer of energy and decision."

3. John Drummond, "James S. Rains," *Missouri Historical Society*, John Drummond File # 57 (ND); Bruce S. Allardice, *More Generals in Gray* (Baton Rouge, 1995), p. 190. The twenty-fifth Missouri Senate district included the counties of Dade, Polk, Cedar and Jasper. It is interesting to note that Rains (and Col. Richard Weightman) filed reports after Carthage listing their division as the "Second Division," rather than the Eighth Division, even though there is little doubt that Rains' command was indeed designated the latter. *OR* 3, pp. 20, 22. Rains' subordinate cavalry officers, including Robert Peyton, James McCown and Robert Boughan all correctly used the "Eighth Division" affiliation. Ibid., pp. 25, 27, 29. This exemplifies the confusion within the ranks of the Missouri State Guard at this early state of the conflict. See also Krick, *Lee's Colonels*, p. 490, and his listing showing Richard Weightman with the "8th Division."

4. McElroy, *Struggle for Missouri*, p. 128; Castel, *General Sterling Price*, p. 26.

5. Snead, *Fight for Missouri*, pp. 215-216; Castel, *General Sterling Price*, p. 26; Adamson, *Rebellion in Missouri*, p. 131; Shalope, *Sterling Price*, p. 167. Price was indeed correct; Lexington did not offer any significant defensive advantages. As if to prove that point, Price captured a Union garrison there on September 19-20, 1861. According to Joseph Crute, *Confederate Staff Officers* (Powhatan, 1982), pp. 38, 159, Thomas Snead served on the staff of Col. John B. Clark, Jr., shortly after the Battle of Carthage. He held many positions on Sterling Price's staff, including: AAG, March and July, 1862; chief of staff, September 1862; A.A.G., March 1864. He resigned from Price's staff on June 23, 1864. His resignation stemmed from his May election to the Confederate Congress from the First Congressional district of Missouri. His career in that legislative body was undistinguished. Warner and Yearns, *The Confederate Congress*, p. 229.

6. Snead, *Fight for Missouri*, pp. 214-216; Shalope, *Sterling Price*, p. 167.

7. Virginia Easley, ed., "Journal of the Civil War in Missouri: 1861 Henry Martyn Cheavens," *MHR*, vol. 56 (1961), pp. 14-15.

8. Ibid., p. 15.

9. Peckham, *Lyon in Missouri*, p. 258.

10. Ibid., p. 258.

11. Adamson, *Rebellion in Missouri*, p. 137-138; *OR* 3, p. 388.

12. Peckham, *Lyon and Missouri*, pp. 259-260; Adamson, *Rebellion in Missouri*, p. 129.

13. Ibid.; Frank J. Welcher, *The Union Army, 1861-1865, Organization and Operations: The Western Theater*, 2 vols. (Bloomington, 1993), vol. 2, pp. 680-681.

14. Peckham, *Lyon and Missouri*, pp. 259-260.

15. Ibid.

16. *Mississippi Blatter*, June 16, 1861.

17. Adamson, *Rebellion in Missouri*, pp. 119-122; Welcher, *The Union Army*, pp. 678-679. The Home Guard troops under McNeil and Gratz were also known as the Unites States Reserve Corps. Ibid. Prior to his departure, Lyon issued orders commandeering the necessary rail cars and clearing the Southwest Branch of the Union Pacific Railroad from St. Louis to its terminus one hundred miles southwest at Rolla.

18. The St. Louis *Missouri Democrat*, June 13, 1861; Ingenthron, *Borderland Rebellion*, pp. 62-63; Adamson, *Rebellion in Missouri*, p. 122; *Westliche Post*, May 8, 1861; Engle, *Yankee Dutchman*, pp. 62-63; Ella Lonn, *Foreigners in the Army and Navy* (Baton Rouge, 1951), pp. 180-181; Adolf E. Zucker, ed., *The Forty-Eighters: Political Refugees of the German Revolution of 1848* (New York, 1950), pp. 186-188. Primm, *Germans for a Free Missouri*, pp. 195-197. The presentation of the flag was a proud event for the 3rd Missouri. The *Westliche Post* reported a large number of spectators gathered at the Arsenal for the ceremony, most of them ladies. The ceremony honoring the newly-made United State banner was led by Mrs. Josephine Weigel of the St. Louis German community. The flag was stitched in double silk. Embroidered across the faces of the red and white stripes were the following words: III. Regiment, MISSOURI VOLUNTEERS, Lyons Fahenwacht (Lyon's Color Guard). Mrs. Weigel presented the flag to Colonel Sigel after a short speech. The arsenal's guns boomed out a salute as Sigel unfurled the flag for display to the gathered crowd. Sigel responded with a short speech thanking the women, promising that his men would never desert the proud flag. After his remarks, Nathaniel Lyon and other dignitaries made a few short speeches. The regimental color guard marched the flag to the top of the hill and the entire regiment lined up in front of it, singing "Die Fahenwacht." Reportedly onlookers were surprised at the regiment's discipline and military bearing, especially since the men had only been in Federal service for a short time.

19. *Missouri Democrat*, June 13, 1861. According to Welcher, *The Union Army*, p. 679, Francis Hassendeubel's battalion left on June 11, followed two days later by Henry Bishoff's battalion and Franz Backoff's artillery.

20. Jay Monaghan, *Civil War on the Western Border* (Boston, 1955), p. 150; *Missouri Democrat*, June 12-14, 1861; Peckham, *Lyon and Missouri* p. 56; Engle, *Yankee Dutchman*, p. 62.

21. Monaghan, *Civil War on the Western Border*, p. 151; Phillips, *Damned Yankees*, p. 227; *Springfield Missouri Mirror*, July 4, 1861; *Anzeiger des Westens*, June 20, 1861.

22. Phillips, *Damned Yankee*, pp. 228-233.

23. *Missouri Democrat*, "News from Lyon's Campaign," July 17, 1861; Welcher, *The Union Army*, pp. 678-679.

24. *Missouri Democrat*, "News from Lyon's Campaign," July 17, 1861.

25. The *Springfield Mirror*, June 28, 1861; William G. Bek., "The Civil War Diary of John T. Buegel, Union Soldier," pt. 1, *MHR*, vol. 4 (1946), p. 311.

26. Ibid., p. 311.

27. "The Civil War Diary of John T. Buegel," p. 311.

28. Ingerthron, *Borderland Rebellion*, p. 89.

29. St. Louis Western Historical Company, *A History of Greene County* (St. Louis, 1883), pp. 286-290; Bek, ed., "Diary of John T. Buegel," p. 311.

30. *A History of Greene County*, pp. 288-290.

31. Ibid., p. 290; *Springfield Mirror*, July 4, 1861, Peckham, *Lyon and Missouri*, pp. 292-294; Phillips, *Damned Yankee*, p. 227; Welcher, *The Union Army*, pp. 678-679.

32. Adamson, *Rebellion in Missouri*, pp. 121-123.

33. *Springfield Mirror*, June 28, 1861; Welcher, *The Union Army*, pp. 678-679.

34. Ibid.; Adamson, *Rebellion in Missouri*, pp. 121-123.

35. Ibid., pp. 121-123; Sweeny's report is substantially different, and makes no mention of the Springfield mounted party. *OR* 3, p. 15.

36. Ibid.

Chapter 5: Unification

1. Snead, *Fight for Missouri*, p. 216-217; Castel, *General Sterling Price*, p. 27.

2. Salem Ford Letter to his Grandchildren, Ford Letter File, Missouri State Historical Society.

3. Elliot Ellsworth, Jr., *West Point and the Confederacy* (New York, 1942), pp. 315, 356, 393-394.; Peterson, *Sterling Price's Lieutenants*, pp. 14-15: William C. Davis, "Lewis Henry Little," William C. Davis, ed. *The Confederate General*, 6 vols. (Lancaster, 1991) vol. 4, pp. 78-79; Salem Ford Letter.

4. Peterson, *Sterling Price's Lieutenants*, pp. 14-15. These West Point-schooled officers included: Brig. Gen. Thomas A. Harris (Second Division), Col. Jesse L. Cravens (Fifth Cavalry Regiment), Lt. Col. Chaplin Good (Third Division), Maj. John C. Landis (First Artillery), Lt. George W. Bates (adjutant, Second Cavalry Regiment, Sixth Division). Ibid. Robert Krick, *Lee's Colonels* (Dayton, 1991), p. 473. In addition to listing valuable information on Army of Northern Virginia line officers, Krick includes an appendix with biographical listings of Confederate field officers from all theaters. This is a valuable and overlooked source. See also *OR* 3,

p. 30. Little is known of Edwin R. Price, who led the 1st Missouri Infantry in John B. Clark's Third Division. According to E. F. Ware, a private soldier in the Federal 1st Iowa, Edwin, nicknamed "stump," was "vain, ambitious, and ordinary; he never amounted to anything." E. F. Ware, *The Lyon Campaign* (Iowa City, 1991), p. 150.

5. Salem Ford Letter.

6. Adamson, *Rebellion in Missouri*, p. 132. It was difficult to differentiate between the Missouri State Guard members and the pro-Union Home Guard forces. The Home Guard was also clad in identically-dyed homespun. Miscellaneous Articles, Wilson Creek National Battlefield Vertical Files.

7. Snead, *Fight for Missouri*, p. 219.

8. Ibid.

9. Kathleen W. Miles, *Bitter Ground: The Civil War in Missouri's Golden Valley* (Warsaw, Mo., 1971), p. 72.

10. Ibid., p. 72.

11. Robert E. Miller, "General Mosby M. Parsons; Missouri's Secessionist General," *MHR*, vol. 80 (October, 1985), pp. 33-57; Warner, *Generals in Gray*, pp. 228-229.

12. Ibid.

13. Snead, *Fight for Missouri* p. 216.

14. E. B. Long, *The Civil War Day By Day* (New York, 1971), p. 87. There is a large disparity in casualties at this small affair. I have used Confederate historian Edward A. Pollard, *Southern History of the War*, 4 vols. (Fairfax, 1968), vol. 1, p. 106. 's numbers,. Federal casualties to be 23 killed, 20 wounded and 23 prisoners. *Dyer's Compendium*, p. 797, lists the Union losses at 15 killed, 62 wounded. The actual numbers probably are somewhere in between the two figures stated.

15. Adamson, *Rebellion in Missouri*, pp. 134-135. Unfortunately, the scarcity of firsthand accounts and reports makes it difficult to definitively set forth the precise routes of retreat, dates, etc., for the two wings of the State Guard. As a result, some dates and times are based upon the best available evidence and common sense.

16. Ibid., p. 136. Jeff Patrick, ed., "Remembering the Missouri Campaign of 1861: The Memoirs of Lieutenant W. P. Barlow, Guibor's Battery, MIssouri State Guard." This unpublished manuscript is scheduled to appear in *Civil War Regiments: A Journal of the American Civil War*, Vol. 5, No. 4 (1997). As of the publication of this book, exact page numbers were not available. Henry Guibor's Battery was formerly organized for service with the Confederacy in Febru-

ary 1862. Joseph Crute, *Units of the Confederate States Army* (Powhatan, 1987), p. 207.

17. Patrick, "Remembering the Missouri Campaign of 1861," note 9. John Bowen, who eventually attained the rank of major general, was one of the South's better tacticians. He fought gallantly in the Vicksburg Campaign and died of dysentery shortly after the city's surrender in July 1863. Faust, *Civil War Encyclopedia*, p. 73.

18. Patrick, "Remembering the Missouri Campaign of 1861"; Snead, *Fight for Missouri*, p. 217; Guibor Battery Roster, National Archives.

19. Patrick, "Remembering the Missouri Campaign of 1861." 20. Despite their improved efficiency, many outside of the artillery did not respect the army's long arm. "The battery quickly acquired a peculiar way of its own. The next day Col. Bob McCulloch joined the column by an intersecting road, at the head of a long string of mounted men, just as our guns were passing. Seeing the way blocked, the old gentleman bawled out `Get out of the way with them artillery wagons!' It has always been a mystery why the brave but kindly old man did not resent my indignant reply of `Go to hell.' Ibid. Also see, Peterson, *Sterling Price's Lieutenants*, pp. 14-15.

21. Snead, *Fight for Missouri*, p. 218; Jon L. *Wakelyn, Bibliographical Dictionary of the Confederacy* (Westport, 1977), pp. 247-248.

22. Snead, *Fight for Missouri*, p. 218; *OR* 3, p. 584.

23. Snead, *Fight for Missouri*, p. 219.

24. Shalope, *Sterling Price*, p. 167; Snead, *Fight for Missouri*, pp. 200-201; Adamson, *Rebellion in Missouri*, p. 133 ; Bevier, *The First and Second Missouri Confederate Brigades*, p. 35. Philip Thomas Tucker, *The South's Finest: The First Missouri Confederate Brigade From Pea Ridge to Vicksburg* (Shippensburg, 1993), p. 3. Although Price proved his popularity by rallying so many men to his banner, they would have better served Southern interests had they been present at Carthage instead of roaming south of the border on a diplomatic mission.

25. Easley, "Journal of the Civil War in Missouri," p. 15; Mills Historical Company, *History of Jasper County* (St. Louis, 1883), p. 231. While the Missouri State Guard used the term "division" to identify its primary components (Rains' Division, Slack's Division, etc.), the term had nothing to do with the size of the unit. Instead, it denoted a particular geographic region of the state from which the men were recruited. The size of the "divisions" varied greatly throughout 1861.

26. John P. Drummond, "Richard Hanson Weightman," Missouri Historical Society, The John Drummond File, No. 64.

27. James E. Payne, "Early Days of War in Missouri," *Confederate Veteran*, 39, pp. 58-59.

28. National Historical Company, *The History of Cass and Bates Counties* (St. Joseph, 1883), pp. 627-628; *History of Henry and St. Clair Counties, Missouri*, p. 503. Thomas Rosser's role during this part of the war is somewhat clouded. Although he commanded the First Regiment in Weightman's brigade, the regiment does not appear to have seen action at Carthage, and may be been unarmed. Richard C. Peterson, *Sterling Price's Lieutenants*, pp. 227-228. Hurst was only a captain at the time of the Carthage battle. He was promoted to colonel on June 19, 1861. Hurst left the State Guard in December of 1861. County histories cited above list Hurst as "murdered" by Union soldiers in June 1862, with little explanation.

29. Ward L. Schrantz, *Jasper County in the Civil War* (Carthage, 1923), p. 20. Hiram Bledsoe's Battery was formed in May of 1861 at Lexington, Missouri, in response to Nathaniel Lyon's activities in St. Louis. The two 6-lb. pieces (plus "Old Sacramento," reputed to be a 9-lb. iron gun) were vintage 1841. A brief editorial in *Confederate Veteran*, 28 (1920), p. 91, discusses the myth that "Old Sacramento" was cast of silver. Another piece, captured at Wilson's Creek, was later added to the battery, which was eventually mustered into Confederate service as Bledsoe's Light Artillery. Carolyn Bartles, *The Forgotten Men* (Shawnee Mission, 1995), p. 24. Bledsoe was a captain on June 11, 1861, and listed his home as being Lexington, Lafayette County, Missouri. There is some confusion about his age. According to Bledsoe's Compiled Service Record, his age at the time of enrollment was 31. When he was wounded at Pea Ridge in early March, 1862, however, he listed his age as 34. For more information on Bledsoe's Confederate service, see Crute, *Units of the Confederate States Army*, p. 205. As artillerists on both sides quickly discovered, light weight artillery was virtually useless by the 1860s, and the Mexican piece was eventually converted into a more traditional 12-lb. gun by boring out the muzzle. This may have been done before Carthage, for Colonel Weightman refers to it as a 12-lb. piece. *OR 3*, p. 22.

30. Ibid., pp. 20, 24; National Historical Company, 1866, *A History of Lafayette County*, p. 411. Peyton's Third Missouri contained several hundred men, although there were only arms and ammunition for about 115 of them by the time of the fight at Carthage, July 5, 1861.

31. Ibid.; *OR* 3, pp. 20, 25. Colonel Cravens apparently was not with the army at Carthage, although he reappears in the record and fought with the Missouri State Guard at Wilson's Creek. Lt. Col. Richard A. Boughan's name is routinely spelled several ways, including "Vaughan" and "Baughan." Although Rains reported him as commanding the Fourth Missouri Cavalry, he in fact led the Seventh Missouri Cavalry. *OR* 3, p. 29. Krick, *Lee's Colonels*, p. 421, gets the regiment right but places Boughan in the "1st Division."

32. *OR* 3, p. 20; *The History of Cass and Bates Counties*, pp. 376-379; John N. Edwards, *Shelby and His Men; or the War in the West* (Waverly, 1993), p. 56. Shelby was born in 1830 in Lexington, Kentucky, and moved to Waverly, Missouri in Lafayette County in 1849. He inherited his father's rope factory as well as his plantation, which made Shelby a rich man. By 1861 he was one of the wealthiest individuals residing along the Kansas-Missouri border. Shelby's sympathies toward the Southern cause grew during the Kansas-Missouri border troubles in the 1850s. Daniel O'Flaherty, *Jo Shelby: Undefeated Rebel* (Wilmington, 1987), p. 66.

33. Peterson, *Sterling Price's Lieutenants*, p. 143; Philip T. Tucker, *The South's Finest*, pp. 5-6. While the majority of Ben Rives' men from the First Cavalry Regiment were from Missouri, over 180 of them hailed from Kentucky, Virginia, North Carolina and Tennessee. Rives was the largest slave holder in Ray County at the outbreak of the Civil War.

34. Carolyn Bartles, *The Forgotten Men*, p. 39; Charles V. Duncan, *John T. Hughes, From His Pen* (Modesto, 1991), pp. 77-80.

35. Miles, *Bitter Ground*, p. 81; 1860 Barton County Census Records.

36. Adamson, *Rebellion in Missouri*, p. 136; Easley, "Journal of the Civil War in Missouri," p. 16.

37. Ibid., pp. 16-17; Van Gilder, "The Story of Barton County from 1858-1972," Carthage Press, n.d., 1972, pp. 10-12.

38. Easley, "Journal of the Civil War in Missouri," pp. 16-17.

39. Ibid., p. 17; Snead, "The First Year of the War in Missouri," p. 268.

40. Van Gilder, "History of Barton County," p. 10.

41. Ibid.; Patrick, "Remembering the Missouri Campaign of 1861."

42. Ibid.

43. Ibid. See note 25, supra, for an understanding of the size and organization of the Missouri State Guard "divisions."

44. Ibid.

45. Ibid.

46 Adamson, *Rebellion in Missouri*, p. 137.

47. Snead, *Fight for Missouri*, pp. 220-223; Adamson, *Rebellion in Missouri*, pp. 137.

48. Ibid., p.132.

49. Adamson, *Rebellion in Missouri*, p.132.

50. Ibid., p.132.

Chapter 6: Sigel's March

1. Carl Wittke, *The German Forty-Eighters in America* (Westport, 1970), pp. 191-192; Charles W. Dahlinger, *The German Revolution of 1848* (New York, 1903), pp. 146-147; Adolf E. Zucker, *The Forty-Eighters: Political Refugees of the German Revolution of 1849* (Columbia, 1950), pp. 280-282; Franz Sigel, "Memoirs," *The Nation*, 76 (January, 1903), pp. 35-36.

2. Adamson, *Rebellion in Missouri*, pp. 121-123.

3. Dahlinger, *Revolution of 1848*, pp. 220-224; Sigel's Papers, "Miscellaneous" Box 3; Sigel, "Memoirs," p. 36; Wittke, in *The Forty-Eighters America*, p. 193; Franz Sigel Collection, Western Reserve Historical Society, Cleveland, Ohio, autobiographical sketch, "Miscellaneous Letters and Memoirs." Engle, *Yankee Dutchman*, pp. 1-23, provides one of the best overviews of Sigel's early years in Europe.

4. Ibid.; Dahlinger, *Revolution of 1848*, pp. 220-224.

5. Ibid., pp. 220-221.

6. Wittke, *The Forty-Eighters in America*, pp. 220-224; Priscilla Robertson's *Revolution of 1848* offers a different account of Sigel's behavior at Rastatt. According to Robertson, Sigel's revolutionary army, stationed outside the fort, was to provide relief to those inside once provisions ran low. Reduced to a three day food supply, two officers left the fort hoping to find Sigel and receive relief. However, they quickly discovered, ". . .Sigel and his army had fled across the Swiss border, throwing down their arms, two weeks previously, and had forgotten, or been unable, to get word into Rastatt."

7. Franz Sigel Collection, Western Reserve Historical Papers, "Miscellaneous Letters and Memoirs"; Lucy M. Schwiener, "The St. Louis Public Schools at the Outbreak of the Civil War," *MHR*, vol. 13 (October, 1956), pp. 10-15; Lawrence E. Griffen, Sr., "The Strange Story of Major General Franz Sigel: Leader and Retreater," *MHR*, vol. 84 (July, 1990), pp. 404-410. Dr. Hammer

served with Sigel in the 1848 Revolution as a surgeon. He not only recruited Sigel to St. Louis but helped lead the 4th Missouri Volunteers, formed in 1861, while Sigel assumed command of the 3rd Missouri Volunteers. Although their careers were intertwined, the two men never served together in the same military campaign. Engle, *Yankee Dutchman*, p. 245n.

8. Lucy M. Schwienher, "The St. Louis Public Schools at the Outbreak of the Civil War," *MHR*, vol. 13 (October, 1956), pp. 10-15; Andreas Dorpalen, "The German Element and the Issues of the Civil War," *MVHR*, vol. 29 (January, 1942), pp. 61-64; *Anzeiger des Westens*, March 22, 1860; Wittke, *The German Forty-Eighters in America*, p. 193; Lawrence Giffen, Sr., "Sigel: Leader and Retreater," pp. 404-410; Franz Sigel Collection, Western Reserve Historical society, Cleveland, Ohio, Autobiographical Sketch, "Miscellaneous Letters and Memoirs."

9. *Anzeiger des Westens*, March 22, 1860.

10. Ibid., December 17, 1860; Engle, *Yankee Dutchman*, p. 46; Western Reserve Historical Society, *"Autobiographical"*; Schwienher, "St. Louis Public Schools at the Outbreak of the Civil War," *MHR*, vol. 13 (October, 1956), pp. 10-22; Engle, *Yankee Dutchman*, pp. 46-47. According to Engle, "Yankee Dutchman" was a positive reference to Sigel's allegiance to the Union; *Daily Missouri Democrat*, April 30, 1861.

11. *History of Greene County*, p. 256; Engle, *Yankee Dutchman*, pp. 62-63; Schrantz, *Jasper County in the Civil War*, pp. 29-31; Shalope, *Sterling Price*, pp. 167-170; Snead, "Early Years," pp. 269-270. In the Ozarks, much of the flat open spaces on the prairie were (and often still are) used for agricultural purposes. Pool's Prairie was probably named after a family that farmed that particular piece of land. Pool's Prairie should not be confused with Cowskin Prairie, the final destination of the Missouri State Guard. Pool's Prairie was about forty miles south of Neosho, while Cowskin Prairie was an additional 60 miles south.

12. Engle, *Yankee Dutchman*, pp. 62-63; Welcher, *The Union Army*, p. 680.

13. Harris and Phyllis Dark, *Springfield of the Ozarks: An Illustrated History* (Woodland Hills, 1981), p. 45.

14. Ibid., p. 46; Adamson, *Rebellion in Missouri*, p. 148; Engle, *Yankee Dutchman*, p. 62. See the Atlas accompanying the Official Records, Plate CLX.

15. Schrantz, *Jasper County in the Civil War*, p. 29; *OR* 3, p. 16.

16. Adamson, *Rebellion in Missouri*, p. 148; Marvin Van Gilder, "Centennial History of the Battle of Carthage," *Carthage Evening Press*, July 4, 1961. Van Gilder's richly detailed but undocumented account is a treasure trove of information that everyone interested in this battle should consult. Unfortunately, the only copy we could obtain was on microfilm. Its poor quality made it difficult to determine the page number upon which specific information is printed, and it was often difficult to determine the spelling of some names. The article is lengthy and broken up in columns. Being able to microfilm only small portions per page compounded our problem. Therefore, subsequent citations to this source may be listed without a page number. Of those listed, some may be incorrect, and we apologize in advance for any confusion this might cause.

17. Welcher, *The Union Army*, pp. 681-682.

18. Van Gilder, "Centennial History of the Battle of Carthage"; *OR* 3, p. 16.

19. Ibid.; *OR* 3, p. 15. Sigel does not mention in his report that he received orders from General Sweeny to concentrate with Colonel Salomon and move against Jackson's army. Instead, he claims that he ordered the concentration and determined the course of action that brought on the July 5 fighting at Carthage. If it were not true, why would he include it in a report prepared for Sweeny's inspection? On the other hand, why would Sweeny claim to have ordered a concentration of forces that came within a hair's breadth of being wiped out if he had not done so? Ibid., pp. 15-16.

20. Ibid., p. 16.

21. Adamson, *Rebellion in Missouri*, p. 149; Van Gilder, "Centennial History of the Battle of Carthage." The first names of Neosho's leaders are unknown.

22. Adamson, *Rebellion in Missouri*, p. 149; Van Gilder, "Centennial History of the Battle of Carthage"; *OR* 3, pp. 16-17.

23. Ibid.

24. Van Gilder, "Centennial History of the Battle of Carthage."

25. Ibid.; *OR* 3, p. 17; Engle, *Yankee Dutchman*, p. 63.

26. Van Gilder, "Centennial History of the Battle of Carthage."

27. Mills and Company, *History of Jasper County*, p. 229; Schrantz, *Jasper County in the Civil War*, p. 30. LaForce established a farm three miles northeast of Carthage even before the town existed. He was one of the most prominent members of the community and represented Jasper County in the State Assembly in 1851. LaForce declared his allegiance to the Union at the out-

break of hostilities. When Sigel retreated from the area, LaForce remained with him, eventually joining the Union Army (Company I, 152nd Illinois Infantry). He remained in his native state of Illinois for much of the war, but returned to Jasper county thereafter and again held several prominent county government positions.

28. Van Gilder, "Centennial History of the Battle of Carthage."

29. Mills and Company, *History of Jasper County*, p. 228.

30. Adamson, *Rebellion in Missouri*, p. 145; Van Gilder, "Centennial History of the Battle of Carthage"; Schrantz, *Jasper County in the Civil War*, p. 31; Mills and Company, *History of Jasper County*, p. 230.

31. Van Gilder, "Centennial History of the Battle of Carthage."

32. Ibid.; Adamson, *Rebellion in Missouri*, p. 145. See the Salem Ford Letter for a mention of the casualties. Claiborne Jackson demonstrated good judgment when he put a stop to Mosby Parsons' attempt to execute a night march, which would have been risky with the Sixth Division's untrained and ill-disciplined troops. In any event, the Missouri State Guard could not have reached the Spring River until long after sunrise. Salem Ford of Slack's Division, however, recalls the event differently, claiming the news reached camp about "day" and that "orders to march immediately" were received. Ford is mistaken. Salem Ford Letter. Despite the widespread commotion in camp that night, not everyone was aware that a skirmish had taken place. Private Cheavens, who does not even mention learning that the Federals were nearby until the morning of July 5, described the nighttime chaos as "a stampede of horses." It is possible, of course, that he was recording a wholly separate event. See note 2, Chapter 7, below. Easley, "Journal of the Civil War in Missouri," p. 17.

33. Van Gilder, "Centennial History of the Battle of Carthage."

34. Ibid.

Chapter 7: First Blood

1. Schrantz, *Jasper County in the Civil War*, p. 31.

2. Easley, "Journal of the Civil War in Missouri," p. 17. Since the official battle reports clearly indicate that the army did not march until 4:00 a.m., we chose to record Cheavens' stampede as an event separate from that that took place after nightfall on July 4, when word of the Spring River skirmish was received.

3. Ibid.; *OR* 3, p. 20.

4. Ibid., p. 17; Van Gilder, "Centennial History of the Battle of Carthage."

5. Ibid.

6. Ibid.; *OR* 3, p. 17.

7. Ibid., pp. 21, 27, 30; Schrantz, *Jasper County in the Civil War*, p. 35; O'Flaherty, *General Jo Shelby*, p. 67.

8. Van Gilder, "History of Barton County," p. 10.

9. Ibid.; Van Gilder, "Centennial History of the Battle of Carthage," p. 11.

10. O'Flaherty, *Undefeated Rebel*, p. 67. Van Gilder, "Centennial History of the Battle of Carthage," p. 11; The lack of canteens may account for much of the straggling during the battle.

11. Ibid.; *OR* 3, p. 21.

12. Easley, "Journal of the Civil War in Missouri," p. 17; *OR* 3, p. 21.

13. Ibid., p. 67; Mills and Company, *A History of Jasper County*, p. 300. Unfortunately, there is no information as to which companies Sigel deployed as skirmishers on July 5. The initial contact between the forces was three miles from the point of the opening artillery bombardment.

14. *OR* 3, p. 17.

15. Ibid.

16. Mills and Company, *A History of Jasper County*, p. 300; Van Gilder, "Centennial History of the Battle of Carthage," p. 13; *OR* 3, p. 17. In Jay Monaghan's *Civil War on the Western Border*, p. 152, the name Coon Creek is frequently used to refer to Dry Fork Creek (also referred to as Bear Creek). Other sources also make this mistake. The real Coon Creek is four miles north of the location where the first shots were exchanged. The State Guard crossed Coon Creek on their march to meet Sigel early that morning.

17. *OR* 3, pp. 17, 20-21; O'Flaherty, *Undefeated Rebel*, pp. 68-69.

18. OR 3, p. 20; Mills and Company, *A History of Jasper County*, p. 301. Van Gilder, "Centennial History of the Battle of Carthage," p. 13. The ridge line upon which the State Guard deployed is so gentle that it is difficult to spot if you are not searching for it.

19. Mills and Company, *A History of Jasper County*, p. 300. Van Gilder, "Centennial History of the Battle at Carthage," p. 13; OR 3, p. 17. The timing of the initial deployment of the armies and the beginning of the battle is open to legitimate debate. James Rains reported that his scouts first located the enemy in force about three miles in advance "about 7 a.m." Weightman claims he deployed for battle "about 8 o'clock," and "The engagement was begun about 8.30 o'clock." This coincides with Rains' estimates. But how could

Rains' men (and the rest of the state troops) have marched so many miles so quickly over such a poor road? Private Cheavens remembered the time as about "9½," meaning 9:30 a.m, (p. 17), while his regimental commander, Ben Rives, claimed the bombardment began about 10:00 a.m. *OR 3*, p. 34. Both John Clark and William Slack, however, claim the battle opened precisely at 11:00 a.m. Ibid., pp. 30, 32. Franz Sigel did not discuss the time in his report. It is impossible to reconcile these widely divergent estimates. A knowledge of the balance of the marching and fighting on July 5 makes it difficult to reconcile estimates that the bombardment began between as early as 8:00–9:00 a.m. Cheavens' and Rives' estimates are probably close to correct, i.e., the bombardment began around 10:00 a.m.

20. Van Gilder, "Centennial History of the Battle at Carthage," p. 13. The command structure of the Missouri State Guard during the early months of the war was poorly defined and almost hopelessly muddled. At Carthage, for example, each of the four division commanders waged the battle as though he were in charge of the army, sending troops hither and yon often without regard to what was taking place on other parts of the field. The issue of who was actually in charge of the State Guard at Carthage illustrates this problem. Although some secondary accounts report that Governor Jackson turned over command of the army to James Rains, we have been unable to find a single firsthand account documenting this fact. Indeed, the silence on this issue in the battle's official reports is deafening. Not a single division leader (Rains, Slack, Parsons or Clark) acknowledged James Rains as the army commander. It is instructive to note that John Clark and Mosby Parsons submitted their reports to Jackson, James Rains submitted his to the army's adjutant-general, and William Slack's is addressed to Gen. Sterling Price. Jackson himself did not leave a report. More evidence is provided by Thomas Snead, Jackson's aide-de-camp at the battle. Neither of his detailed post-war accounts suggest or confirm that Jackson turned over command to anyone, a situation surely his aide-de-camp and friend would have discussed. In fact, Snead states that the governor gave orders for the army to advance once the fighting began, a statement we reject as unsubstantiated by other credible evidence. Although Rains' report appears first in the *Official Records*, which might denote his position as commander of the army, someone's report has to be printed first. Curiously, not a single battle report mentions Jackson once the battle begins, even though the affair lasted from early

morning until nightfall and covered more than ten miles of ground. Reports after Boonville blasted Jackson for remaining in the rear and for not being present with his men. Did he do the same thing at Carthage? The similarities between Jackson's actions at Boonville, where we know he turned over field command to John Marmaduke and then remained in the rear, and at Carthage, where no evidence of any change of command exists, are interesting.

Our conclusion is that Jackson was *probably* in charge of the army and abdicated his battlefield responsibilities by staying in the rear and letting his subordinates fend for themselves. Snead's semi-contrary account smacks of his close friendship with Jackson. Until firsthand sources document otherwise, there is no other conclusion that can be reached.

21. Parrish, *A History of Missouri*, 3, p. 48; Allardice, *More Generals in Gray*, p. 190.

22. *OR* 3, pp. 20, 22-23; Schrantz, *Jasper County in the Civil War*, pp. 32-33; The exact placement of Capt. F. M. McKinney's detachment of sixteen is unclear. Similarly, although Weightman makes mention of Rosser as "commanding," it is unclear whether he means Rosser's own First Regiment, or the brigade, although it is almost certainly the former. No further mention is made of the First Regiment during the battle. Perhaps its members were unarmed and coalesced with Governor Jackson in the rear.

23. *OR* 3, pp. 20, 22-23, 27. Lt. Col. Richard Boughan's name is misspelled in the reports as "Vaughan [Baughan]," another example of the State Guard's organizational confusion. For a map of the road's bow-like turn, see the *OR* Atlas, Plate XXXIII, number 6.

24. Snead, *The Fight for Missouri*, pp. 224-225. Snead's careless handling of the alignment places several units in the wrong place, include Guibor's Battery of artillery.

25. *OR* 3, pp. 23, 32.

26. Ibid., pp. 23, 35. General Clark had changed positions with Parsons as regards their divisional marching order. Ibid., p. 30. Other writers may have overlooked this small but significant fact tucked away in Clark's report.

27. Ibid., p. 30.

28. Ibid.

29. Van Gilder, "Centennial History of the Battle at Carthage," p. 16; Salem Ford Letter.

30. Miscellaneous Articles, "Wilson's Creek National Battlefield Park Vertical Files," (n.a., n.d.).

31. *OR* 3, p. 17. The large arc in the Lamar-Carthage Road, as previously described, caused most of the initial fighting at Carthage to take place east of the road.

32. Ibid., p. 17; Schrantz, *Jasper County in the Civil War*, p. 35; Van Gilder, "Centennial History of the Battle of Carthage," p. 12.

33. Salem Ford Letter; William P. Barlow, "Guibor's Battery in 1861," *Daily Missouri Republican*, August 1, 1885. See also, Patrick, "Remembering the Missouri Campaign of 1861," for the editor's insightful comments and additions.

34. Van Gilder, "Centennial History of the Battle of Carthage," p. 12.

35. Ibid., p. 13.

36. *OR* 3, p. 20-21; Mills and Company, *A History of Jasper County*, p. 234. Much of the land where the fighting initially started is still owned by Gresham family descendants.

37. Van Gilder, "Centennial History of the Battle of Carthage," p. 13.

38. *OR* 3, pp. 21, 23; Allardice, *More Generals in Gray*, pp. 190-191.

39. Van Gilder, "Centennial History of Carthage, " p. 13.

40. Ibid. *OR* 3, pp. 18, 24.

41. *OR* 3, pp. 30, 32. See not 19, supra, for a discussion of what time the battle began.

42. Ibid.; *OR* 3, pp. 17, 21, 23, 30, 32, 35.

43. Ibid., p. 30, 35. Lieutenant Barlow of Guibor's Battery supports Parsons' version. "As soon as we were ready, Guibor galloped over to Gen. Parsons and asked permission to open the fight. It was given. I carefully pointed the right piece, Guibor nodded his head, [and] bang went the first gun for Missouri." Patrick, "Remembering the Missouri Campaign of 1861."

44. Archy Thomas, "Letter to the Editor," Western Historical Manuscript Collection, Curtis Laws Wilson Library, University of Missouri-Rolla; Barlow, "Guibor's Battery in 1861"; Patrick, "Remembering the Missouri Campaign of 1861."

45. Ibid.

46. *OR* 3, 30, 35. Rosser was not in command of any separate artillery battery at Carthage. He may have enjoyed an informal assignment as the army's artillery chief. This issue again speaks to the disorganized state of the militia army.

47. Barlow, "Guibor's Battery in 1861"; Patrick, "Remembering the Missouri Campaign of 1861."

48. Ibid.

49. Easley, "Journal of the Civil War in Missouri," p. 18; Otto C. Lademann, "The Battle of Carthage," *War Papers Read before the Commandery of the State of Wisconsin, Military Order of the Loyal Legion of the United States* (Milwaukee, 1914), vol. 4, pp. 133-134; W. D. Vandiver, "Reminiscences of General John B. Clark," *MHR*, vol. 20 (January 1926), pp. 223-235; *OR* 3, p. 30.

50. Salem Ford Letter.

51. Ibid. Although sheer speculation, Ford's detailed description probably would have mentioned the shell bounding amongst the unarmed rabble lurking behind the army if such a thing had occurred, leading one to believe that wherever Jackson was hoarding his unarmed "reserve," it was not immediately behind Slack's Division.

52. *OR* 3, p. 34.

53. Ibid., pp. 21, 23, 35-36; Easley, "Journal of the Civil War in Missouri," p. 19. Private Cheavens also commented on the artillery. One shot "struck one of Sigel's guns in the muzzle, splitting it from muzzle to vent," he claimed, although he certainly was not in a position to determine such a thing. The private also wrote that "One of their men, a surgeon, prisoner, was afterwards in Bledsoe's company. When Bledsoe described a shot of his which was aimed at a certain man's knee but hit the horse instead, 'Dat vas my horse; you nearly cot me' [he answered]. A pair of shoes with the feet were found, but not the man corresponding, till over a week later, when he was found by the creek bank, having lived on grass and berries. He got well, I am told, having dressed his own wounds. A dead man with rings on was found by a marauder. Not being able to get them off, he bit off the fingers." Ibid., pp. 19-20; Archy Thomas letter.

54. Ibid., pp. 23, 35.

55. Ibid., p. 21. Note that Rains' report, written immediately after the battle, contradicts Thomas Snead's account, *Fight for Missouri*, pp. 225-226, which was written long after the war, that Governor Jackson *ordered* Rains to advance. Not one of the division commanders, including Rains, mention that Jackson *ordered* anyone to do anything once the battle got underway. It is also interesting to note that Rains ordered his senior cavalryman, Colonel Peyton, to transfer some of his troops to serve under an inferior officer, namely Jo Shelby. Peyton dispatched one company under "Captain Dook." *OR* 3, p. 27. See also, O'Flaherty, *General Jo Shelby*, p. 6 7.

56. *OR* 3, pp. 27-28.

57. Ibid., p. 29.

58. Ibid., pp. 26, 29.

59. Ibid., pp. 17, 21.

60. Ibid., p. 34; Easley, "Journal of the Civil War in Missouri," p. 18. It appears that virtually all of Rives' losses for the entire day took place during these few minutes.

61. *OR* 3, p. 34; Easley, "Journal of the Civil War in Missouri," p. 18. Cheavens and his handful of comrades remained behind to care for the corpse, "washing and laying him out. . ." By this time the artillery duel had ended and the fighting had passed on. Cheavens noted that Captain Stone died "about "3 o'clock." Since the private did not regain the army until its last action near Carthage, about nightfall, he probably spent several (unproductive) hours with Stone's corpse. The surgeon that attended Stone was probably Capt. John Marshall Allen, who was appointed to his post on June 21, 1861. While it is unclear to which house Captain Stone was removed, in all probability it was the Widow Smith home.

62. OR 3, p. 34.

63. Ibid., p. 35. Colonel Ben Brown arrived in Ray County, Missouri, during its formative years and played a significant role in developing the area. He served as state senator for the 10th District and in 1862 still considered himself as the president of that body. When hostilities commenced, Colonel Brown organized a regiment and marched to Lexington to offer its services. (No Author), *The History of Ray County* (St. Louis Historical Company, 1883), p. 386.

64. Schrantz, *Jasper County in the Civil War*, p. 36; Snead, *Fight For Missouri*, p. 226; Adamson, *Rebellion in Missouri*, pp. 150-151. The impact of the 2,000 unarmed men led by Governor Jackson is another good story relating to Carthage, albeit without much if any substance. Some writers delight in perpetuating this dramatic tale. The governor's decision to move the men inadvertently causes Sigel to believe the entire mounted (but unarmed) body is moving around his flank. The alarmed Sigel thereby retreats, triggering his ultimate defeat. It is more likely than not that this episode did not occur as they would have us believe. Thomas Snead, Jackson's aide-de-camp, speaks of it in passing, although not one other contemporary source mentions it. Is it possible that none of the State Guard division leaders would comment in their reports on such a massive movement of men—half as large as the entire Southern line of battle? Snead and others would have us believe that the shift was part of the

reason for Sigel's retreat. Indeed, Sigel could have used the mass movement as another excuse for withdrawing. He does not do so. Instead, his report unequivocally mentions only the Southern cavalry moving beyond his flanks (as opposed to the mass of mounted men *behind* the Rebel army). It is valid to question whether Sigel could have even seen such a move at this stage of the engagement. He was, after all, on lower ground, powder smoke would have obscured his vision, and Jackson was in the rear of the Rebel line of battle. Even assuming that Jackson moved the large body of men and that Sigel witnessed it, the Federal commander would not have acted any differently. The pressure applied by Rains' cavalry on one flank and Rives and Brown on the other was itself enough to force his retreat. Given Jackson's mysterious absence during the entire battle, perhaps the story was nurtured to rehabilitate his non-existent role.

65. *OR 3*, p. 17.
66. Ibid.
67. Ibid., pp. 17, 34.
68. Ibid., p. 17.
69. Barlow, "Guibor's Battery in 1861."
70. Ibid.
71. *OR 3*, p. 18.
72. Ibid.
73. Ibid.
74. Ibid.

Chapter 8: Dry Fork Creek

1. Van Gilder, "Centennial History of the Battle of Carthage," p. 2.
2. Ibid., p. 2
3. Ibid., p. 2.
4. *OR 3*, p. 38.
5. Ibid., pp. 21, 23.
6. Ibid., pp. 30, 35-36.
7. Ibid., pp. 30-31.
8. Ibid., p. 31.
9. Ibid., p. 23.
10. Ibid., p. 36.

11. Ibid., p. 18; Archy Thomas letter. Adamson, *Rebellion in Missouri*, p. 151, claims that Sigel's retreat across Dry Fork was conducted "in the face of a hard-pressing. . .enemy." This is obviously untrue, for had it been otherwise, how could Sigel have crossed his men and guns over the single ford without loss?

12. Ibid., p. 18.

13. Ibid., p. 18; Van Gilder, "Centennial History of the Battle of Carthage," p. 15.

14. Ibid., p. 15.

15. *OR* 3, pp. 23-24, 33, 35. Salem Ford's fairly detailed letter excludes all reference to the Dry Fork Creek assaults—the heaviest fighting of the battle. It is reasonable to assume that either he missed this part of the action, or that Slack's men came up too late to participate, although Slack's report states otherwise.

16. Ibid., pp. 23-24.

17. Ibid., pp. 31, 36.

18. Ibid., p. 36.

19. Van Gilder, "Centennial History of the Battle of Carthage," p. 15.

20. *OR* 3, pp. 27-28.

21. Ibid.

22. Ibid., p. 24; Van Gilder, "Centennial History of the Battle of Carthage," p. 15.

23. *OR* 3, p. 24. Sigel claims in his report that one of the Southern guns "burst." Ibid., p. 19. While none of the State Guard reports or accounts confirm this claim, it is possible that Sigel is referring to the powder keg that exploded near Bledsoe in the Dry Fork Creek fighting.

24. Ibid., pp. 31, 35-36.

25. Ibid., pp. 31, 36.

26. Archy Thomas letter; Bevier, *History of the First and Second Missouri Brigades*, p. 38.

27. *OR* 3, p. 24.

28. Ibid., p. 36.

29. Ibid., pp. 24, 32-33. The evidence is sketchy as to where and when Slack's Division attacked at Dry Fork. His men probably went in west of the Lamar-Carthage Road at some point after Weightman's advance began.

30. Ibid., p. 24, 31. The exact alignment of Burbridge and Price is unknown.

31. Ibid., p. 18. Contrary to Sigel's claims, the Missouri State Guard did not lose any color bearers during the day long Carthage fight. The Rebel infantry attacks at Dry Fork Creek, however, marked the most intense period of fighting during the battle. The majority of the Southern casualties sustained during the day fell near the timber-fringed banks of the creek. This phase of the fighting impressed so many of the participants that, prior to the 1900s, the day-long engagement was commonly known as the Battle of Dry Fork (as opposed to the Battle of Carthage).

32. *OR* 3, pp. 21, 29.

33. Van Gilder, "Centennial History of the Battle of Carthage," p. 16; Lademann, "The Battle of Carthage," p. 135.

34. *OR* 3, pp. 31, 33, 36.

35. Bevier, *History of the First and Second Missouri Brigades*, p. 38.

36. *OR* 3, pp. 21, 24.

Chapter 9: Retreat

1. Van Gilder, "Centennial History of the Battle of Carthage, p. 15; Lademann, "The Battle of Carthage," p. 135.

2. *OR* 3, p. 34.

3. Ibid.

4. Ibid. Although Colonel Rives reported that his line was drawn *north* of Buck's Branch Creek, credible Federal evidence—and common sense—places his men south of the creek. Forming a line with a stream immediately in the rear with only one ford would have been sheer folly.

5. *OR* 3, p. 18. According to Thomas Snead in *The Fight for Missouri*, Clark and Parsons had managed to cross the creek and "[Christian] Essig thereupon gave the order to retire." Snead's account contains several factual errors, and almost certainly Sigel would not have entrusted a battery commander with such a responsibility.

6. Van Gilder, "Centennial History of the Battle of Carthage, p. 15; Lademann, "Battle of Carthage," p. 135; *OR* 3, p. 18.

7. Ibid.

8. Ibid., p. 34.

9. Ibid., p. 24.

10. Lademann, "Battle of Carthage," p. 135.

11. Ibid. While Lademann's account is the best we have of this action, it must be read with caution. He was clearly a strong partisan of Francis Hassendeubel's and not a fan of Franz Sigel's, which may have colored his memory of the encounter between those officers.

12. Ibid.

13. *OR* 3, p. 18; Lademann, "Battle of Carthage," pp. 135-136.

14. Ibid., p. 136. One secondary account, Marvin Van Gilder, *Crisis at Carthage: A Historical Journal*, (Carthage Press, 1997), which appears to be a reprinting of Van Gilder, "Centennial History of the Battle of Carthage," claims that the fight at Buck's Branch included bayonet-wielding hand-to-hand fighting that "felled" many horses and sent Southerners tumbling to the ground. In addition this account cites an unnamed "unofficial report" that the Federals captured 45 prisoners and 80 horses. Neither Lademann's "Battle of Carthage," pp. 135-136, nor the detailed reports of Franz Sigel or Ben Rives confirm such claims, and in fact contradict them on several counts. While it makes a good story, there was no hand-to-hand fighting at Buck's Branch Creek.

15. Ibid., p. 34. Unfortunately, neither Colonel James McCown nor Col. Ben Brown filed after-action reports. For Weightman's comments, see ibid., p. 24.

16. Ibid., p. 18.

17. Van Gilder, "Centennial History of the Battle of Carthage," p. 15.

18. Ibid., p. 31.

19. Ibid., pp. 31, 33, 36. Clark is referring to the artillery fire being "about one mile in our advance," not the distance to Carthage.

20. Lademann, "Battle of Carthage," p. 136.

21. *OR* 3, p. 28. It is possible that Rains stopped to confer with other division commanders because the fighting had ended and Sigel had abandoned his Dry Fork Creek position.

22. Ibid., p. 21. The import of the halt ordered by General Rains has uniformly been overlooked by previous historians. Few have bothered to inquire how it came to pass that cavalry could not catch up and pass infantry and wagons on flat terrain. Rains' temporary halt south of Dry Fork, at least in part, answers that question.

23. Ibid. It is unknown what became of Colonel Brown's regiment during the remainder of the battle.

24. Ibid., p. 18; Van Gilder, "Centennial History of the Battle of Carthage," p. 17.

25. Ibid.; *OR* 3, p. 18.

26. Ibid., pp. 18, 21, 26, 28, 29.

27. Ibid., pp. 21, 26, 28, 29. Snead, *Fight for Missouri*, p. 227, claims that "Sigel continued his retreat in good order, closely followed by a rabble of State troops and harassed on all sides by their mounted men, who did not, however, dare to attack his compact ranks." Southern battle reports demonstrate that Snead's account is grossly erroneous as well as misleading. Adamson, *Rebellion in Missouri*, pp. 151-152, is more closely aligned with the truth. "The retreat continued in good order, followed at a distance by skirmishers. When they buzzed too close, Sigel would employ his expert use of artillery to brush them off."

28. Van Gilder, "Centennial History of the Battle of Carthage," p. 17; Schrantz, *Civil War in Jasper County*, p. 38. Assuming that the berry-picking story is wrapped around a kernel of truth, it is possible that the soldiers harvested the fruit when Rains left his cavalry and rode east, as Peyton later claimed, to confer with other commanders of the Missouri State Guard. If so, no undue delay resulted. Peyton does not mention a word about blackberries. It is interesting to note that none of the other Southern commanders who left reports mention any meeting with Rains during the battle, and even Rains does not discuss leaving his command (no doubt an intentional omission).

29. *OR* 3, p. 18.

30. Van Gilder, "Centennial History of the Battle of Carthage," p. 17; *OR* 3, p. 18.

31. Ibid.

32. *OR* 3, p. 21.

33. Ibid., pp. 26, 28; Van Gilder, "Centennial History of the Battle of Carthage," p. 17.

34. *OR* 3., p. 18.

35. Ibid.; Van Gilder, "Centennial History of the Battle of Carthage," p. 17.

36. *OR* 3, p. 18; Van Gilder, "Centennial History of the Battle of Carthage," p. 17.

37. Interview with Thomas C. Hood, *Carthage Evening Press*, July 4, 1911; Van Gilder, "Centennial History of the Battle of Carthage," p. 17.

38. *OR* 3, p. 18.

39. Easley, "Journal of the Civil War in Missouri," pp. 18-19.

40. *OR* 3, pp. 24, 33; Van Gilder, "Centennial History of the Battle of Carthage," p. 17.

41. Ibid.

42. Ibid.

43. Ibid.

44. Ibid.

45. Ibid.

46. *OR* 3, pp. 36-37.

47. Van Gilder, "Centennial History of the Battle of Carthage," p. 17.

48. *OR* 3, pp. 24-25.

49. Ibid., pp. 24-25, 33; Van Gilder, "Centennial History of the Battle of Carthage," p. 17.

50. Ibid.; *OR* 3, p. 18.

51. Ibid., pp. 24-25; Van Gilder, "Centennial History of the Battle of Carthage," p. 17. State Guardsman Archy Thomas mentions an interesting incident regarding Col. James Pritchard, which may have taken place at this juncture in the fighting. Pritchard, who commanded John Hughes' regiment at Carthage, came out of some brush "in advance of his men [and] was fired at by (it is said) from 40 to 50 men concealed in a corn field, but his command was `Come on boys here they are.' When his boys in quick and regular order came forth from the brush and fired into the Federals in the corn leaving 15 dead in the corn and running the rest out, the Federals again took up the line of running and firing." The report of the 15 dead Federals is, of course, quite an exaggeration. The fighting did leave some Southern casualties. "In this contest (in and around the town) it was that young T. McCain received a flesh wound in the thigh and Wm. Morrow was knocked down by a ball grazing his head above the ear, and that I Arch Thomas received a slight wound in the arm." Based upon this evidence, it is reasonably clear that Thomas served with Slack's Division. Archy Thomas Letter.

52. *OR* 3, p. 25.

53. Van Gilder, "Centennial History of the Battle of Carthage," p. 18; *OR* 3, p. 25.

54. *OR* 3, p. 37.

55. Salem Ford Letter; Archy Thomas letter.

56. Van Gilder, "Centennial History of the Battle of Carthage," p. 17.

57. Ibid., p. 17.

58. *OR* 3, p. 37.

59. Archy Thomas letter; Van Gilder, "Centennial History of the Battle of Carthage," p. 18.

60. Ibid.

61. Van Gilder, "Centennial History of the Battle of Carthage," p. 18. According to Van Gilder, Nichols was mounted at the time of the battle. Sigel makes no mention of the loss of the color bearer, and Van Gilder does not explain why the color bearer of an infantry regiment was mounted. The story may be largely apocryphal.

62. *OR 3*, p. 37.

63. Ibid.

64. Ibid., p. 33.

65. Easley, "Journal of the Civil War in Missouri," p. 19; *OR 3*, p. 33.

67. Ibid.

68. Ibid.; *OR 3*, p. 33.

69. Ibid., pp. 25, 31.

70. Ibid., p. 33, 34.

71. Ibid., p. 34.

72. Lademann, "Battle of Carthage," pp. 136-137. Sigel is referring to Capt. John E. Strodkamp, whose name is correctly spelled on both the Muster Roll for the Third Missouri, Company E, as well as that officer's Compiled Service Records, National Archives.

73. Ibid. It is impossible to say with any certainty who Lademann and his comrades were confronting. If his memory is correct, the likelihood is that the officer was from Col. John Graves' 2nd Regiment of Colonel Weightman's command.

74. Ibid.

75. Ibid., p. 137.

76. Ibid.

77. OR 3, p. 38.

78. Ibid.

79. Ibid., p. 40.

80. Ibid.

81. Ibid.; Faust, *Civil War Encyclopedia*, p. 461.

82 Ibid.

83. Ibid., p. 40.

84. Ibid., pp. 38-39.

85. Ibid., p. 38.

Chapter 10: The Wake

1. *OR* 3, p. 19. Sigel's claim that a Southern gun "burst" may be an honest mistake. See supra, Chapter 8, note 23. While he also mentioned the loss of but one wagon, William Slack reported that his men captured two wagons "loaded with tents and other quartermaster's stores," and Colonel Rives also reported a captured wagon. Slack also claims to have captured eight prisoners. Ibid., p. 33. Sigel is silent on this point.

2. Ibid., p. 19. Federal muster roles, housed in the National Archives, tabulate 18 killed, 53 wounded and five captured. Muster Rolls, Third and Fifth Missouri Volunteers, National Archives.

3. Franz Backoff (spelled "Backof" by Sigel in his report, *OR* 3, p. 19) was a fellow soldier with Sigel in the 1848 Revolution. The diminutive artillerist, who stood less than five feet tall, was detested by many of the enlisted men. Considered to be cruel and heartless, he would often scream profanities at the soldiers from the back of his horse. John Snyder File, Bibliographic Sketches, Missouri Historical Society.

4. Ibid., p. 25.

5. Ibid., p. 33.

6. Ibid., pp. 31-32, 37. One veteran Missouri researcher who wishes to remain anonymous claims that muster rolls and other written organizational memoranda prepared later in the war mention earlier wounds received at Carthage that are not accounted for in the official reports. It is this researcher's contention that the Missouri State Guard suffered substantially higher casualties than officially listed, but that the militia's organizational disarray made it difficult for its officers to accurately list losses. It is also probable that many of the army's "walking wounded"—those able to continue to serve without hospitalization—were not listed among the wounded.

7. Ibid., pp. 20-37; Patrick, "Remembering the Missouri Campaign of 1861." At least one secondary account, Van Gilder, "Centennial History of the Battle of Carthage," p. 23, declares the Federals captured 44 Southerners in the day-long fighting. He does not cite a source for this remarkable figure. We have been unable to substantiate it, and no firsthand accounts corroborate Van Gilder. If Franz Sigel had taken such a sizable body of the enemy he surely would have mentioned that fact in his official report. Southern battle reports do not reference large numbers of missing soldiers (in fact they mention only one). It is possible that the informality of the

Missouri State Guard organizations made it difficult to determine who, if anyone, was actually missing. We know that a sizable number of men became separated from their units during and after the fighting, and many of these men might have simply left and gone home. Based upon *known* sources, however, the reference to 44 captured Southerners is simply not credible.

8. *Carthage Evening Press*, June 27, 1990, p. 21; ibid., Hood interview, July 4, 1911. He took part in the fighting at Pea Ridge, Arkansas, although we do not know the unit with which he served. He eventually joined the 1st Arkansas Cavalry, which was comprised of pro-Union sympathizers from southwest Missouri. This regiment filtered through Southern lines to assist the Union cause. Originally from Newark, Ohio, Caffee moved to Jasper County in 1857. After the war he returned to Carthage, quit his medical practice and opened a drugstore.

9. Ibid. Assuming for the sake of argument that the newspaper interview is accurate (it was given fifty years after the fact), the obvious question is what became of the remains of the amputated limbs? Despite substantial research on this issue, we were unable to verify Thomas Hood's claim or find any subsequent reference to the burial trench. It is thus fair to conclude that, if there were buried body parts, they were not exhumed at a later date or news of this discovery would have surfaced. The area described by Hood probably would have been excavated to accommodate the larger foundation for the new courthouse. News accounts, however, do not mention the discovery of human remains. Is it reasonable to assume that such a burial in a small town would go unmarked by the townspeople and forgotten? Or is it more probable that the story is merely the innocent embellishment of a tale told too many times?

10. Van Gilder, "Centennial History of the Battle of Carthage," p. 20. The Hood's moved to Fort Scott, Kansas.

11. Ibid., p. 20.

12. Ibid., p. 20. This may be on the only known reference to the blackberry incident, although only the speaker, and not the source of the quote, is cited.

13. Easley, "Journal of the Civil War in Missouri," p. 19; Archy Thomas letter.

14. Van Gilder, "Centennial History of the Battle of Carthage," p. 20.

15. *OR* 3, p. 38; Lademann, "Battle of Carthage," pp. 138-139.

16. Ibid.

17. *OR* 3, p. 15.

18. Ibid.

19. Ibid.

20. Easley, "Journal of the Civil War in Missouri," p. 19; Archy Thomas letter; Salem Ford letter.

21. Easley, "Journal of the Civil War in Missouri," p. 19; Salem Ford Letter.

22. Easley, "Journal of the Civil War in Missouri," p. 20. Snead, *Fight for Missouri*, p. 219.

23. Ibid., p. 219-220; Patrick, "Remembering the Missouri Campaign of 1861."

24. Ibid.

Bibliography

MANUSCRIPTS

Chicago Historical Society, Chicago, Illinois
    Franz Sigel Collection
Library of Congress, Washington D.C.
    O. D. Finley to Montgomery Blair, Box 29
Missouri Historical Society, St. Louis, Missouri
    Brauckman Scrapbook
    Civil War Collection
    Drummond File num. 57
    Ford Letter File, 1876
    John Snyder File
    Western Historical Manuscript Collection
The National Archives, Washington D.C.
    Compiled Service Records
    Muster Rolls of the 3rd U.S. Missouri Volunteers
    Muster Rolls of the 5th U.S. Missouri Volunteers
Muster Rolls of the Missouri State Guard
State Historical Society of Missouri, Columbia
    Champ Clark Papers
    Western Historical Manuscript Collection
Curtis Laws Wilson Library, Rolla, Missouri
    The Archy Thomas File
Western Reserve Historical Papers, Cleveland, Ohio.
    Sigel Papers
Wilson's Creek National Park Vertical Files
    Miscellaneous Articles File (unidentified sources)

OFFICIAL PUBLICATIONS

Kennedy, Joseph C. G. *Population of the United States in 1860 compiled from the Official Returns of the Eighth Census.* Washington D.C.

History of Cass and Bates Counties, 1883. National Historical Co., St. Louis

History of Cooper County, 1882. National Historical Co., St. Louis

History of Henry and St. Clair Counties. 1885. National Historical Co., St. Louis

History of Greene County, 1883. St. Louis Western Historical Co.

History of Ray County, 1883. St. Louis Western Historical Co.

History of Vernon County, 1883. St. Louis Western Historical Co.

United States War Department. *The War of the Rebellion, A Compilation of the Official Records of the Union and Confederate Armies.* 70 volumes in 128 parts. Washington D.C., 1890-1901.

United States War Department. *Atlas to Accompany the Official Records of the Union and Confederate Armies.* Washington, D. C.: Government Printing Office, 1891-1895.

NEWSPAPERS

Anzeiger des Westens
Carthage Evening Press
Carthage Press
Daily Missouri Republican
Kansas City Business Journal
Missouri Democrat
Missouri Republican
Missouri Statesman
Mississippi Blatter
Springfield Mirror
Westliche Post

PUBLISHED PRIMARY SOURCES

Barlow, William P. "Guibor's Battery in 1861," *Daily Missouri Republican,* St. Louis, 1885.

Bek, William G. "The Civil War Diary of John T. Buegel, Union Soldier, part 1." *Missouri Historical Review.* 40 (July, 1946)

Boyce, Joseph. "What Flag Was This?" *Confederate Veteran,* 40 vols. Vol. 27 (1919).

Boyd, A. "Hiram Bledsoe," *Confederate Veteran*, 40 vols. Vol. 28 (1930).

Carter, Harvey L. and Norma L. Peterson, "William S. Stewart Letters, January 13, 1861 to December 4, 1862." *Missouri Historical Review*. 62 (January, 1967).

Duncan, Charles V. *John T. Hughes, From His Pen*. Modesto, 1991.

Easley, Virginia, ed. "Journal of the Civil War in Missouri, 1861: Henry Martyn Cheavens." *Missouri Historical Review*. 56 (October, 1961).

Lademann, Otto C. "The Battle of Wilson's Creek." *War Papers, Read before the Commandery of the State of Wisconsin, Military Order of the Loyal Legion of the United States*, 1914.

Thomas, Archy. "Letter to the Editor," *Western Historical Manuscript Collection*, Curtis Laws Wilson Library, University of Missouri-Rolla.

PUBLISHED SECONDARY SOURCES

Adamson, Hans C. *Rebellion in Missouri*. Philadelphia: The Chilton Company, 1961.

Alden, Henry M., Guernsey eds. *Harper's Pictorial History of the Civil War*. New York: Fairfax Press, 1977.

Allardice, Bruce S. *More Generals in Gray*. Baton Rouge: Louisiana State Press, 1995.

Anders, Leslie, ed. *Confederate Roll of Honor: Missouri*. Warrensburg: West Central Missouri Genealogical Society and Library, 1989.

Anderson, Galusha. *A Border City During the Civil War*. Boston: Little, Brown and Company, 1908.

Bailey, Anne J. "The Abandoned Western Theater: Confederate National Policy Toward the Trans-Mississippi Region." *Journal of Confederate History*, 5 (1990).

Barnes, John. "Boonville: The First Land Battle of the Civil War." *Infantry Journal*. 35 (December, 1929).

Barr, Alwyn. "Confederate Artillery in Arkansas." *Arkansas Historical Quarterly, 21 (1962)*.

Bartles, Carolyn. *The Forgotten Men*. Shawnee: Two Trails Genealogy Shop, 1995.

Bevier, R. S. *First and Second Missouri Confederate Brigades, 1861-1865*. St. Louis: Bryan, Brand Co., 1879.

Blum, Virgil C. "The Political and Military Activities of the German Element in St. Louis, 1859-1861." *Missouri Historical Review* , 42 (January, 1948).

Boatner, Mark M. *The Civil War Dictionary*. New York: David McKay Co., 1959.

Boyce, Joseph. "The Flags of the First Missouri Confederate Infantry." *Missouri Historical Society,* St. Louis, Missouri.

Britton, Wiley. *Civil War on the Border.* New York: G. P. Putnam's Sons, 1899.

Brownlee, Richard S. *Gray Ghosts of the Confederacy.* Baton Rouge: Louisiana State University Press, 1958.

Cain, Marvin E. *Lincoln's Attorney General: Edward Bates of Missouri.* Columbia: Uni versity of Missouri Press, 1965.

Castel, Albert. *A Frontier State at War, 1861-1865.* Lawrence: Kansas Heritage Press, 1958.

—. *General Sterling Price and the Civil War in the West.* Baton Rouge: Louisiana State University Press, 1968.

Clark, Kimball. "The Epic March of Doniphans Missourians." *Missouri Historical Review,* 80 (January, 1986).

Conrad, Howard L. *Encyclopedia of St. Louis.* St. Louis, 1901.

Cook, George. "Neosho. . .Its Part in the Confederate Dream." *Gateway Magazine,* 2 (Spring, 1981).

Covington, James W. "The Camp Jackson Affair, 1861." *Missouri Historical Review,* 55 (April, 1961).

Crute, Joseph H., Jr. *Confederate Staff Officers.* Powhatan, 1982.

—. *Units of the Confederate State Army.* Pohatan, 1987.

Current, Richard N. ed. *Encyclopedia of the Confederacy.* 4 volumes. New York: Simon and Schuster, 1993.

Cutrer, Thomas W. *Ben McCulloch and the Frontier Military Tradition,* Chapel Hill, 1993.

Dahlinger, Charles W. *The German Revolution of 1848.* New York, 1972.

Dark, Harris and Phyllis. *Springfield of the Ozarks: An Illustrated History.* Woodland Hills: Windsor Publications, 1981.

Davis, William C. ed. *The Confederate Generals.* Lancaster, 1991.

Dictionary of American Biography. New York: Charles Scribner's Sons, 1937.

Dorpalen, Andreas. "The German Element and the Issues of the Civil War." *Mississippi Valley Historical Review,* 29 (January, 1942).

DuBois, J.R.L. *Historical Review,* 60 (July, 1966).

Dunson, A. A. "Notes in the Missouri Germans on Slavery." Missouri Historical Review, 59 (January, 1964).

Dyer, Frederick H. A Compendium of the War of the Rebellion. Dayton, 1978.

—, Robert L. *Boonville: An Illustrated History.* Boonville: Petitanoui Publishing, 1982.

—, Thomas. "The Liberty Arsenal." *The Western Campaigner: Journal of the Missouri Civil War Reenactors Association.* (June, 1995).

Edwards, John N. *Shelby and His Men: Or the War in the West*. Cincinnati: Miami Publishing Company, 1867.

Ellsworth, Elliot Jr. *West Point and the Confederacy*. New York, 1942.

Engle, Stephen D. *Yankee Dutchman: The Life of Franz Sigel*. Fayetteville: University of Arkansas Press, 1993.

Gannon, Gerald. "The Harney-Price Agreement." *Civil War Times Illustrated*, 23 (December, 1984).

Giffen, Lawrence E. "The Strange Story of Major General Franz Sigel." *Missouri Histor ical Review*, 84 (July, 1990).

Goodrich, James W. "Gottfried Dudden: A Nineteenth Century Missouri Promoter." *Missouri Historical Review*, 75 (January, 1980).

Gottschalk, Philip. *In Deadly Earnest: The Missouri Brigade*. Columbia: Missouri River Press, Inc., 1991.

Grover, Benjamin Whiteman. "Civil War in Missouri." *Missouri Historical Review*, 7 (Ocotober, 1913).

Harvey, Charles M. "Missouri from 1849-1861." *Missouri Historical Review*, 2 (October, 1907).

Holcombe, Return Ire, and F. W. Adams, compilers. *An Account of the Battle of Wilson's Creek, or Oak Hills*. Springfield: Dow and Adams, 1883.

Holland, Dorthy G. "The Planter's House." *Bulletin of the Missouri Historical Society*, 28 (January, 1972).

Hopewell, John M. *The History of Camp Jackson*. St. Louis, Missouri, 1861.

Hurt, Douglas R. *Agriculture and Slavery in Missouri's Little Dixie*. Columbia, 1995.

Ingenthron, Elmo. *Borderland Rebellion: A History of the Civil War on the Missouri-Arkansas Border*. Branson: Ozark Mountaineer, 1980

Johnson, Robert Underwood, and Howard L. Conrad, eds. *Battles and Leaders of the Civil War*. New York: Thomas Yoseloff, 1956.

Kirkpatrick, Arthur Roy. "The Admission of Missouri to the Confederacy." *Missouri Historical Review*, 55 (July, 1961).

—. "Missouri in the Early Months of the Civil War." *Missouri Historical Review*, 55 (April, 1961).

—. "Missouri on the Eve of the Civil War." *Missouri Historical Review*, 55 (January, 1961).

Knox, Thomas W. *Campfire and Cotton Field: Southern Adverntures in time of War*. Philidelphia: Jones Brothers and Company, 1865.

Krick, Robert K. *Lee's Colonels*. Dayton, 1991.

Laughlin, Sceva B. *Missouri Politics During the Civil War*. Salem, Oregon: Sceva B. Laughlin, 1930.

Long, E. B. *The Civil War Day by Day*. New York, 1971.

Longacre, Edward G. "A Profile of General Justus McKinstry." *Civil War Times Illustrated*, 17 (July, 1978).

Lonn, Ella. *Foreigners in the Union Army and Navy*. Baton Rouge: Louisiana State University Press, 1951.

Lyon, William H. "Claiborne Fox Jackson and the Secession Crisis in Missouri." *Missouri Historical Review*, 58 (July, 1964).

McDonough, James L. *Schofield: Union General in the Civil War and Reconstruction*. Tallahassee: Florida State University Press, 1972.

McElroy, John. *The Struggle for Missouri*. Washington D.C.: The National Tribune Company, 1909.

Malin, James C. "The Proslavery Background in the Kansas Struggle." *Mississippi Valley Historical Review*, 10 (December, 1923).

Maxwell, Lewis. "Confederate Artillerists Henry Guibor." *Confederate Veteran* (January-Febuary, 1989).

Meyer, Duane G. *The Heritage of Missouri*. St. Louis: River City Publisher, 1971.

Miles, Kathleen W. *Bitter Ground: The Civil War in Missouri's Golden Valley*. Warsaw: The Printery, 1971.

Mills and Company. *The History of Jasper County*. Des Moines: Mills and Company, 1883.

Miller, Robert E. "Daniel Marsh Frost, C.S.A." *Missouri Historical Review*, 85 (July, 1991).

Miller, Robert E. "General Mosby M. Parsons: Missouri's Secessionist General." *Missouri Historical Review*, 80 (October, 1985).

Monaghan, Jay. *Civil War on the Western Border*. Boston: Little, Brown and Company, 1955.

Moore, John C. *Confederate Military History: Missouri, 17 vols.* (Wilmington, 1988), vol. 12.

Nichols, James L. *The Confederate Quartermaster in the Trans-Mississippi*. Austin: University of Texas Press.

Noe, F. R. "Scattered Remnant of a Company." *Confederate Veteran*, 11 (1903).

O'Flaherty, Daniel. *General Jo Shelby: Undefeated Rebel*. Chapel Hill: University of North Carolina Press, 1954.

Parrish, William E. *David Rice Atchison of Missouri: Border Politician*. Columbia: University of Missouri Press, 1961.

—. *Turbulant Partnership: Missouri and the Union, 1861-1865*. Columbia: Universty of Missouri Press, 1963.

—. Charles T. Jones, and Lawrence O. Christensen. *Missouri: The Heart of a Nation*. Columbia: University of Missouri Press, 1980.

Payne, James E. "Early Days of Civil War in Missouri, *Confederate Veteran*, 39 (1921).

Peckham, James. *General Nathaniel Lyon and Missouri in 1861.* New York: American News Company, 1866.

Peterson, Richard C., James E. McGhee, Kip A. Lindberg, and Keith I Daleen. *Sterling Price's Lieutenants: A Guide to Officers and Organization of the Missouri State Guard 1861-1865.* Shawnee Mission: Two Trails Press, 1995.

Philips, Christopher W. *Damned Yankee: The Life of General Nathaniel Lyon.* Columbia: University of Missouri Press, 1990.

Philips, Christopher W. "The Court Martial of Lieutenant Nathaniel Lyon." *Missouri Historical Review,* 81 (April, 1987).

Pollard, Edward A. *Southern History of the War,* 4 vols. (Fairfax, 1968).

Primm, James Neal. *Germans for a Free Missouri: Translations from the St. Louis Free Radical Press, 1857-1862.* Columbia: University of Missouri Press, 1993.

Reavis, Logan Uriah. *The Life and Military Services of General William Selby Harney.* St. Louis: Bryan, Brand and Company, 1878.

Reilly, Robert M. *United States Military Small Arms 1816-1865: Federal Firearms of the Civil War.* New Jersey: The Gun Room Press, 1970.

Ripley, Warren. *Ammunition of the Civil War.* Charleston: The Battery Press, 1984.

Robbins, Peggy. "The Battle of Camp Jackson." *Civil War Times Illistrated,* 20 (June, 1981).

Robertson, Priscilla. *Revolution of 1848.* London, 1971.

Roed, William. "Secessionist Strength in Missouri." *Missouri Historical Review,* 72 (July, 1978).

Rombauer, Robert J. *The Union Cause in St. Louis in 1861.* St. Louis: Nixon-Jones Printing Company, 1909.

Rorvig, Paul. "The Significant Skirmish: Battle of Boonville, June 17, 1861." *Missouri Historical Review,* 86 (January, 1992).

Rutherford, P. "The Carthaginian Wars." *Civil War Times Illustrated,* (February, 1987).

Ryle, Walter H. *Missouri: Union or Secession.* Nashville: Geoge Peabody College for Teaching, 1931.

St. Peters, Robert. *Memorial Volume of the Diamond Jubilee of St. Louis Universtiy, 1829-1904.* St. Louis, 1904.

Scarpino, Phillip V. "Slavery in Callaway County Missouri:1845-1855." *Missouri Historical Review,* 71 (October, 1976).

Schofield, John M. *Forty Six Years in the Army.* New York: The Century Company, 1897.

Schrantz, Ward. *Jasper County, Missouri in the Civil War.* Carthage: Carthage Press, 1923.

Schrantz, Ward. "The Battle of Carthage." *Missouri Historical Review*, (January, 1937).

Schwienher, Lucy M. "The St. Louis Public Schools at the Outbreak of the Civil War." *Missouri Historical Review*, 13 (October, 1956).

Shalhope, Robert E. *Sterling Price: Portrait of a Southener*. Columbia: Bryan, Brand and Company, 1878.

Scharf, J. Thomas. *History of St. Louis City and County*, Two Volumes. Philedelphia: L. H. Everts, 1883.

Shea, William L., and Earl J. Hess. *Pea Ridge: Civil War Campaign in the West*. Chapel Hill: University of North Carlina Press, 1992.

Shoemaker, Floyd C. *A History of Missouri and Missourians*. Columbia: Walter Ridge way Publishing Company. 1922.

—. *Missouri's Struggle for Statehood*. Jefferson City: The Hugh Stephens Printing Co., 1916.

—. "Missouri: Heir of Southern Tradition and Individuality." *Missouri Historical Review*, 36 (July, 1942).

Smith, Donnal V. " The Influence of the Foreign Born of the Northwest in the Election of 1860." *Mississippi Valley Historical Review*, 19 (September, 1932).

Smith, Edward. *Borderland in the Civil War*. New York: McMillian Company, 1927.

Smith, William E. *The Francis Preston Blair Family in Politics*. New York: McMillan Company, 1933.

Snead, Thomas L. *The Fight for Missouri from the Election of Lincoln to the Death of Lyon*. New York: New York, 1886.

—. "The Early War in Missouri." *Battles & Leaders of the Civil War*, vol. 1, pp. 262-277.

Sunder, John E. "The Early Telegraph in Rural Missouri, 1847-1859." *Missouri Histori cal Review*, 51 (October, 1956).

Trexler, Harrison A. "Slavery in the Missouri Territory." *Missouri Historical Review*, 3 (April, 1909).

Tucker, Philip Thomas. *The South's Finest*. Shippensburg, 1993.

VanDiver, W. D. "Reminiscences of General John B. Clark." *Missouri Historical Review*, 20 (January, 1926).

Van Gilder, Marvin. "A Centennial History of the Battle of Carthage," *Carthage Evening Press*, 1961.

Wakelyn, Jon L. *Biographical Dictionary of the Confederacy*. Conneticut: Westport, 1977.

Wallace, Doris D. "The Political Campaign of 1860 in Missouri." *Missouri Historical Review*. 70 (January, 1976).

Ware, Eugene F. *The Lyon Campaign*. Topeka: Crane and Company, 1907.

Warner, Ezra J. *Generals in Blue: Lives of the Union Commanders*. Baton Rouge: Louisiana State University Press, 1964.

—. *Generals in Gray: Lives of the Confederate Commanders*. Baton Rouge: Louisiana State University Press, 1959.

—, and Buck Yearns. *Biographical Register of the Confederate Congress*. Baton Rouge, 1975.

Webb, W. L. *Battles and Biographies of Missourians*. Hudson-Kimberly Publishing Company, 1903.

Welcher, Frank J. *The Union Army, 1861-1865, Organization and Operations: The Western Theater*. 2 vols. Bloomington, 1993.

Winter, William. *The Civil War in St. Louis: A Guided Tour*. St. Louis: 1994.

Wittke, Carl. *Refugees of the Revolution: The German Forty-Eighters in America*. Westport: Greenwood Press, 1970.

Wurthman, Leonard B, Jr. "Frank Blair: Lincoln's Congressional Spokesman" *Missouri Historical Review*, 64 (April, 1970).

Zucker, Adolf E., editor. *The Forty-Eighter's: Political Refugees of the German Revolution of 1848*. New York, 1950.

THESES, DISSERTATIONS AND UNPUBLISHED ARTICLES

Burks, Walter W. *Thunder on the Right*, University of Missouri at Kansas City, 1962.

Patrick, Jeff. "Remembering the Missouri Campaign of 1861: The Memoirs of Lieutenant W. P. Barlow, Guibor's Battery, Missouri State Guard."

INDEX

An Interview with David Hinze

conducted by Theodore P. Savas

TPS: My initial concern when you told me you were writing a book on Carthage was whether or not a small battle west of the Mississippi River deserved a full-length book. Why does it?

DCH: Because what happened in Missouri in early 1861 set the stage for the remainder of the war in both that state, which was a critical border region, and much of the Trans-Mississippi Theater.

TPS: Fair enough. Give us an overview of the situation in Missouri on the eve of the Civil War.

DCH: Missouri was a state of divided loyalties. By 1860 the eastern counties, primarily centered around St. Louis, were more economically aligned with Northern states than the western or interior regions. St. Louis also had a large immigrant population, primarily German, and far fewer slaves than the inland counties. The Germans were also staunchly abolitionist in their leanings. But, Missouri had a pro-Southern governor in Claiborne Fox Jackson, who was elected on a moderate plank. He publicly steered a moderate course while privately preparing to slip the state into the Confederate fold if and when that time arose. Each side drilled militia units, and each prepared for war. Their focus was the Federal arsenal in St.

Louis. Whoever controlled it could effectively equip an army and thus dominate any opponent.

TPS: What were the repercussions of Fort Sumter in Missouri?

DCH: That was the triggering mechanism for war in Missouri. After Fort Sumter, as arsenals and supply depots across the South fell to Southerners, Federal Congressman Frank Blair, with Nathaniel Lyon, launched preemptive strikes against the growing Missouri state militia. The first was at Camp Jackson. That fiasco erupted in bloodshed in the streets of the city and galvanized opposing points of view. Fort Sumter led to Camp Jackson, and the pretense of peace within the state evaporated. Lyon's move solidified Federal control over the arsenal and kept valuable munitions out of the hands of Governor Jackson's private army.

TPS: Describe the events immediately leading up to the July 5, 1861, engagement at Carthage.

DCH: After an attempt to mediate the situation failed, Governor Jackson issued a call to arms and formed the Missouri State Guard. This state militia army (I want to emphasize *state*) coalesced in the interior counties, a pro-Southern area popularly known as "Little Dixie." The State Guard was led by a popular ex-governor and Mexican War hero, Brig. Gen. Sterling Price. Unfortunately for the Southerners, Price got sick and went home, leaving behind a poorly-equipped and untrained army under the command of the governor. Jackson was a crafty politician without an ounce of military sense. [Nathaniel] Lyon moved quickly up the Missouri River and defeated the Rebels at Boonville on June 17. This little skirmish—which was a lot more important that most people realize—forced the state militia to fall back in two separate columns, one from Boonville and the other from Lexington, deep into the southwestern corner of the state. It was Jackson's hope that he could unite his two wings and eventually stop the Federals.

TPS: Essentially he was trading space for time?

DCH: Yes. He really had no other choice.

TPS: *How did Lyon respond to Jackson's withdrawal?*

DCH: Lyon was aware that a Confederate army—and the distinction is important, because Jackson's men were *state* troops; they did not belong to the Confederacy—was forming in northern Arkansas. Lyon had to keep that army and the Missouri State Guard apart. He was a very aggressive and capable general and he designed an aggressive and pretty bold strategy to deal with Jackson.

TPS: *What was his plan?*

DCH: His plan was to follow the State Guard and catch it from behind or shepherd it into the corner of the state while a second column under Brig. Gen. Thomas Sweeny marched southwest out of St. Louis to cut off Jackson and possibly destroy him. Lyon's wing was to play the role of the hammer, and Sweeny the anvil. It was a classic pincer strategy.

TPS: *For that early in the war, Lyon demonstrated offensive acumen on a large strategic scale.*

DCH: Yes, he was very aggressive and bright. He could have marked time after Boonville and not risked his growing reputation, but he wanted to destroy Jackson. That was his goal and he moved to implement it.

TPS: *But the Federal plan ultimately failed. Why?*

DCH: In a word, logistics. Primarily it was because Lyon, while a good tactician, was not well schooled in matters of supply. Few generals were that early in the war. He didn't understand how difficult it was to feed and equip an army campaigning in the field far from its base of supplies. His departure south from Boonville was delayed because of too few wagons and bad weather, and Tom Sweeny got mired down for much the same reason in St. Louis and Rolla. Sweeny's column eventually moved southwest through the railhead at Rolla and on to Springfield, but Sweeny remained in the rear dealing with his supply problems. His senior officer stepped in and led about 1,100 men out of Springfield after the Missouri State Guard. His name was Col. Franz Sigel.

TPS: Was Sterling Price back with the state army at this juncture?

DCH: No, and he was sorely missed. "Old Pap" Price had recovered but was riding south into Arkansas to try and get General Benjamin McCulloch's Confederates to march into Missouri to help the state troops.

TPS: How large was Jackson's command at this time?

DCH: The two state troop columns merged north of Carthage at Lamar on July 3. Jackson's army now numbered about 6,000 men, but only about 4,000 were armed. These are just rough numbers. Organizational records are nonexistent.

TPS: Ok. So Sigel marches north and finds Jackson's army. . .

DCH: Much to his discomfiture! (laughter) There was a small skirmish on the night of July 4-5 along Spring River, which tipped off both commanders their opponent was in the vicinity. Sigel marched his men early the next day, about 1,100 strong and eight field pieces, through Carthage and into the prairie to defeat Jackson. Jackson also had his men on the road early, about 4:00 a.m. The two sides met early on the morning of July 5 about nine or ten miles north of town.

TPS: Describe the initial phase of the battle.

DCH: Carthage was more of a series of engagements, a running battle that covered about twelve hours and more than ten miles before it ended. The Missouri State Guard aligned for battle on a slight ridge across Sigel's axis of advance—across the Lamar-Carthage Road—and waited. The terrain was almost flat prairie land, so they could see Sigel coming for some distance. Jo Shelby gave a good account of himself in front of the state militia, his first engagement of the war. Sigel, even though he was badly outnumbered, marched his men right up to the enemy and deployed. It was all very Napoleonic in form and style. Both sides exchanged artillery fire for about half an hour from a distance of 800 yards. During that time Southern cavalry, which was placed on both wings, separated from the main body and attempted to envelop Sigel, who had no cavalry of his own.

TPS: *The realization of what was happening to him must have come as quite a shock!*

DCH: (laughing). More than he ever let on. He also had thirty-two baggage wagons a couple miles behind him, and he was miles from any support. His primary concern was to protect his wagons and extricate his men.

TPS: *How did he get out of such a tight spot?*

DCH: That's an interesting question and we spend a substantial amount of the book discussing the issue. He withdrew from the initial fighting at just about the last moment he could do so. He then deployed a small but powerful rear guard at Dry Fork Creek, a mile or so behind his first position of the morning. Dry Fork is a deep stream with wooded and steep banks and just one ford. It was perfectly suited for a rear guard defense. Christian Essig and his four artillery pieces were directed to hold the ford with the assistance of four companies of infantry. Sigel essentially utilized his superior firepower just long enough and effectively enough to hold the Southerners at bay while he slipped his wagons and the majority of his infantry toward Carthage.

TPS: *And even with a large arm of cavalry and relatively open terrain the Southerners could not catch him? That is just incredible!*

DCH: That is one of the mysteries of the battle. It is indeed incredible, although no one has seriously tried to explain why. The simple answer is that the cavalry was poorly handled—and I am being generous. General James S. Rains, the Eighth Division commander of the Missouri State Guard, led his troopers personally, and he did not have a clue as to what he was doing. Walk the terrain with battle reports in hand and it doesn't take long to figure out Rains (and most of the cavalry leaders) were in way, way over their heads. Sigel's artillery had earlier stunned the horsemen more than they let on in their reports and drove both wings farther out, allowing him time to disengage south to Dry Fork. The Southern infantry was also disrupted from the artillery fire and had a problem getting started after him.

TPS: What happened at Dry Fork?

DCH: The real pitched fighting of the battle took place there. A classic artillery duel was waged between Hiram Bledsoe and Essig; Bledsoe and his crew took a terrible pounding. When the Southern infantry was relatively well aligned, a strong assault was launched against the creek. The men fought at close range for about half an hour over the wooded banks until Sigel's men finally fell back. The fighting was so fierce that many of the men called the day-long fight the battle of Dry Fork instead of Carthage.

TPS: Was Sigel driven from Dry Fork or did he retire?

DCH: Well, we're not sure. Sigel says he learned he was flanked by cavalry and withdrew, although that may only be part of the story. I personally believe he was flanked by infantry crossing the creek and decided to withdraw.

TPS: But the Federals actually were flanked farther south by cavalry?

DCH: Yes, that's true, in what turned out to be the best opportunity for the Rebels to defeat Sigel and capture his entire column.

TPS: So what happened?

DCH: Colonels Benjamin Rives and Ben Brown and some 500-700 troopers had managed to cross Dry Fork, slip around Sigel's right flank deep into his rear and take a position behind a small stream that cut across Sigel's route of retreat. Buck's Branch Creek, like Dry Fork, had only one narrow and very muddy ford. If the Southerners could hold the ford for any length of time, their infantry, which was just a couple miles back, could strike Sigel from behind. It was a perfect situation for them and a terrible predicament for Sigel. The ford was a real logistical bottleneck, and the Southerners were present in sufficient numbers to cause a real problem.

TPS: And yet Sigel managed to escape. . .

DCH: This is a really fascinating part of the story and I don't want to spoil it for the readers. Suffice it to say that he wiggled out of a very tightly-drawn box. The man had lots of luck on retreats!

TPS: . . .and reach Carthage?

DCH: Eventually, yes, but it was a close-run affair.

TPS: Which officers handled themselves with distinction on the Southern side? Obviously not Rains!

DCH: (laughing). No, not Rains, or Ben Rives for that matter. I think Colonel Richard Hanson Weightman contributed largely to the victory. He led a brigade in Rains' Division like a veteran and did a great job. I think he was the best infantry commander on the field. He kept it together pretty well and drove his men forward relentlessly. If he hadn't been killed at Wilson's Creek, I think he would have gone on and done great things. Mosby Parsons also performed very well at the head of his division. He went on and carved out a very respectable career. The Confederacy misused Parsons. He was very capable.

TPS: Like Rains, you don't have much good to say about Governor Jackson.

DCH: Well, whatever we wrote we tried to be objective and even-handed. Jackson is a real enigma. He disappears from the written record as soon as the battle is ready to begin. In fact, not once is he mentioned in any of the nine Southern reports that cover a twelve to seventeen hour span. There is this story that has gained credence over the years, largely local lore, that Jackson turned over command of the army to James Rains just before the fight. Karen [Farnham] and I believed it until we studied all the battle reports and realized there isn't a single shred of evidence to support that and quite a bit that disproves it. In fact, we went into this project with lot's of preconceived notions because of what others had written, and much of it is simply wrong.

TPS: So Rains did not command the army. That is just a myth?

DCH: We think so, yes. Like all battles, Carthage has a bushel full of them.

TPS: Anyone stand out on the Federal side?

DCH: Francis Hassenduebel, who led a battalion of the Third Missouri, seems to have contributed significantly to the end result. Christian Essig handled his guns very well throughout the day. You know, it is interesting that Sigel chose Essig for the toughest task of the day [holding Dry Fork Creek], and then ignored him in his battle report! Sigel credited instead the head of his artillery, Franz Backoff. We're not sure, but we think Backoff was just "along for the ride," so to speak, at Carthage. He was also a crony of Sigel's from the old country.

TPS: What is your analysis of Sigel's generalship during the campaign?

DCH: Sigel's performance was typical of his pre-Civil War career in Europe, where he fought with the German Revolutionaries in 1848. He was trained at a Prussian academy and Sigel was a text book type of general. Whenever situations became fluid or changed dramatically from his preconceived notions of how the fighting should develop, he usually had no contingent plan other than to withdraw.

But, he could keep his head pretty well during retreats. He was a soldier full of contradictions.

TPS: He struck me as being incredibly overconfident.

DCH: Sigel was very overconfident and he badly underestimated the danger posed to his regiments by the Missouri State Guard. I think he knew Jackson's army was a semi-organized rabble, but it was still a dangerous enemy. Sigel thought that training and good artillery would overcome numbers, but in this battle they tended to neutralize each other.

TPS: So Sigel gets a mixed review. . .

DCH: (sigh). His initial blind search out of Springfield was foolhardy. Look, he was out seeking a battle in enemy territory with an enemy that he knew outnumbered him. I think he was counting on sheer discipline to win the day at Carthage, and the terrain was perfect for a European-style battle that he favored. Sigel bashing is a popular sport among Civil War historians, and I will grant you that he demonstrated on several fields that he was not a capable field commander. He bungled the beginning of the fight at Carthage about as badly as you can . . .

TPS: But his retreat was well performed. . .

DCH: Yes it was. He fought the rest of the day as well as anyone could have done under very trying and stressful circumstances. He utilized his strengths and exploited the terrain to extricate his men and wagons.

TPS: What would have happened, in a larger sense, if Sigel had defeated Jackson's men—if it had been another Boonville?

DCH: Well, if either Lyon or Sigel had eliminated Governor Jackson's Missouri State Guard or soundly defeated it in the field again, the war in Missouri would have been radically different. Pro-Southern morale would have sunk like a stone, reinforcements would have been hard to come by and the state would have remained in Federal hands on a far more firm footing than it did. The Battle of Wilson's Creek [August 5, 1861] would not have taken place and Lyon would not have been killed. Many writers overlook Lyon because he was removed from the equation so early in the war, but his passing was a big, big loss to the Union. He demonstrated superior skills as a field commander. He had a lot to learn, but he was willing to fight.

TPS: So why hasn't anyone written a book about the campaign and battle until now?

DCH: This was a difficult project. There are very few firsthand sources on the battle, which is particularly vexing if you want to base your work on them and not secondary materials. We have spent years researching this action and little, relatively speaking, has come to light. Almost nothing exists in the Library of Congress, and the National Archives gave up nothing but a few muster rolls and compiled service records. Similarly, letters and diaries and the like are few and far between.

TPS: So the after-action reports were doubly valuable to you.

DCH: Yes, but so many of those are missing. None of the reports prepared by Sigel's subordinates have been found, which means the Federal perspective is largely told through Sigel's very biased pen and a couple of quasi-reliable reminiscences. Half of the Southern reports are missing. It was also very early in the war, just about two weeks prior to the fighting at Bull Run. The battle was fought on the edge of the frontier, removed from large population centers. . .there were not many witnesses.

TPS: In other words it wasn't near Washington or Richmond?

DCH: Exactly. And, no reporters were traveling with either army.

TPS: Did the Battle at First Bull Run steal some of the limelight?

DCH: Compared to Carthage, Bull Run was a immense affair. And it was fought on the doorstep of the North's capital. News of the battle shoved Carthage into undeserved shadows. Wilson's Creek and Lyon's death compounded the situation.

TPS: Was the fight at Carthage the first Southern victory of the war?

DCH: Actually, yes it was. It was the first real land engagement as well, the South's first true field victory. It went a long way toward buoying the Southern cause in the Trans-Mississippi. . .

TPS: What about Philippi or Big Bethel?

DCH: Well, at Philippi there was no pitched fighting and far fewer men involved. You hear a lot about Big Bethel, and the opposing forces at Bethel outnumbered those on the field at Carthage. What you don't hear is that only a small portion of each side managed to get into the fight [at Big Bethel]. Plus, it was not part of a large land campaign with the possibility of affecting the course of the war in the area in which it was fought.

TPS: What other ramifications came about after Carthage?

DCH: The men of the Missouri State Guard gained valuable experience and went on to form the nucleus of the First and Second Missouri brigades. As you known, these were two of the premier combat units of the war. Franz Sigel's defeat also allowed the linkage of Price's Missourians—and I reemphasize *state* militia—and McCulloch's Confederate army. This combined force defeated Lyon a month later at Wilson's Creek. Carthage also kept the Granby lead mines in Southern hands, and kept Southern morale up, at least for a while.

TPS: You spoke earlier of Sigel's strength in artillery and the Southern advantage in horsemen. I found the battle fascinating from the perspective of mobility versus firepower.

DCH: In many respects that is what this battle was all about. Sigel had two well-drilled and disciplined artillery batteries, eight guns in all, against seven light (primarily 6-pound) Mexican War-vintage Rebel pieces with poorly-trained crews and inferior homemade ammunition. Not much of a match. . .

TPS: The exchange at Dry Fork Creek proved that.

DCH: Yes it did. Sigel also had a powerful infantry component. Most of his soldiers fielded rifled muskets or .69 caliber smooth bores, while the State Guard had a wide assortment of arms, from squirrel rifles and shotguns to pistols and hunting knives. So Sigel had more firepower and discipline. The key ingredient he lacked was cavalry. He did not have any and was burdened with a large train of wagons which slowed him down even more. The State Guard, on the other hand, had about 1,000 horsemen positioned on each wing of the army and generally open or partially wooded terrain over which to maneuver.

TPS: Did mobility win the day?

DCH: It is not as clear cut as that. The mobility and speed of the State Guard cavalry turned Sigel's flanks and forced his retreat several times, but decisive victory eluded the Southerners.

TPS: Defined as the capture or destruction of Sigel's small force?

DCH: Yes. Federal artillery—especially Essig's pieces—preserved Sigel's career and allowed him to survive. Complete or near-complete destruction was well within Southern reach on two or three occasions. Sigel was literally sitting in Governor Jackson's palm and he was unable to close more than one finger at a time. And Sigel kept wriggling out of each situation. That he was able to do so was largely attributable to inexperienced Southern cavalry leadership and well-applied Federal firepower.

TPS: The Missouri State Guard was really a colorful organization. How effective as a fighting force was it at Carthage?

DCH: We really need more firsthand accounts to make that judgment, and we don't have them. So much of what happened is speculation and logic. It's important to remember that the State Guard, at this early stage, was barely organized. It was a militia body of inexperienced troops led by inexperienced, and in many cases inept, leaders. The rank and file endured significant hardships and still fought remarkably well. This is especially true when you realize they were untrained, poorly-equipped and haphazardly armed. Certainly the State Guard gave a good account of itself.

TPS: So whatever weaknesses it had started at the top?

DCH: Yes. The rank and file went on to prove themselves as superb soldiers. Jackson, by virtue of his gubernatorial capacity, was the army's leader at Carthage. What most people ignore is that he failed to take any role in the fighting. Some of the writing produced on this battle, Thomas Snead's [Jackson's aide-de-camp] in particular, is often little more than a thin attempt to cover up for Jackson's negligent handling of the army. I think the answer is pretty clear. He left his four division commanders to fight on their own hooks, and three of the four did a pretty good job. Don't forget, they were also inexperienced.

TPS: Anything else you would like to add about either the battle or your book?

DCH: Yes, a couple things. First, readers should keep in mind that the situation here, I believe, was unique. You have Federal troops under Nathaniel Lyon and Franz Sigel engaging state troops—militia—under the command of a state governor. The Missouri State Guard was not part of the Confederate army. That fact alone makes this engagement significant. Imagine one of today's governor's leading armed men against our army. It was an amazing situation.

TPS: Yes, it was. And second?

DCH: I have studied this battle for years and Karen and I have walked the ground many, many times. We started this project believing certain things because we had read or heard about them for so long. After studying the battle reports and other firsthand accounts, we realized much of it was either simply wrong or open to serious debate.

TPS: For example?

DCH: Well, the Southern divisional alignment was different than we had been led to believe, and several dramatic stories about the battle turned out to be impossible.

TPS: In other words, your interpretation of the fighting differs substantially from conventional accounts?

DCH: Yes. But in all matters we strove to be objective and thoughtful in our interpretations and conclusions. Ultimately whether we agree or disagree with another writer or historian is irrelevant. Our goal is to focus attention on the early war in Missouri. If we can successfully do so, everyone benefits, and more scholars will pay attention to the war in the Trans-Mississippi Theater.

TPS: I am going to set you up here. This is your first book. How are you going to handle readers who take you to task for your conclusions?

DCH: Everyone is entitled to their own opinions, of course. We tried to base all of our conclusions on the best available documentary evidence. Some of it is admittedly very sketchy. Assuming they read the book and *then* disagree about something, I would only ask that they explain their positions and show me manuscript or other sources that support their contentions. This is still a labor of love under construction, and if anyone has anything to share, we would appreciate hearing from them.